OXFORD EARLY CHRISTIAN STUDIES

General Editors

Gillian Clark   Andrew Louth

THE OXFORD EARLY CHRISTIAN STUDIES series includes scholarly volumes on the thought and history of the early Christian centuries. Covering a wide range of Greek, Latin, and Oriental sources, the books are of interest to theologians, ancient historians, and specialists in the classical and Jewish worlds.

Titles in the series include:

Ascetic Eucharists
Food and Drink in Early Christian Ritual Meals
Andrew McGowan (1999)

St Symeon the New Theologian and Orthodox Tradition
Hilarion Alfeyev (2000)

Asceticism and Anthropology in Irenaeus and Clement
John Behr (2000)

The Old Latin Gospels
A Study of Their Texts and Language
Philip Burton (2000)

Paulinus Noster
Self and Symbols in the Letters of Paulinus of Nola
Catherine Conybeare (2000)

The Cult of Saint Thecla
A Tradition of Women's Piety in Late Antiquity
Stephen T. Davis (2001)

Eunomius of Cyzicus and the Nicene Revolution
Richard Paul Vaggione, O.H.C. (2001)

Ambrose: *De Officiis*
Edited with an Introduction, Translation and Commentary
Ivor J. Davidson (2002)

St John Damascene
Tradition and Originality in Byzantine Theology
Andrew Louth (2002)

Augustine's Commentary on Galatians
Introduction, Text, Translation, and Notes
Eric Plumer (2002)

The Ancient Traditions of the Virgin Mary's Dormition and Assumption
Stephen J. Shoemaker (2002)

The Early Development of Canon Law and the Council of Serdica
Hamilton Hess (2002)

The Commentaries of Origen and Jerome on St Paul's Epistle to the Ephesians
Ronald E. Heine (2002)

Grace and Christology in the Early Church

DONALD FAIRBAIRN

OXFORD
UNIVERSITY PRESS

OXFORD
UNIVERSITY PRESS

Great Clarendon Street, Oxford OX2 6DP

Oxford University Press is a department of the University of Oxford. It furthers the University's objective of excellence in research, scholarship, and education by publishing worldwide in

Oxford New York

Auckland Bangkok Buenos Aires Cape Town Chennai Dar es Salaam Delhi Hong Kong Istanbul Karachi Kolkata Kuala Lumpur Madrid Melbourne Mexico City Mumbai Nairobi São Paulo Shanghai Singapore Taipei Tokyo Toronto

Oxford is a registered trade mark of Oxford University Press in the UK and in certain other countries

Published in the United States by Oxford University Press Inc., New York

First published 2003

British Library Cataloguing in Publication Data
Data available

Library of Congress Cataloging in Publication Data
Data applied for

ISBN 0-19-925614-4

1 3 5 7 9 10 8 6 4 2

Typeset by Regent Typesetting, London
Printed in Great Britain
on acid-free paper by
T.J. International Ltd.
Padstow, Cornwall

To my parents,
Donald (Sr.) and Frances Fairbairn

PREFACE

Without a doubt the central affirmation of the Christian faith is that Jesus Christ is both divine and human. On this truth all Christians are agreed, since indeed one who denies this can scarcely bear the name 'Christian' in any meaningful sense at all. But in what sense may one say that the man Jesus was and is God? This question has proved to be a source of debate throughout Christendom's two millennia, and the debate has been especially prominent in the last 200 years, as a proliferation of new exegetical and theological approaches to the New Testament has produced a bewildering array of pictures of Christ.

How is one to choose among so many different modern christologies, most of which claim to be faithful to the biblical witness? Many Christians would agree that the doctrinal writings and creeds of the early Church should play a major role, perhaps even a normative role, in our efforts to evaluate the modern christologies that confront us. This prominent role is related to an idea or sentiment that could be called 'historical authority'. If there was a single dominant way of understanding Christ's deity and humanity in the early Church, and if a certain modern view is consistent with that early consensus, then that modern view gains such historical authority. On the other hand, if there was no such early consensus but rather a variety of ways of describing Christ's person, then one could argue that no modern view deserves preferential consideration, but rather that many (or even all) views may stake a claim to validity. Modern interpreters who wish to see their own views as following in the footsteps of historic Christianity will naturally hunger for historical authority to back up their positions, and they are likely to look for a strong consensus in the early Church. In contrast, interpreters who wish to distance themselves from the Church's historical dogma or even to discredit it will be prone to find no consensus in the early Church, no view of Christ that could claim such universal adherence in its own time that it would virtually force us to adopt a similar view now.

Partly because of this issue of historical authority, the post-Enlightenment debate over Christ's deity and humanity has focused not only on the New Testament itself, but also on the Church's christological controversies, especially the early fifth-century controversies that determined the language the Church would use subsequently to talk about Christ. The modern proliferation of christologies appears in a very different light if the early Church espoused a single consensus view of Christ's person than it does if the fifth century espoused no consensus or only a very minimal consensus. Accordingly, the christological controversies are of far more than merely historical interest to contemporary Christians. To some degree, those controversies will judge our varied efforts to describe Christ's person, and the issue of what we may say, or should say, about our Saviour is at stake.

Was there, then, a consensus in the early Church regarding Christ's person? Does the fact that there was intense disagreement and controversy imply that there was no consensus, that there were several well-represented ways of looking at christology? Did different regions in Christendom see Christ in different ways? Or did the controversies constitute disagreements between a substantial majority on one hand and a few dissenters on the other? I am convinced that in order to answer these questions with any accuracy, one must look not merely at christology itself, but at the broader soteriological issues that lie behind christology. In particular, I believe that one especially helpful issue is the question of grace, and in this book I hope to show that there was an intimate relation between the early Church's understanding of grace and its description of Christ's person. In the process, I also hope to substantiate the view that there was a substantial consensus in the fifth-century Church about the person of Christ, a consensus that then serves as a starting point from which to evaluate our modern christologies.

I suppose that one could justifiably call any extended academic research project a pilgrimage, and that appellation is certainly accurate in the case of this one. The three years I spent in Cambridge preparing the dissertation from which this book came represented the culmination of a much longer process of reflection that led me into the study of Christian theology, into the study of the early Church, and into a doctoral course. I would like to thank a few of the people whose influence provided the guideposts directing me along the path I have taken.

First, Dr John Carson of Erskine Theological Seminary, whose lectures on historical soteriology in the spring of 1987 planted the seeds that I later nurtured into the idea that salvation consists of God's sharing with us the relationship he has between the persons of the Trinity. It was largely Dr Carson's lectures that gave me the theological underpinnings to recognize the significance of Cyril's use of *oikeiotes*, which figures so prominently in this book.

Second, Dr Craig Blomberg and Dr William Klein of Denver Seminary, whose encouragement helped to keep alive my dream of doing doctoral study at a time when my work in Ukraine made it seem as if I would not have the opportunity to pursue that goal. Their advice also proved invaluable as I found my way through the process of considering and applying to graduate schools.

Third, Dr Lionel Wickham, my supervisor in Cambridge, who realized much sooner than I did what I was seeking and who took my unfocused interest in grace in the Church fathers and directed me to the connection between grace and christology. His outstanding early supervision provided the framework enabling me to make the discoveries that form the heart of this book. I am also indebted to him for his assistance in checking the accuracy of quotations from patristic literature preserved only in Syriac.

Fourth, Professor Thomas Torrance of Edinburgh, whose enthusiastic correspondence provided great encouragement for my study of Cyril.

Finally, Professor Winrich Löhr (now of Hamburg) and Dr Andrew Louth of Durham, the examiners for my dissertation, who offered invaluable suggestions for transforming the thesis into a book.

I hope you will find the book you hold in your hands to be a piece of credible historical scholarship that throws some helpful light on the complex issues the Church faced in the early fifth century. But much more than this, I hope you will find the book to be a piece of devotional scholarship that reflects in a small way the enormous privilege God has granted me to reflect, under the tutelage of the early Church, upon the mystery of Emmanuel, the Word made man.

D.F.

Erskine Theological Seminary
Due West
South Carolina
March 2002

CONTENTS

LIST OF TABLES

ABBREVIATIONS

ABR	*Australian Biblical Review*
ACO	*Acta conciliorum oecumenicorum*, ed. E. Schwartz (Berlin, 1914 ff.)
ACW	Ancient Christian Writers, ed. Quasten and Plumpe (Westminster, Md., 1946–)
ANFa	*The Ante-Nicene Fathers* (New York, 1886–7)
Arm.V.	Armenian Version
AThR	*Anglican Theological Review*
Aug.	*Augustinianum*
AugSt	*Augustinian Studies*
BAGD	Bauer, Arndt, Gingrich, Danker, *A Greek–English Lexicon of the New Testament and Other Early Christian Literature* (Chicago, 1957; rev. 1979)
CCist	*Collectanea Cisterciensia*
CCSL	Corpus Christianorum Series Latina (Turnhout, 1954–)
ChH	*Church History*
CistS	*Cistercian Studies*
CPG	*Clavis Patrum Graecorum* (Brepols-Turnhout, 1974–87)
CPL	*Clavis Patrum Latinorum*, 3rd edn. (Brepols, 1995)
CSEL	*Corpus Scriptorum Ecclesiasticorum Latinorum* (Vienna, 1866 ff.)
DHGE	*Dictionnaire d'histoire et de géographie ecclésiastique* (Paris, 1912–)
Diss.	Unpublished dissertation
DR	*The Downside Review*
DSp	*Dictionnaire de spiritualité ascétique et mystique, doctrine et histoire* (Paris, 1937–)
DThC	*Dictionnaire de théologie catholique* (Paris, 1903–40, 1951–72)
EOr	*Echos d'Orient*
E.T.	English Translation

EThL	*Ephemerides Theologicae Lovaniensis*
FaCh	The Fathers of the Church (Washington, DC, 1947–)
Fr.T.	French Translation
FrancSt	*Franciscan Studies*
Ger.T.	German Translation
Gk.V.	Greek Version
GOTR	*Greek Orthodox Theological Review*
Gr.	*Gregorianum*
HeyJ	*Heythrop Journal*
IJT	*The Indian Journal of Theology*
IThQ	*The Irish Theological Quarterly*
JECS	*Journal of Early Christian Studies*
JEH	*Journal of Ecclesiastical History*
JThS	*Journal of Theological Studies*
Lampe	G. W. H. Lampe, *A Patristic Greek Lexicon* (Oxford, 1961)
Lat.V.	Latin Version
LewSh	Lewis and Short, *A Latin Dictionary* (Oxford, 1879)
LoF	*Library of the Fathers of the Holy Catholic Church*, ed. Pusey *et al.* (Oxford, 1838–85)
LSJ	Liddell, Scott, Jones, *A Greek–English Lexicon* (Oxford, 1843; 9th edn. 1940, suppl. 1996)
LXX	Septuagint
MSR	*Mélanges de science religieuse*
NPNF	*A Select Library of the Nicene and Post-Nicene Fathers of the Christian Church*, ed. P. Schaff (New York, 1887–1900)
NS	New Series
ODCC	*Oxford Dictionary of the Christian Church*, 3rd edn. (Oxford, 1997)
OCP	*Orientalia Christiana Periodica*
PBR	*The Patristic and Byzantine Review*
PG	*Patrologia, series graeca et latina*, ed. J. P. Migne (Paris, 1847–66)
PL	*Patrologia, series latina*, ed. J. P. Migne (Paris, 1841–64)
ProEccl	*Pro Ecclesia*
REByz	*Revue des études byzantines*

RechAug	*Recherches augustiniennes*
RevSR	*Revue des sciences réligieuses*
RHE	*Revue d'histoire ecclésiastique*
RSPhTh	*Revue des sciences philosophiques et théologiques*
RSR	*Recherches de science réligieuse*
RThom	*Revue Thomiste*
SC	Sources chrétiennes, ed. Lubac and Daniélou (Paris, 1941–)
ScEc	*Sciences ecclésiastiques*
SCH	*Studies in Church History*
SJTh	*Scottish Journal of Theology*
Sobornost	*Sobornost: Incorporating Eastern Churches Review*
StPatr	*Studia Patristica* (Berlin (vols. i–xvi), Oxford (vols. xvii–), 1957–)
SVTQ	*St Vladimir's Theological Quarterly*
Syr.V.	Syriac Version
TDNT	*Theological Dictionary of the New Testament* (Grand Rapids, Mich., 1964–76)
Theol(A)	*ΘΕΟΛΟΓΙΑ*
TRE	*Theologische Realenzyklopädie* (Berlin, 1976–)
TS	*Theological Studies*
TU	*Texte und Untersuchungen* (Berlin, 1897–1976)
TynB	*Tyndale Bulletin*
VigChr	*Vigiliae Christianae*
Vulg.	Vulgate
ZKG	*Zeitschrift für Kirchengeschichte*
ZNW	*Zeitschrift für die neutestamentliche Wissenschaft und die Kunde der älteren Kirche*
ZThK	*Zeitschrift für Theologie und Kirche*

NOTE ON QUOTATIONS AND REFERENCES

Throughout the text of this book, I cite patristic sources by abbreviations of the standard Latin titles used in *CPG* and *CPL*. These references generally come in parentheses at the end of a citation or quotation. In each case, references to book, chapter, section, or fragment number follow the divisions in the edition I cite. In order to aid the reader in locating the passage, I also give in brackets the page number(s) where the citation may be found in that edition (or, in the case of works long enough to span more than one volume, the volume number followed by the page number). I refer the reader to section one of the Bibliography for further information.

Throughout the book, all direct quotations of patristic sources are given in English translations for which I bear responsibility. In some cases the translations are completely my own, and in other cases I have used available translations and have made modifications as appropriate. The entry for each patristic source in the bibliography indicates translations I have consulted, if any, and the reader should understand that I am indebted—to a greater or lesser degree—to the translations listed. In particular, I am indebted to Boniface Ramsey's excellent translation of Cassian's *Conlationes* in ACW 57. Please remember that all page references to patristic writings are to the edition of the Greek or Latin text, *not* to the page number of any translation.

In the case of writings by Diodore, Theodore, and Nestorius preserved only in Syriac, my exposition follows the best available modern translations (German in the case of Diodore, since there are no English translations; and French in the case of Theodore and Nestorius, since the available English translations are considerably poorer than the French). Accordingly, the English quotations in the text are my renderings of the German or French, and they have been checked against the

Syriac by Dr Lionel Wickham. All page references are to these German and French versions, rather than to the Syriac texts or the inferior English translations.

I often include material in either parentheses or brackets within patristic quotations. Parentheses enclose noteworthy portions of the Greek or Latin text lying behind my translation, and brackets enclose explanatory material that I have added, such as a phrase that is implied but not stated in the text. When a patristic quotation includes a quotation from or clear allusion to a biblical passage, I italicize the biblical quote, and I indicate the reference of the biblical text either in brackets within the patristic quotation or in my discussion of the passage.

Citations from secondary literature are placed in notes and consist of the author's name and a shortened form of the title of the book or article (or, rarely, an abbreviation such as LSJ), followed by the page numbers. In cases where I quote directly from secondary literature not available in English (and thus listed in the bibliography in its original language), the translations are my own.

I

Grace and the Central Issue of the Christological Controversy

> And the Word became flesh and dwelt among us, and we beheld his glory, glory as of the Only-Begotten from the Father, full of grace and truth.
>
> (John 1: 14)

> Although he existed in the form of God, he did not consider equality with God something to be grasped, but he emptied himself by taking the form of a servant and being made in human likeness.
>
> (Phil. 2: 6–7)

These two biblical texts proclaim what is at once both the central truth of the Christian faith and perhaps its most controversial affirmation. God has become a man. The one who was equal with God has taken upon himself the form of a servant. In the man Jesus who has lived among us, we see the glory of the Father's only Son. As early as AD 325, this affirmation was enshrined prominently in the Creed of Nicaea, even though the Council of Nicaea dealt not with the incarnation per se, but with the full deity of God the Son. The Creed affirms not only that 'we believe in one God, Father all-sovereign, maker of all things seen and unseen; and in one Lord Jesus Christ, the Son of God', but also that this Son of God 'for us men, and for our salvation, came down, and was incarnated, and was made man, suffered, and arose on the third day'.

The prominence given to the incarnation in the Creed of Nicaea set in motion a series of intense theological discussions that led to serious controversies about christology. These controversies were eventually resolved (to some degree) at the Council of Chalcedon in AD 451, whose Definition of Faith determined the language which the vast majority of the Christian

Church has used to speak about Christ ever since. However, the development that produced the Creed of Nicaea, the Nicene-Constantinopolitan Creed (AD 381), and the Chalcedonian Definition raises a question that is extremely important for our understanding of the history of Christian doctrine: Was the uniformity that the creeds and definitions fostered a natural one reflecting something essential to the Christian faith and agreed on throughout the Church, or was it an artificial unity forced upon the Church by imperial pressure? To put it differently, did the Church arrive at its great creedal statements because it believed that only these statements could express its faith adequately, or did it devise these statements simply because imperial policy demanded confessional uniformity as a way of promoting political unity?

In dealing with this question, one must be quick to admit that imperial policy *did* play a significant role in the development of the creedal statements. Constantine himself called the Council of Nicaea in AD 325, only thirteen years after his conversion, and it is generally agreed that he had only a limited understanding of the theological differences between Arius and the Nicaeans. He insisted on a single statement of faith, but he seemed to have little idea what that statement should include. The Council of Constantinople in AD 381 served to cement the link between imperial policy and ecclesiastical affairs even further by promoting the episcopal see of Constantinople, the imperial capital, to the same level of honour as the sees of Rome and Alexandria. Neither Rome nor Alexandria accepted this realignment, and much of early fifth-century Church history can be understood in terms of the political clash between the older sees on one hand and the upstart see of Constantinople, backed by imperial might, on the other. The Council of Ephesus in AD 431 actually consisted of two competing councils, and in the aftermath both sides poured a great deal of effort (and even money) into the task of gaining the Emperor's approval. At Chalcedon in AD 451, the bishops were reluctant to write a new creedal statement, and it was only under imperial pressure that they produced the Chalcedonian Definition at all.

That ecclesiastical pronouncements in the fourth and fifth centuries were influenced by imperial politics cannot be disputed. The question, though, is how this influence is to be interpreted. Did imperial pressure force the Church to adopt creedal statements even though such creedal uniformity was not really essential to the Christian faith? Did such creedal statements produce only a surface unity while masking deep divisions in the way Christians understood Christ? Or was there a genuine consensus about the person of Christ, a consensus that was *brought to light* under imperial prodding but not *imposed* by that pressure? As I mentioned in the Preface, the presence or absence of a genuine consensus in the early Church has a great deal of significance for modern work in the field of christology. If the Definition of Chalcedon actually represents a single view of Christ (rather than a political compromise among competing views), and if this view represents a genuine consensus among Christians who believed that only this statement could adequately express the Christian faith, then Chalcedon can legitimately stand in historical judgement on modern christologies. In that case, only those christologies that are clearly consistent with that fifth-century consensus can claim the historical authority that comes from representing the faith of the early Church, and those who hold to other christologies must admit that they have departed from the early Church's faith. But if there was no genuine theological consensus behind Chalcedon, then one may perhaps conclude that the early Church did not believe doctrinal formulation to be essential to the Christian faith, and thus that no single view of Christ should carry historical authority. Clearly, then, the question of whether there was a genuine *theological* consensus underlying the *political* unity forged in most of the Christian world in the fifth century is a crucial one, both for the understanding of historical theology and for contemporary expressions of the Christian faith.

Unfortunately, there is no scholarly agreement on the question of whether there was such a theological consensus. The two great christological controversies of the fifth century (the Nestorian controversy leading to the Council of Ephesus in AD 431 and the Eutychian controversy leading to Chalcedon two decades later) are often portrayed as clashes between two rival schools of thought based in Alexandria and Antioch. Modern interpreters have been divided on the issues of how far apart these two Eastern schools were theologically, whether the Western Church's christology was closer to that of Antioch or Alexandria, and how one should view the Reunion Formula of AD 433 and the Chalcedonian Definition in relation to these two schools of thought. Part of the reason for this disagreement is that there is no clear consensus among modern commentators about what the central issue of the christological controversies was. Some scholars argue that while Antiochene and Alexandrian christology differed in emphasis, the differences did not strike at the heart of Christian faith, and these interpreters insist that the controversy had more to do with political or personal rivalry and with misunderstanding than with significant, irreconcilable doctrinal differences. Other scholars see the theological divergence as being more crucial and argue that the central issue was the question of whether one began with the two elements in Christ or with his single person. Still others view the controversy as a clash between different sets of theological concerns, and these commentators argue that the central issue was that of God's direct, personal presence in the world.

Accordingly, any insight into the question of whether there was a fifth-century consensus about Christ and what the consensus was depends on a clear understanding of what the central issue of the controversy was. If political rivalry was actually the root of the conflict, then we can know very little about what sort of consensus there was. In that case, the fact that prominent churchmen chose to fight about politics instead of theology could imply that there was a substantial consensus that was obscured by political infighting, that there was a minimal consensus but that this was considered to be all that was necessary, or that there was actually very little consensus but that little was thought necessary. Conversely, if the question of beginning with unity (Alexandria) or duality (Antioch) in describing Christ was the central issue, then it may well appear that both sides were equally represented, and one could justifiably conclude that there was little consensus. However, if God's direct personal presence in the world was the central issue, then perhaps the entire categorization of the conflict in terms of equally represented 'schools' is misleading, since all but a handful of thinkers insisted on God's personal presence with us through the incarnation.

In this study, I will attempt to clarify the question of what the central issue in the controversy was, and therefore also the question of whether there was a substantial theological consensus in the fifth-century Church. I will do this by examining the relation between divine grace and christology in the works of Cyril of Alexandria and John Cassian, as they responded to the thought of Theodore and Nestorius. I hope to demonstrate that in the fifth-century Church, a given writer's depiction of Christ's person was, to a large degree, an expression of his charitological and soteriological concerns. I will seek to show further that there was a sharp contrast between the understanding of grace that guided Theodore and Nestorius on one hand, and that which shaped the christology of Cyril and Cassian on the other. In addition, I believe that a study of grace and christology will help to show that the controversy was concerned primarily with the third of the issues above, the question of whether God personally entered human history through the incarnation. By considering the controversy from this perspective, I hope to lend support to the view that the dispute was not a clash between two rival schools, each of which was significantly represented in the fifth-century Church, but rather that a few people were opposing the theological consensus of a substantial majority. Accordingly, I will usually refer not to 'Antiochene' and 'Alexandrian' schools or movements, but to Theodorean and Cyrillian modes of thought about grace and christology.[1] I hope to substantiate the view that the Cyrillian way of looking at grace and the person of Christ was not Cyril's alone but was shared by most of the early Church, both Eastern and Western.

Therefore, as I introduce this study I will survey modern scholarship on the christological controversy by examining which issue scholars believe to have been the central question in dispute. I will then offer my reasons for believing that a study of grace and christology will help to evaluate the controversy and my rationale for concentrating on Cyril and Cassian. Finally, I will introduce two key ideas related to the understanding of grace and christology, concepts that will figure significantly in the course of this study.

[1] The exception to this is that I will use the words 'Antiochene' and 'Alexandrian' when I refer to the thought of scholars who themselves use these categories.

1.1. SCHOLARLY OPINIONS ON THE CENTRAL ISSUE OF THE CONTROVERSY

The discussions surrounding Christ's person encompassed an array of interrelated issues, and everything from imperial politics to popular piety to eucharistic doctrine played a part. But in spite of this diversity of concerns, most scholars regard one or another issue as the central one, the vantage point from which to view the entire controversy. As we have seen above, a given scholar's interpretation of the relation between the various modes of christological thought is closely tied to that interpreter's belief about what the central issue was.

1.1.1. Politics, Personal Rivalry, and Theological Misunderstanding

Certainly one of the important factors in the Nestorian controversy was the rivalry that I have already mentioned between the established sees of Rome and Alexandria on one hand and the relatively new see of Constantinople on the other, and a number of scholars have seen political and personal friction as the main driving force behind the dispute. Loofs and Schwartz assert that Cyril's animosity towards Constantinople was aroused when he learned that some Egyptian monks had brought charges against him before the imperial court. Cyril's focus on doctrinal issues, Loofs and Schwartz claim, was an attempt to deflect attention away from the charges levelled against him.[2] Loofs insists that Cyril could have come to terms with Nestorius as easily as he did with John of Antioch later, had he not had a vested interest in discrediting Nestorius. He concludes, 'More than the heretic Nestorius, the "Saint" but really very unsaintly Cyril is to be held responsible for the Nestorian controversy.'[3] Schwartz is even more direct when he makes the famous claim: 'The motive which drove Cyril to the point of beginning the controversy with Nestorius was not dogmatic opposition. In his preaching Nestorius brought forth no innovations, but only the teaching which Diodore of Tarsus and Theodore of Mopsuestia had

[2] Loofs, *Nestorius and His Place*, 41; Schwartz, *Cyrill und der Mönch Viktor*, 3–6.

[3] Loofs, *Nestorius and His Place*, 41.

advocated nearly two generations earlier, but without being suspected as heretics.'[4]

Other scholars, while not agreeing that political and personal factors *alone* were the cause of the controversy, nevertheless argue that both sides were within the realm of orthodoxy and that misunderstanding played a large role. Sellers insists that Antioch and Alexandria were fighting for the same christological principles but that they were unable to see their commonality because each side read the other's unfamiliar terminology in its own way. He asserts that if the two sides had come to Ephesus to learn instead of to argue, each might have seen the value of the other side, and together they might have come to an agreement on terminology.[5] Similarly, Prestige writes of Cyril and Nestorius: 'Never have two theologians more completely misunderstood one another's meaning. They approached the subject from widely different angles, but in substance they were not wholly and irreconcilably opposed.'[6]

These scholars and others who assert that the controversy was due largely to theological misunderstanding and personal/political rivalry generally believe that any christology that asserted the unity of Christ's person and the duality of his divine and human elements was sufficiently orthodox. While Cyril and his followers placed more emphasis on the unity of Christ and Nestorius and Leo accented the distinction between the natures, these emphases did not actually conflict, and each was necessary to complement the thought of the other. In this understanding, the entire controversy was a tragic story of animosity between men whose thought was actually in substantial agreement.[7]

1.1.2. Beginning with Duality or with Unity

In contrast, the majority of modern scholars believe that while political considerations and misunderstanding were important,

[4] Schwartz, *Cyrill und der Mönch Viktor*, 3.

[5] Sellers, *Two Ancient Christologies*, 208–14, 233.

[6] Prestige, *Fathers and Heretics*, 264. Cf. Mahé, 'Les Anathématismes de Cyrille', 542, who argues that both Antioch and Alexandria were within the realm of orthodoxy. Cf. also Guillet, 'Les Exégèses d'Alexandrie et d'Antioche', 297–8, who asserts that in spite of their differences of emphasis, the two sides were consistent with each other.

[7] See Sellers, *Two Ancient Christologies*, pp. vii–viii, for a clear statement of this idea.

the theological differences between Cyril and Nestorius were nevertheless significant. These commentators argue that the central issue was whether one began with Christ's duality or unity, and many hold that only by beginning with duality can one do justice to Christ's full humanity and to the historical depiction of him in the Gospels. From this vantage point, Cyril's 'one nature' formula looks suspicious, and scholars are likely to regard Theodorean christology as more faithful to Scripture than Cyrillian thought is. Raven asserts that Cyril's doctrine was not significantly different from that of Apollinarius and that in fact, they and most of the early Church operated with an inadequate conception of Christ's humanity. In contrast, Raven finds in Theodore a clear acknowledgement of the importance of history and a more biblical stress on the true humanity of Christ and the significance of that humanity for our salvation.[8] Similarly, Greer asserts that Theodore's dualistic christology derives from the Antiochene exegetical interest in the historical person of Jesus, in contrast to the more Platonic notions that led Alexandrian theologians to emphasize static ontology over history.[9]

Scholars who adopt this perspective generally see the making of a clear distinction between the deity and humanity of Christ and the use of concrete terms to describe his humanity as indications of a belief in his full (independent) humanity. Since the West adopted these ways of writing about Christ, these interpreters usually view Western christology as being more Theodorean than Cyrillian. Harnack argues that Celestine held to Nestorius' view of two natures united without confusion, and thus that the pope betrayed his own faith by siding with Cyril during the controversy. He regards Leo's *Tome* as close to Nestorianism and insists that Cyril would have repudiated parts of it.[10] Similarly, Amann writes that Cassian and the West were much closer to Nestorius than to Cyril, and he even claims that if Cyril had seen Cassian's *De Incar. Dom.*, he would have declared it to be Nestorian.[11]

[8] Raven, *Apollinarianism*, 231, 279–80, 297–8.

[9] Greer, *Theodore of Mopsuestia*, 110–11, 151.

[10] Harnack, *History of Dogma*, iv. 182–3, 204–5. Cf. Braaten, 'Modern Interpretations of Nestorius', 252.

[11] Amann, 'Nestorius et sa doctrine', 100. Cf. Studer, '*Una Persona in*

Scholars who argue that the question of whether one begins with the duality or unity of Christ was the central issue often assert that the Reunion Formula and the Chalcedonian Definition were essentially Antiochene, rather than Cyrillian. Harnack states that the Reunion Formula permanently prohibited Greek piety from using the 'one nature' slogan which alone could express its faith. Of Chalcedon he writes that the participants could accept Leo's *Tome* only by deluding themselves into thinking that Cyril had said much the same thing.[12] Similarly, Samuel asserts that Cyril's slogan 'out of two natures' and Leo's/Chalcedon's 'in two natures' were contradictory and that the latter was Nestorian,[13] and Gregorios sees Chalcedon as depicting the person of Christ symmetrically, as a union of equal divine and human natures to make a personal being.[14]

1.1.3. The Reality of God's Personal Presence in the World

Finally, there are scholars who argue that the central issue of the controversy was the question of whether God himself entered the world personally through the incarnation. Bethune-Baker argues that while the Antiochenes were right to emphasize the full humanity of Christ, they failed to grasp the fundamental truth that God himself had entered into the experiences of human life. In this way, he claims, they deprived the incarnation of most of its meaning.[15] Grillmeier makes much the same

Christo', 454, who asserts that Augustine and Leo see the one person as the result of the union, not the christological starting point. Also, both Dewart, 'The Influence of Theodore on Augutine', 132, and McGuckin, 'Did Augustine's Christology Depend on Theodore?', 50, see a close similarity between Theodore's and Augustine's christology, although McGuckin denies Dewart's claim that the similarity is the result of direct Theodorean influence on Augustine.

12 Harnack, *History of Dogma*, iv. 197, 219.

13 Samuel, 'One Incarnate Nature', 51.

14 Gregorios, 'The Relevance of Christology Today', 107. I should point out that Samuel and Gregorios (both non-Chalcedonian Orthodox) reject Chalcedon precisely because they believe it begins with the two natures of Christ, rather than starting with the unity as Cyril has done. They agree with the Western scholars whom I have cited that the central issue of the controversy was whether one began with duality or with unity, but they disagree on the question of where one *should* start.

15 Bethune-Baker, *Early History of Christian Doctrine*, 275. I should note that in another work Bethune-Baker backs away from this judgement by writing that

point when he argues that Cyril's great contribution to the debate was his clear expression of the unity of the subject of Christ.[16] Perhaps the clearest statement of this view comes from O'Keefe, who argues that the Nestorian controversy was a debate not about terminology or about the completeness of Jesus' humanity, but about the fullness of God's presence in the world. O'Keefe argues that Nestorius' thought was governed by the assumption that God was immutable and thus could not suffer and that while Cyril generally shared that assumption, his study of Scripture had convinced him that the Son had in fact suffered, so he should not balk at saying so.[17] O'Keefe concludes by writing: 'The Antiochenes clung to a mediated presence, while Cyril, albeit with plenty of qualification, announced that God's presence in the world was unmediated and direct: Jesus is the "one incarnate nature of the Word." Jesus is the second Person of the Trinity.'[18]

These scholars and others who see the direct personal entrance of the Logos into the world as the central issue almost invariably regard Western christology, the Reunion Formula, and the Chalcedonian Definition as being closer to Cyril's thought than to that of Nestorius. Galtier asserts that Cassian, Celestine, Cyril, John of Antioch, and Leo all affirmed that the Son himself descended into the virgin's womb and was born according to the flesh. He claims that this was the faith of the Church and that what was new with Leo was not the idea of his christology but simply his two-natures terminology.[19] Florovsky asserts that although Chalcedon did not use Cyril's language, the council deliberately reflected his faith while phrasing it in more precise

Nestorius was orthodox and was deposed for personal rather than doctrinal reasons. See Bethune-Baker, *Nestorius and his Teaching*, 198–9.

[16] Grillmeier, *Christ in Christian Tradition*, 476–7. Cf. Sullivan, *The Christology of Theodore*, 283–8; Romanides, 'Cyril's "One Physis" and Chalcedon', 159.

[17] O'Keefe, 'Impassible Suffering?', 41, 45–6. Much earlier Hodgson, 'The Metaphysic of Nestorius', 54–5, had written that Cyril 'would no more question the antithesis between godhead and manhood than would Nestorius, but where the truth was too much for his system, he preferred the truth to the system'.

[18] O'Keefe, 'Impassible Suffering?', 58–9.

[19] Galtier, *L'Unité du Christ*, 69–70, 75, 85. Cf. van Bavel, *Recherches sur la christologie*, 38–9; Diepen, 'L'*Assumptus Homo* patristique', 38–43; and Grillmeier, *Christ in Christian Tradition*, 409, all of whom argue that in Augustine's later writings, he saw the single person of Christ as the Logos himself.

terminology through the introduction of a distinction between *physis* and *hypostasis*.[20] Kelly writes that Chalcedon's 'one and the same' language had never been heard in Antiochene circles and that Cyril's insistence on the unity of Christ lay behind this language.[21] Norris argues that the Chalcedonian Definition is intelligible only in terms of Cyril's subject-attribute scheme for describing Christ and that it unequivocally reaffirms Cyril's faith in the unicity of subject in Christ. He insists that Chalcedon excludes not only Nestorius' christology, but also the common idea that the one subject of Christ was a combination of divine and human natures.[22]

This brief survey shows that the way modern interpreters evaluate the fifth-century christological controversy is linked quite closely to their assumptions about what lay at the centre of the dispute. Furthermore, the questions of whether there was a consensus view of Christ, how strong that consensus was, and whether the consensus view was more like that of Cyril or Theodore/Nestorius also appear in a different light depending on which issue one sees as being the central focus of the controversy. Therefore, it is critical that interpreters be able to evaluate these varied assessments of the controversy's central focus. Was it primarily a matter of misunderstanding and political rivalry, of different theologies derived from starting with unity vs. diversity in Christ, or of divergent convictions about whether God the Logos was personally and immediately present in Jesus? In the following section, I will argue that the relation between grace and christology provides a helpful key for identifying the central issue, and therefore for interpreting the controversy as a whole.

20 Florovsky, *The Byzantine Fathers of the Fifth Century*, 288, 297–9.

21 Kelly, *Early Christian Doctrines*, 342.

22 Norris, 'Toward a Contemporary Interpretation of the Chalcedonian *Definition*', 74. Cf. Romanides, 'Cyril's "One Physis" and Chalcedon', 87, 101–2; Meyendorff, *Christ in Eastern Christian Thought*, 22–4; and McGuckin, *St. Cyril of Alexandria*, 237–40, all of whom see Chalcedon in decidedly Cyrillian terms, as an affirmation of the Logos as the single subject of Christ. Grillmeier, *Christ in Christian Tradition*, 552–3, offers a concurring opinion when he writes that the Definition centred around the person of the Logos in Cyrillian fashion but also drew the features of Christ's manhood with unmistakable clarity.

1.2. GRACE AND THE INTERPRETATION OF THE CHRISTOLOGICAL CONTROVERSY

It is well known that much patristic discussion about the person of Christ was motivated by a concern to safeguard the accomplishment of redemption and that differing conceptions of salvation contributed to the christological controversy. If a patristic writer believes that salvation is largely a human task, a matter of achieving the vocation that God has set before us, then he is likely to see Christ as the leader who has first achieved the human calling and now assists us to follow him. Therefore, Christ must not simply be fully human, but his humanity must also have a measure of autonomy and must receive prominence in one's conception of his person, in order for his achievement of redemption to be of any saving significance for us. On the other hand, if a patristic writer sees salvation as more of a divine rescue operation, an act of God to deliver people from a morass from which they cannot extricate themselves, then he is more likely to argue that only if God the Son was truly and personally present on earth is salvation possible. In this case, the writer is not likely to be as concerned with distinguishing the deity and humanity of Christ as he is with maintaining that Christ is 'God with us' in the fullest possible sense. God's presence in Christ must be a direct, personal presence, not a mediated one.

Among these soteriological concerns, one that is intimately linked to christology in the thought of the early Church is the concept of divine grace. Theodore uses the idea of grace or *eudokia* as his basis for explaining the christological union, and Nestorius follows him in making this the foundation of his thought. Cyril writes frequently that Christ must be a Son by nature in order to make us sons by grace, and he asserts that Christ could not give us grace if he were not the very source of grace. As Cassian refutes Nestorius' christology in *De Incar. Dom.*, his first line of attack is to equate Nestorian thought with Pelagianism. Since christological thought was bound up with the understanding of grace in all three major regions involved in the controversy, an examination of the relation between grace and christology should be helpful in identifying the central issue on which that controversy hinged.

1.2.1. The Focus of this Study: The Christological Sense of Grace

However, this assertion immediately raises the question of what one actually means by grace. The word is so broad that it can be used to refer to virtually everything pertaining to the divine–human relationship. In order to provide direction for this study and to prevent it from being engulfed by the plethora of ideas that fall under the umbrella of grace, I would like to make a distinction between what I will call the christological sense of grace and the anthropological sense. By christological grace, I mean the issue of what (or whom) God gives people through the incarnation and atoning work of Christ. By anthropological grace, I mean the issue of how God leads us to receive and to retain this gift.[23]

The anthropological aspect of grace is primarily concerned with the relation between the gift of freedom that God has already given to humanity at creation and the gifts of faith and perseverance that he gives in salvation. Does God's grace work with human freedom in a co-operative way as a person comes to faith in Christ and remains in the faith, or does grace somehow overcome or transform the human will in this process? Of course, this question is closely connected to the issues of how the fall has affected human freedom, whether and how the atonement restores freedom lost in the fall, and whether there is a sequential relation between God's election of people to salvation and his foreknowledge of who will come to him. Most Western scholarly discussions of salvific grace in the patristic period revolve around the Pelagian and Semi-Pelagian controversies and deal with what I am calling anthropological grace. The question is not one of what God gives us in Christ, but rather of the relation between God's gracious action and our free will (or lack thereof) as he leads us through Christian life. Because Western scholars construe grace largely in anthropological terms, they generally write the history of the early fifth-century Church in two distinct sections, one dealing with christology (in

[23] Of course, these two senses of the word 'grace' hardly exhaust its theological meaning, since both of them deal with what could be called broadly 'salvific grace', and they do not include God's gifts that he bestows on all people at creation (what is sometimes called 'common grace').

which the concern is largely terminological) and the other dealing separately with grace.[24]

In contrast, what I call christological grace is more closely related to the question of what salvation actually is, what Christ gives the Christian. Virtually all patristic writers understood salvation to include immortality and incorruption, but there was disagreement about whether these qualities belong properly to a perfected humanity or to God himself. Thus there was a question of whether grace consisted of Christ's giving the Christian power, aid, and assistance in reaching that perfect human condition, or whether God gave the believer participation in his own immortality and incorruption. Furthermore, the patristic idea of deification led many to argue that salvation consisted not just of immortality, but also of union with God, and in this case grace could be seen as God's giving himself to Christians through Christ. Naturally there were various ideas concerning what union with God meant and therefore what it meant for God to give himself to us in grace. This aspect of grace is much more closely related to christology than anthropological grace is. How a given writer answers the question of what or whom God gives us in Christ has a direct bearing on what he will say about the person of Christ, about who Christ must be (and is) in order to give us this grace. Accordingly, I will focus on the christological aspect of grace and will touch on the anthropological aspect only intermittently.

1.2.2. The Subjects of this Study: Theodore, Nestorius, Cyril, and Cassian

For the bulk of this study I will concentrate on those writers who contributed to the Nestorian controversy and the Council of Ephesus in AD 431. I believe that in spite of the procedural and diplomatic chaos that surrounded Ephesus, that council did provide the opportunity for the Church's understanding of grace and christology to crystallize. I am convinced that this process of crystallization both revealed what the Church had long believed about grace and christology and solidified the mindset with

[24] A glance at virtually any survey of early Christian doctrine will confirm this point: e.g. Harnack, *History of Dogma*, who entitles Book 1 'The Dogma of the God-Man' and Book 2 'The Dogma of Sin, Grace, and the Means of Grace'. Cf. Pelikan, *The Christian Tradition*; Kelly, *Early Christian Doctrines*.

which the Church later dealt with the Eutychian controversy and formulated the Chalcedonian Definition. Accordingly, an exposition of the relation between grace and christology at Ephesus should throw into relief the background to Chalcedon and help to clarify the potential ambiguities of the Chalcedonian Definition.

As already noted, the writers on whom I will concentrate are Cyril of Alexandria and John Cassian. The choice of Cyril can hardly be surprising. Whether one reveres or despises him, one cannot dispute that he was the major player in the controversy and the ancient Church's pre-eminent christological doctor.[25] Furthermore, in spite of the vast scholarly literature on Cyril's christology and the frequency with which modern interpreters have pointed out the link between his portrait of Christ and his soteriological concerns,[26] there has been no study of which I am aware specifically dedicated to his views on christological grace.[27] I will argue in Chs. 3 and 4 that Cyril's portrayal of Christ is so directly linked to his understanding of grace that one can justifiably assert that for Cyril, Christ is grace.[28]

In contrast, my choice of Cassian probably requires some justification. If one seeks to understand the relation between grace and christology in the early Latin Church, the natural starting points would seem to be the writings of Augustine and Leo. I will mention Leo briefly in the conclusion, but my desire to focus on Ephesus removes him from prominent consideration. My reasons for choosing Cassian to the exclusion of Augustine are three: two strategic and one practical. The first strategic reason is that although Augustine was still alive in early 430 when Leo (then archdeacon of Rome) asked Cassian to write

[25] Wickham, *Cyril: Select Letters*, p. xi, declares, 'The patristic understanding of the Incarnation owes more to Cyril of Alexandria than to any other individual theologian.'

[26] e.g. H. Chadwick, 'Eucharist and Christology', Gebremedhin, *Life-Giving Blessing*, and Welch, *Christology and Eucharist*, all of whom link Cyril's christology to his eucharistic doctrine. Cf. Russell, *Cyril of Alexandria*, 14, 40, 45–6, who argues for the closest possible connection between Cyril's single-subject christology and his transformational spirituality.

[27] Perhaps Weigl, *Die Heilslehre des Cyrill*, comes closest to this, since he devotes a substantial portion of his work on Cyril's soteriological teaching to his doctrine of grace. However, most of his discussion concerns what I call anthropological grace.

[28] Wickham, 'Symbols of the Incarnation in Cyril', 44, makes this claim.

against Nestorius, Leo chose the monk rather than the illustrious bishop. This may well have been simply a pragmatic decision (Cassian's Greek was much better than Augustine's, and the monk was closer to Rome as well), or it may have had to do with suspicion in Rome that Augustine was becoming too extreme in his teaching on predestination. Whatever the case, Leo chose the monk, and Cassian was the only Westerner who contributed a doctrinal writing to the Nestorian controversy. My second strategic reason is that I think Cassian's writings provide insight into the way the Western Church as a whole understood christology. Lacking Augustine's brilliance (and the corresponding peculiarities), Cassian may represent more accurately what the choir, rather than the soloist, was singing. My more practical reason for writing on Cassian is that bringing Augustine into the study would overwhelm the other voices that deserve to be heard. In contrast to the monumental amount of attention scholars have given to Augustine's thought, commentators have almost ignored Cassian's christological work. There is a sizeable body of literature about Cassian's monastic thought and a smaller one dealing with his part in the semi-Pelagian controversy, but to my knowledge there was no published book-length study of *De Incar. Dom.* in the twentieth century.[29] For these reasons, I will devote Chs. 5 and 6 to the relation between Cassian's concept of grace and his christological thought and will argue that his doctrine agrees very closely with the major lines of Cyril's teaching.

In order to provide a picture of the ideas that Cyril and Cassian were opposing, I will consider Theodore's and Nestorius' concepts of christological grace in Ch. 2. Nestorius' extant writings deal almost exclusively with what one could call technical christology, the terminology used to describe the relation between Christ's two *physeis* within his single *prosopon*. He writes very little about the understanding of grace and salvation that undergirds his christology, but what he does write shows

[29] There are two unpublished theses devoted to *De Incar. Dom.*: Brand, 'Le *De incarnatione Domini* de Cassian', and Kuhlmann, 'Eine dogmengeschichtliche Neubevertung'. O. Chadwick, *John Cassian*, and others have brief sections dealing with Cassian's role in the christological controversy. But as we shall see, the consensus among these scholars and others is that the work is of little value and contributed nothing positive to the christological controversy.

that for the most part, Nestorius follows his teacher Theodore. Thus I will look primarily at Theodore's writings, which reveal far more clearly than those of Nestorius the relation between their common understanding of grace and their christology.

After I have dealt with the thought of Cyril and Cassian in response to Theodore and Nestorius, I will widen my scope in the conclusion of this work by briefly considering several other significant figures from the same time period: John Chrysostom and John of Antioch in the East, and Leporius, Celestine, and Leo in the West. In doing so, I will suggest that the Cyrillian way of understanding grace and christology was, in fact, reflective of the faith of virtually the entire early Church.

1.3. KEY ISSUES RELATED TO CHRISTOLOGICAL GRACE

Although I will concentrate on the fifth century, I will also introduce two issues from the earlier history of the Church that had a great impact on the development of patristic charitology and christology. Differing approaches to these issues contributed markedly to the divergence of Theodorean and Cyrillian modes of thought, and thus it will be helpful to consider briefly the progress of these ideas in the first four Christian centuries.

1.3.1. The Structure of Salvation: Three Acts or Two?

Harnack states that in the early Church, there were two competing views of sin and salvation. The first viewed redemption as a restoration of man to the original condition from which he had fallen, and the second saw salvation as an elevation of man from a primitive natural state to a higher condition.[30] I will label the first of these views a three-act scheme of salvation and the second a two-act scheme. The three-act scheme sees humanity as created (the first act) in a state of immortality and fellowship with God and views the fall (the second act) as a radical departure from the good condition in which God had originally placed Adam and Eve. Salvation (the third act) is understood primarily

[30] Harnack, *History of Dogma*, iii. 279–80. Cf. Greer, *Theodore of Mopsuestia*, 22–3.

as a restoration of people to the original condition of perfect fellowship. This way of understanding salvation, then, sees the key acts or movements as *creation*, *fall*, and *restoration*.[31] In contrast, the two-act view sees humanity's original created state (the first act) more as one of opportunity than as one of perfection. God created people with the capacity for immortality and fellowship with himself and gave them the vocation of obtaining these things. This view places less emphasis on the fall than a three-act scheme does, and it sees redemption (the second act) as the work of the incarnate Christ in leading humanity to a higher level, assisting people in fulfilling their vocation, rather than as a restoration to a previous condition. This scheme sees the key acts as *creation* and *elevation*.[32]

One can trace these different understandings of the overall structure of salvation back at least to the late second century, when (paradoxically) they both find expression in the work of Irenaeus of Lyons. Irenaeus generally seems to see sin and salvation in terms of a radical fall from a perfect condition and a restoration to that condition. In *Dem. Praed.*, he writes that the first man was immortal and would have remained so if he had kept God's commandment, but if he did not keep it, he would become mortal and dissolve into the earth (*Dem. Praed.* 14–15 [53–5]). Similarly, in Book 5 of *Adu. Haer.*, Irenaeus argues that although people belonged to God, they were unjustly taken captive by Satan, and Christ freed them from that captivity and redeemed them as his own property (*Adu. Haer.* 5.1.1 [153.16–20]). While discussing the reason for the Logos' assumption of flesh, he writes that people had perished, and since what had perished consisted of flesh and blood, he too had to take flesh and blood in order to save them (*Adu. Haer.* 5.14.2 [153.186–8]). These passages show an emphasis on the fall (a transgression, a death, and a captivity) and indicate that salvation is basically a restoration to the original condition, and thus they represent what I call a three-act view of salvation.[33]

[31] One should not take this to imply that salvation gives Christians *nothing* more than humanity possessed at creation. In this scheme, salvation is *primarily*, but *not exclusively*, a restoration. I will discuss the nuances of this point in sect. 3.1.

[32] This does not mean that in this scheme there is no view of the fall at all. I will discuss this point further in sect. 2.1.

[33] Cf. *Adu. Haer.* 3.18.2 [211.344–5], in which Irenaeus describes Christ's

On the other hand, Book 4 (in which Irenaeus defends the existence of human free will against Gnostic fatalism) contains more of a two-act portrayal of salvation. Irenaeus argues that God did not give perfection to humanity at creation, since as infants people would not have been able to receive that perfection. He views Christ's life, especially his growth from boyhood to manhood, as a way of prodding us out of our own infancy into adulthood (*Adu. Haer.* 4.38.2 [100.948–50]). Irenaeus summarizes: 'Now it was necessary that man should first be created; and having been created, should receive growth; and having received growth, should be strengthened, and having been strengthened, should abound, and having abounded, should become mature, and having become mature, should be glorified, and having been glorified, should see his Lord' (*Adu. Haer.* 4.38.3 [100.956]).[34] In these passages, Irenaeus views salvation as a progression, under Christ's guidance, from an original state of childishness and imperfection to a condition of maturity. One could argue that Irenaeus' dominant idea is that salvation is a restoration to the original condition, but when his concern is with the preservation of human freedom, he slides (probably unconsciously) into a view that emphasizes the free action of man in elevating himself to a higher condition.

Origen's thought, like that of Irenaeus, also exhibits a tension between two-act and three-act understandings of salvation. He clearly believes that the original and final conditions of rational creatures are the same; the souls began and will end as incorporeal, eternal intelligences. But he locates the original and final states outside the realm of this universe, outside history. The souls were eternally existent in a disembodied condition, and after their pre-cosmic fall, they descended into this

work as that of reconstituting (*replasmari*/*ἀναπλασθῆναι*) our nature and making us partakers of the salvation which we could not gain ourselves because we had fallen under sin. Cf. also *Adu. Haer.* 3.19.1 [211.374].

[34] In *ANFa* i. 522, Rambaut takes *conualescere* to mean 'recover' and adds in brackets 'from the disease of sin', thus suggesting a three-act scheme. But the word can be used in the sense of 'to grow strong' or 'to gain strength', as well as 'to recover' (see LewSh 461), and the Greek fragment has ἀνδρωθῆναι, 'to reach adulthood' (reflected in my translation 'become mature' in the text). Thus it is virtually certain that Irenaeus' idea here is one of progress to a new condition, not recovery of one previously held. See Brown, 'On the Necessary Imperfection of Creation', 19–20 n., for a fuller explanation.

universe that God created for them and became corporeal.[35] Accordingly, Origen argues that when these souls are born corporeally as human beings, they are already mortal, mutable, and fallen, and during the souls' lives in this physical world, their task is to rise to perfection and union with God. Commenting on the words 'image' and 'likeness' in the creation account (Gen. 1: 26–7), Origen writes:

> Now the fact that he said, *He made him in the image of God*, and was silent about the likeness, points to nothing else but this, that man received the honour of God's image in his first creation, whereas the perfection of God's likeness was reserved for him at the consummation. The purpose of this was that man should acquire it for himself by his own earnest efforts to imitate God, so that while the possibility of attaining perfection was given to him in the beginning through the honour of the image, he should in the end through the accomplishment of these works obtain for himself the perfect likeness.
>
> (*De Princ*. 3.6.1 [268.236])

Therefore, if one considers the overall picture of Origen's thought, the extra-historical and historical careers of the souls together comprise a three-act scheme of salvation: an originally perfect condition, a fall into the historical, corporeal realm, and the rise from that realm back to an eternal, incorporeal state of perfection. But if one looks at human history, at the portion of Origen's thought that concerns *this* universe, then the picture is two-act: human beings are created only in the image of God and are not yet perfected or immortal. We are then called to achieve perfection, to mount up to a higher condition, which Origen associates with the likeness of God.

Although these two strands of thought regarding the overall structure of salvation appeared in tension in the works of Irenaeus and Origen, most later writers leaned decidedly towards one or the other. Athanasius' writings contain only very few passages that might imply that he sees people as created in an imperfect condition with the goal of aspiring to a higher state.[36] His dominant idea is that humanity was created in possession of immortality (although he makes clear that we possessed this as a

[35] Origen understands the καταβολή or foundation of the cosmos to be the descent of the newly fallen souls from their previous condition to this universe (*De Princ*. 3.5.4 [268.224–6]). Cf. *De Princ*. 1.8.1 [252.220–2].

[36] e.g. *Con. Gen*. 4–5 [10–14].

gift of grace, not by nature) and fell from that state through disobedience. Salvation is thus a restoration to a condition basically like that in which we were created.[37] As we shall see, the divergence between these two understandings of salvation was of crucial significance in the development of soteriology and christology. Theodore adopted a two-act scheme of salvation inherited from one strand of Irenaean and Origenist thought, whereas Cyril followed Athanasius in emphasizing the other strand, a three-act scheme. Theodore's and Cyril's conceptions of christological grace, and thus also of the person of Christ, were closely connected to their different understandings of the structure of salvation.

1.3.2. The Personal Subject in Christ

The entire fifth-century Church confessed that Christ was a single *prosopon*, but one of the difficult questions related to the Nestorian controversy is what a given writer meant by this. In order to approach this question, I think it will be helpful to introduce two terminological distinctions. First, I will distinguish between the idea of a synthetic union of deity and humanity in Christ and that of a composite union, and second, I will differentiate between the idea of *prosopon* as a semantic subject and the idea of *prosopon* as a genuine locus of personality. By a synthetic union, I mean a union in which God the Logos added humanity to his own person, so that the one *prosopon* of Christ is the Logos himself. In this view of the incarnation, Christ is a synthesis of deity and humanity in the sense that he includes both elements, but he is not a composite because these two elements were not building blocks from which his person was constructed; his person already existed as the eternal Son. On the other hand, by a composite union, I mean either the combining of divine and human natures to create the *prosopon* of Christ, or the conjoining or uniting of two personal subjects (the Logos and the man) so that they can be called a single *prosopon*. In both of these views, the *prosopon* of the union comes into existence at the incarnation, and so that *prosopon* is a genuine composite.

The second terminological distinction has to do with whether the one *prosopon* is actually the centre of Christ's identity or

[37] e.g. *Con. Gen.* 2–3 [4–10], 8 [18–22]; *De Incar. Ver.* 3 [138–42], 5 [144–6].

whether it is simply a grammatical term, a set of words such as 'Christ', 'Lord', and 'Son' which can apply equally to the Logos and the assumed man. The modern use of the word 'person' revolves around the idea of a subject of consciousness or a psychological nerve centre, and some scholars argue that the early Church did not possess such an idea.[38] Be that as it may, patristic thinkers did have a concept of the centre of one's identity, the subject that guides one's actions, even though they did not understand this as the *ego* of modern psychology. The question in the patristic period was not where the centre of consciousness lies, but rather who acts and to whom the experiences of life happen. In the case of Christ: Who is born, God the Son, or the man Jesus? Who suffers? Who dies? These questions relate to the issue of where the personal subject of Christ is located.

However, a given patristic writer might or might not express this locus of identity with the word *prosopon*. Therefore, when a writer insists that Christ is a single person, it is important to ask where he sees the personal subject in Christ, the acting subject, to be located. If a patristic writer believes that the incarnation was brought about by the addition of humanity to the Logos' own person, then he will see the divine Logos himself as Christ's personal subject. If a writer believes that the incarnation consisted of combining divine and human natures in order to create a personal being, he will see the personal subject of Christ as some sort of divine–human composite. But if he believes that the incarnation was the conjunction or union of two personal beings, he will probably see the personal subject of Christ as the assumed man himself. In this last case, it is likely that a writer will see the *prosopon* of Christ as a composite, but this *prosopon* will be simply a grammatical or semantic subject, a term that can be used to refer to the corporate entity, the association that encompasses both the assumed man and the Logos. One might illustrate this semantic unity (with only a modicum of caricature) through the analogy of a firm composed of two partners, one of whom is never actually seen but whose influence is continually felt in all the firm's decisions. The visible partner is analogous to the man Jesus, yet the Logos is the one who stands behind

[38] Turner, *Jesus the Christ*, 61, argues that in patristic christology, 'person' was a logical idea, not a psychological concept, and the idea of consciousness played no part in it.

important decisions in the man's life, and the words 'Christ', 'Son', and 'Lord' refer to the corporate unity created by the co-operation between the two. The unity is a semantic one because the one name 'Christ' signifies the pair of partners, but the actual personal centre of Christ's being, in this understanding, is the man Jesus himself.[39]

During this study, when I use the word 'composite' to describe the christological union, I will be referring either to the idea that two natures were combined to make a personal being or to the idea that two personal beings were united or conjoined so as to be called a single *prosopon*. I will not use the word 'composite' to refer to the view that the Logos took humanity into his own person. Moreover, when I use phrases such as 'acting subject' and 'personal subject', I will be referring not to the question of what a given writer means by the one *prosopon* of Christ, but to the issue of where he sees the locus of Christ's identity to lie. I will argue that the question of this personal subject in Christ was one of the most crucial issues in the controversy. In order to help us understand the significance of this issue in the fifth century, I would like to sketch the earlier history of another concept that strongly influenced the various portrayals of the personal subject in Christ, namely the question of whether one may ascribe the human events of his life (particularly his birth, suffering, death, and resurrection) to the divine Logos.

One of the most strongly held ideas in Middle Platonic thought was that God was completely transcendent and separate from change or suffering. In fact, by the end of the second century, this sense of God's transcendence was even stronger than it had been in Plato's time, since the Demiurge/Logos began to be seen as a separate god from the One, a lesser agent who mediated between the transcendent One and the created world.[40] While many modern thinkers have criticized such a

[39] McKinion, *Words, Imagery, and the Mystery of Christ*, 103, describes a semantic or corporate unity similarly, calling it a collective unity of two constituents.

[40] Dillon, *The Middle Platonists*, 7. In the same work, 155–6, Dillon points out that the 1st-cent. philosopher Philo was the first author to call God 'unnameable', 'unutterable', and 'incomprehensible under any form'. He suggests that Philo was following Eudorus of Alexandria, under whose influence such a radically transcendent view of the One entered Greek philosophical thought.

strong view of God's transcendence, virtually no patristic theologian did so. Prompted by biblical assertions that God does not change,[41] early patristic writers almost always interpreted the ideas of God's transcendence and immutability in much the same way pagan philosophical thought did. What was open to question, however, was the relation between the Logos and the supreme God, the Father. Many patristic writers unconsciously relegated the Logos to a slightly lower status than God. As a result, in the second and third centuries there was little hesitation to ascribe change and suffering to the Logos, since he was not himself the impassible God, the Father. Thus many writers located the personal subject of Christ with the divine Logos himself.[42]

This subtle subordination of the Logos to the Father did not become apparent until Arius and his followers argued that if the Logos was involved in the sufferings of Christ, he must be a creature, rather than being of the uncreated substance of the Father. In response to this challenge, the Council of Nicaea declared that the Son was consubstantial with the Father (*ὁμοούσιος τῷ πατρί*), and Athanasius and others spent most of the fourth century insisting that the Logos could bring salvation to humanity only if he was just as fully God as the Father was. The securing of this truth solved one major problem but exposed another, that of how to explain the incarnation in a way that made clear that the Logos, like the Father, was impassible. Sullivan aptly summarizes the Arian challenge to orthodoxy in a well-known syllogism, whose major premise is that the Logos is the subject even of the human operations and sufferings of Christ. The minor premise is that whatever is predicated of the Logos must be ascribed to him according to nature. Thus the conclusion is that the nature of the Logos is limited and affected by the human operations and sufferings of Christ.[43] In order to refute this Arian logic, Athanasius and others disputed the minor premise by making a distinction between what could be

[41] e.g. Num. 23: 19–20, Mal. 3: 6, Jas. 1: 17.

[42] See Irenaeus' statement: 'We should indeed not imagine that Jesus was one and Christ another, but should know him to be one and the same' (*Adu. Haer.* 3.16.2 [211.294]). Cf. Tertullian's assertion: 'Was not God truly crucified? Since he was truly crucified, did he not truly die? Was he not truly raised, since of course he truly died?' (*De Car.* 5 [16]).

[43] Sullivan, *The Christology of Theodore*, 162.

predicated of the Logos *as God* and what could be predicated of him *as man*. Eustathius of Antioch and Diodore of Tarsus sought to attack the major premise by arguing that the man Jesus, not the Logos, was the subject of Christ's human sufferings.[44]

Athanasius' approach to the Arian challenge is evident throughout his writings. As he states the central theme of *De Incar. Ver.*, he clearly establishes that all events of Christ's life are to be predicated of the Logos: 'Although he was by nature incorporeal and was the Logos, yet through the mercy and goodness of his Father he appeared to us in a human body for our salvation' (*De Incar. Ver.* 1 [136]). This passage depicts Christ's personal subject as the Logos himself, who existed in both an incorporeal mode before the incarnation and an embodied one afterwards.[45] In *Con. Arian.* Athanasius interprets Phil. 2 in such a way that the humiliation and exaltation refer to the Logos. He died and was exalted 'as man, so that he is said to take, as man, that which he always had as God, in order that such a gift of grace might also reach to us' (*Con. Arian.* 1.42 [100a]). Through arguments such as these, Athanasius sought both to preserve the unity of substance between the Logos and the Father and to assert that the Logos was the subject of all Christ's experiences, while still insisting that the Logos did not suffer or die in his own nature; he died as man.

In contrast, Diodore's approach to the Arian challenge was to argue that the Logos was not the subject of the human events in Christ's life. If the extant fragments of his writings reflect his intent with any accuracy, Diodore clearly held to a divisive christology. He argues that the one born from Mary changed and grew in human fashion, was weary, hungered, thirsted, and was crucified, but the Logos born from the Father before eternity underwent neither change nor suffering (*Frag.* 19 [37–9]). Diodore rejects the idea that the Logos underwent two births, asserting instead that he 'was indeed born from the Father by nature, but the temple that was born from Mary was certainly made from her womb itself' (*Frag.* 22 [41]).[46] Furthermore, he

44 Ibid. Cf. Wilken, 'Tradition, Exegesis, and the Christological Controversies', 128–30; Greer, *The Captain of our Salvation*, 175.

45 Cf. *De Incar. Ver.* 18 [176], where Athanasius insists, 'The body . . . was no one else's but the Lord's.'

46 Cf. *Frag.* 28 [45].

frequently comments that it is absurd to try to reconcile the divine and human attributes of Christ as if both belonged to the same Logos: one who is eternal cannot have been born recently, one who is infinite cannot have a body, and one who is immortal cannot die.[47]

Diodore's sharp distinction between the Logos and the assumed man led to the charge that he taught a doctrine of two sons, and he responds to this charge by writing: 'So we do not say two sons of one Father, but one Son of God by nature, God the Word. Now he who is from Mary is David's by nature, but God's by grace. Moreover, we shall also concede that the two are one Son, in an irrevocable principle' (*Frag.* 30 [47]). In the next fragment he elaborates further: 'The man who is from Mary is a son by grace, but God the Word is indeed a Son by nature. That which is by grace is not by nature, and that which is by nature is not by grace. There are not two sons. Let the sonship, glory, and immortality that are by grace suffice for the body which is from us' (*Frag.* 31 [47]). These passages indicate that for Diodore, the reason there are not two sons is that the man born from Mary is not naturally a Son of God at all; he participates in the sonship and glory of the Only-Begotten. Similarly, the Logos does not actually take part in the man's human experiences; he is somehow united to the one who undergoes these. To use the terminology I established at the beginning of this section, the one *prosopon* of Christ is a grammatical subject, a way of referring to the Logos and the assumed man as a corporate unity, even though they are distinct personal entities. In contrast to the *prosopon*, the genuine personal subject of Christ (that is, the one who actually is born, suffers, and dies) is the assumed man, and the Logos is not personally involved in these events. This idea becomes startlingly apparent when Diodore argues that the Logos abandoned the body of Christ (that is, his humanity) at the time of the crucifixion. He writes, 'For the statement, *My God, my God, why have you forsaken me?* [Matt. 27: 46], not only does not belong to God the Logos, but I do not doubt that it belongs to the body, that he cried out because he was forsaken' (*Frag.* 18 [37]).

As a result, the fourth-century struggles with Arianism and

[47] e.g. *Frag.* 4 [25–7], 5 [27], 6 [27], 11 [31], 16 [33], etc.

the Church's clear acknowledgement that the Logos was equal to the Father brought to the surface the theological tension between the idea that only the Logos could save humanity and the idea that God the Logos was completely transcendent. Those who emphasized the first of these over the second insisted on the direct personal presence of the incarnate Logos in the world and made a distinction between two ways in which different events should be predicated of the Logos. On the other hand, those who stressed the second idea tended to distinguish between the Logos and the assumed man in the *prosopon* of Christ. This set the stage for a divergence between a christology that saw the Logos as the single subject of Christ and one that held that the *prosopon* of Christ was a composite but implied that the true personal subject of Christ was the assumed man himself. These different ways of responding to Arianism and of understanding the structure of salvation helped to shape the milieu in which the early fifth-century visions of grace and christology crystallized. With these ideas in mind, I will now turn to the thought of Theodore and Nestorius.

2

Christ as the Uniquely Graced Man in Theodore and Nestorius

The two ideas that I briefly surveyed in sect. 1.3 are intimately linked in the thought of Theodore of Mopsuestia and Nestorius. Both men espouse what I call a two-act salvation scheme: they see humanity's natural condition as one of mortality and imperfection and view salvation as an advance to a higher, perfect state. Furthermore, they see salvation not so much as an elevation to *divine* life but rather as progress towards perfect *human* life, and this allows them to adopt a christology that distinguishes sharply between the Logos and the assumed man. What binds this two-act salvation scheme and a divisive christology together is Theodore's and Nestorius' concept of grace, an idea driven by the belief that God gives people those gifts (power, aid, and co-operation) that they will need in order to advance from the age of mortality to that of perfection. The relation between the assumed man and the Logos is a special case of the grace by which God interacts with people in general: God the Logos gives that man the power and co-operation he needs to be our pioneer in the march to the perfect age.

Therefore, in this chapter I will attempt to set the stage for my discussion of Cyril and Cassian by examining the concept of grace that lies behind, and that one could say even *constitutes*, Theodorean/Nestorian christology. While Nestorius was the one who actually ignited the christological controversy, scholars agree that he did little to advance the thought of Theodore and that it was largely the latter's theology that lay behind the dispute,[1] and therefore I will concentrate on Theodore. I will look first at his understanding of the two ages as the basis for his

[1] e.g. Harnack, *History of Dogma*, 4.181; Prestige, *Fathers and Heretics*, 291–2; Sullivan, *The Christology of Theodore*, 288; McGuckin, 'The Christology of Nestorius', 97.

thought, and then I will examine his concept of the divine–human interaction in grace, his depiction of Christ as the supreme example of that gracious interaction, and his portrayal of Christ as a unique case of grace. I will then consider Nestorius' thought briefly in order to demonstrate his substantial agreement with his teacher. For this survey, I will rely on the dogmatic works of both writers: Theodore's *De Incar.* and *Hom. Cat.* (both written about the time he became bishop of Mopsuestia in 392), and Nestorius' letters and sermons from the time of the controversy (428–31) and his later reflections in *Lib. Her.* (completed shortly before the Council of Chalcedon in 451).[2]

2.1. THEODORE'S VISION OF THE TWO *KATASTASES*

There can be little doubt that the fundamental idea of Theodore's theology is that of the two ages, or what he calls the two *katastases*.[3] His vision of humanity's movement from the first

[2] Scholars have raised questions about the authenticity of the fragments of Theodore's *De Incar.* and certain sections of Nestorius' *Lib. Her.* Devreesse, *Essai sur Théodore*, argues that the fragments used to condemn Theodore at the Council of Constantinople in 553 were deliberately falsified, and he is followed by McKenzie, 'Annotations on the Christology of Theodore'. Sullivan, *The Christology of Theodore*, disagrees, arguing that the florilegium of Theodorean citations was compiled before 438 and that the compiler would hardly have falsified the selections when Theodoret still possessed the originals. Sullivan is followed by Galtier, 'Théodore de Mopsueste'. Sullivan's case seems to have gained general acceptance, since scholars writing on Theodore after the early 1960s have used the fragments with confidence. I will use the fragments of *De Incar.* on the grounds that they represent the strand of thought that Cyril and others heard, even if they reflect a distorted version of what Theodore actually intended. In the case of Nestorius' *Lib. Her.*, Abramowski, *Untersuchungen zum Liber Heraclidis*, argues that the entire dialogue (Nau, 5–81) is the work of a later 'Pseudo-Nestorius' and that the conclusion of the work is interpolated in several places. She is followed by Turner, 'Nestorius Reconsidered', and *CPG* (1975), 125. On the other hand, Scipioni, *Nestorio e il concilio de Efeso*, argues for the authenticity of the entire dialogue, and he is followed by Chesnut, 'The Two Prosopa'. I will cite only those sections of the work that everyone regards as authentic, in order to avoid using material that may derive from a post-Chalcedonian environment.

[3] In its intransitive use, *κατάστασις* refers to a settled, orderly condition. Christian writers use it to refer to the moral or mental condition of a person or to

katastasis (an age of mutability, corruption, and sin) to the second age (one of immutability, incorruption, and perfection) underlies his entire exposition of the Christian faith in *Hom. Cat.* Specifically, Theodore places a great deal of emphasis on the changes that will take place in believers in the future, rather than on changes that have already taken place. He assigns the new creation (2 Cor. 5: 17) to a future age, not primarily to the present:

> Death and corruption have ceased, passions and mutability have passed away. The life of the new creation has been made manifest, and we all hope to attain to it at our resurrection from the dead. For at the resurrection from the dead God will make us new instead of old, and incorruptible and immortal instead of corruptible and mortal.
> (*Hom. Cat.* 1.3 [5])

This focus on the future age also shines clearly as Theodore discusses baptism. He writes, 'It is this Church that he [Paul] calls *the body of Christ* [e.g. 1 Cor. 12: 23]; it receives communion with him symbolically in this world through the regeneration of baptism, but in the world to come, that communion will be present truly and effectively' (*Hom. Cat.* 10.17 [271]). Later Theodore explains that just as each person receives two natural births, he also receives two spiritual births. The first natural birth is from semen, which bears no resemblance to the real human being, and the second is from the woman after the person has been fashioned. He continues:

> It is in this same way that we are also generated. First we are semen in baptism, not yet generated by resurrection in the immortal nature into which we expect to be changed, and not receiving its form. But when we have been formed and fashioned in Christian conduct by faith and hope in the good things to come, and when we have awaited the time of resurrection, then according to the decree of God, we will receive from the dust a second birth and will obtain an immortal and incorruptible nature. (*Hom. Cat.* 14.28 [459–61])

Here it is apparent that for Theodore, baptism is the germ of a reality that is reserved for the future. Baptized believers do not yet possess the reality of the life that will be theirs in the future;

his state in relation to God, to a political or ecclesiastical system, to a way of life, or to a dispensation. See LSJ 913; Lampe, 720. Theodore's use of the word is closest to this last, since for him, κατάστασις refers to one or the other of two major conditions of human life, two dispensations or ages.

they have only its conception.[4] Theodore is convinced that the reality to which we aspire as Christians is primarily future, not present,[5] and as a result he sees Christian life as a journey towards that reality, towards the second *katastasis*. Virtually all scholars agree that this vision of the two ages is the foundation of Theodore's theology.[6]

While the centrality of the two-ages concept in Theodore's thought is clear, the relation of these two *katastases* to mankind's original condition is not entirely evident. In most cases, he apparently regards the first age as the natural human condition and the second (future) age as a thoroughly new, higher condition. During a discussion of baptism in the name of the three trinitarian persons, Theodore indicates the reason why the triune God is the source of the benefits of the future age: 'It is not possible that one should be the cause of our first creation and another the cause of this second formation, which is much more excellent than the first' (*Hom. Cat.* 14.14 [431]). The first (present) condition is good, since Theodore attributes creation to the Trinity without reservation, but the second is a much better condition.[7] Here, as in most of his thought, Theodore sees the movement of history from an initial state of mutability in which sin and mortality are latent, to a final, perfected condition of immutability and immortality. Seen in this way, Theodore's idea of the two ages constitutes what I call a two-act salvation scheme, and this understanding of salvation as an elevation from a lower condition to a higher one is what most scholars regard as his primary idea.[8]

However, Theodore vacillates (as Irenaeus has done previous-

[4] One should not take this to mean that Christians have no present participation *at all* in the future life of incorruption. Abramowski, 'Zur Theologie Theodors', 274, has shown (arguing against the position of de Vries, 'Der "Nestorianismus" Theodors', 120) that the type (baptism) contains the reality because it participates in that reality.

[5] Cf. *De Incar.* 7 [296]; *Hom. Cat.* 1.4 [7–9], 11.8 [297], 14.6 [413–15], 14.10 [423–5], 14.27 [457–9], all of which locate the reality of the Christian's new life in the future age.

[6] e.g. Devreesse, *Essai sur Théodore*, 89; Norris, *Manhood and Christ*, 160; Hay, 'Antiochene Exegesis and Christology', 21.

[7] Cf. *Hom. Cat.* 3.9 [65].

[8] e.g. Gross, *La Divinisation du chrétien*, 263–5, 272; Vööbus, 'The Theological Anthropology of Theodore', 117–19; Dewart, *The Theology of Grace of Theodore*, 36–7.

ly) between this view and one in which the first *katastasis* is a fallen age (a view that would be consistent with a three-act scheme of salvation). While discussing the soul's need for healing, he writes:

> Sin had first to be removed, since it was the cause of death, and then death had to be nullified along with it. But if sin were not removed, we would necessarily remain in mortality, and we would sin because of our mutability; and if we sinned, we would again be under punishment, and the power of death would consequently continue.
>
> (*Hom. Cat.* 5.10 [115])

Here Theodore indicates that people's present mortal condition is the result of sin and that the removal of sin is the atonement's primary purpose. Such a statement appears to indicate that the present (first) *katastasis* is one that followed a fall from an originally sinless condition. However, Theodore points out that if sin were not removed, we would continue to sin in our mutability, a phrase that could imply that he sees our sinfulness (and hence the first *katastasis*) as a result of the very fact that people were mutable at creation. Slightly later, Theodore continues:

> In this way the body would be freed from death and corruption. Now this could happen if Christ first made the soul immutable and delivered it from the impulses of sin, so that by acquiring immutability we became free from sin. Indeed, the abolition of sin would effect the abolition of death, because as a result of the abolition of death, our bodies could continue indissoluble and incorruptible.
>
> (*Hom. Cat.* 5.11 [117])

Here the soul's sinfulness is the result not of some act of turning away from God but of a natural mutability that makes it subject to sin. The way Christ removes sin, then, is by making the soul immutable. Thus sin is a natural part of the human constitution in the first age, and the second *katastasis* is a higher age that is free from the sin, mutability, and corruption in which humanity was created. As a result, even in this passage where Theodore seems to imply that the first age is a fallen one, he still reverts to his dominant idea that the limitations of the first age (and even the tendency to sin) are the natural result of creation.

Several scholars have noted the tension in Theodore's understanding of the two *katastases*. Devreesse argues that the apparent contradiction is the result of the fraudulent alteration of texts and that the genuinely Theodorean passages invariably see the first *katastasis* as the result of the fall, not the result of God's having created humanity mortal.[9] However, as we have seen, the idea that mortality is a part of mankind's initial condition is present not merely in the fragments of *De Incar*. but also in *Hom. Cat.* Since the latter was preserved by Theodore's followers, it is unlikely that falsification of texts could account for the tension, especially since the two-act view that Devreesse attributes to alteration of texts is the dominant view in Theodore's writings. More likely is the suggestion of Greer and Norris that the tension reflects the presence of competing strands of thought in the early Church and that both these strands surfaced in Theodore's writings.[10] Norris attempts to reconcile these competing ideas by appealing to God's foreknowledge. Since God knew that death was the fit penalty for sin and that people would sin, he created humanity mortal from the beginning, so that after man's rebellion, the just penalty would supervene. Norris concludes, 'Mortality is chronologically prior to sin; but sin is logically prior to mortality: and this is true, not merely in the case of Adam, but also in the case of his posterity, whose mortality is at once a natural inheritance from the First Man, and punishment for the sin which, after the manner of Adam, each commits for himself.'[11]

Whether or not one accepts Norris's effort to reconcile these competing ideas about sin and mortality, it should be clear that, for Theodore, the second age is a higher condition, not a return to the original created state. The idea that sin was prior to mortality rarely appears in Theodore's thought, and when it does appear, it is never more than a logical concept. It does not point to an actual *time* when humanity was sinless and immortal, and therefore there was no initially perfect condition to which salvation could restore us.[12] Even if the first age can be called a

9 Devreesse, *Essai sur Théodore*, 102–3.

10 Greer, *Theodore of Mopsuestia*, 22–5; Norris, *Manhood and Christ*, 177–8.

11 Norris, *Manhood and Christ*, 184. In developing this argument, Norris cites passages from Theodore's *Pecc. Orig.* 3 [332–3] and *Frag. Gen.* 3.17 [640c–1a], which indicate that if God had meant to create Adam immortal, he would have remained so in spite of his sin.

12 It is possible to envision a pre-temporal and pre-cosmic state of immortality, as in Origen's cosmology, but Theodore's writings betray no hint of such an idea.

fallen condition, the fall was not a historical event (not an 'act', to use the terminology I have adopted), and the current sinful state is the only condition humanity has ever known thus far. Regardless of why people were created mortal, it is clear that Theodore believes they were so created, and their task is to aspire to a higher age of immortality and spiritual perfection. Understood in this way, Theodore's vision of the two *katastases* provides the groundwork for the development of his concept of grace. The focus of his thought is the future condition, and God gives gifts to people in the present *katastasis* in order to help them attain to the second age.

2.2. THEODORE'S UNDERSTANDING OF GRACE IN THE CHRISTIAN LIFE

In the light of Theodore's emphasis on the two *katastases*, it is hardly surprising that his understanding of grace is linked closely to the second age. We have already seen that in his treatment of baptism Theodore connects the sacrament with a future reality, and during this discussion he ties divine grace to this future age as well. He explains to the candidate for baptism, 'From him you possess here the firstfruits, because you now receive symbolically the enjoyment of those future benefits. But hereafter you will receive the entire grace, and from it you will become immortal, incorruptible, impassible, and immutable' (*Hom. Cat.* 14.27 [457–9]). Here 'the entire grace' is not so much the gift of an immortal and immutable condition as it is the *means* by which Christians may gain this condition ('*from it* you will become . . .'). Theodore's desire to safeguard the free human obedience by which we attain to the second age prevents him from declaring in an unqualified way that the benefits of that age are gifts.[13] The immortality of the second age is something that we gain through our obedience to God, even though it is ultimately granted by God himself. In order to preserve the human role in progressing to the second *katastasis*, he states that grace is primarily something *by which* we attain to such a condition, rather than the gift of that condition itself.

[13] Theodore's accent on human free will is universally recognized. See Florovsky, *The Byzantine Fathers of the Fifth Century*, 208–9; Romanides, 'The Debate over Theodore's Christology', 168; Greer, *Theodore of Mopsuestia*, 25.

2.2.1. *Grace and the March to the Second* Katastasis

What then is this grace, this means of attaining to the second *katastasis*? Theodore's basic idea is that it is aid or power that God gives during the first *katastasis* to assist our efforts. Theodore likens baptism to natural birth, that gives a person the capacity to speak and act but does not grant him the reality of speech and action. Each person must develop these realities himself. He writes:

> The recipient of birth in baptism possesses in himself all the potential of the immortal and incorruptible nature and possesses all its faculties. But he is not now able to put them into action, to make them work, or to show them forth, until the moment fixed by God for us arrives, when we will rise from the dead and be given complete actuality and perfect incorruptibility, immortality, impassibility, and immutability. For here he receives through baptism the potential of the very things whose actual realization he will receive when he is no more a natural man but has become completely a spiritual man. (*Hom. Cat.* 14.10 [423])

Although Theodore does not use the word 'grace' in this passage, his treatment of baptism clearly ties his thought here to what he writes in the passage I have just discussed. Through baptism, God gives a person the potential to live the life of the second age, but he does not place one in that age directly. Rather, just as God allows one to develop the ability to speak using the natural capacities he has given, so also he allows a person to develop the life of the second age using the spiritual capacities he has given. God's gift of this power, this ability to live the life of the second *katastasis*, is grace.

While considering the Eucharist, Theodore writes that if Christians sin shamelessly, the sacrament will bring condemnation on us, but if we seek to do good works, our involuntary sins will not injure us: 'Indeed, the body and blood of our Lord, and the grace of the Holy Spirit thence given to us, give us aid in doing good works and invigorate our minds by driving away from us all our ill-considered thoughts and by suppressing sins in every way' (*Hom. Cat.* 16.34 [589]). Here Theodore links grace and divine aid. Our task is to be obedient to God and to do good works, and through the Eucharist the Holy Spirit gives us the aid we need to live in a way consistent with the second *katastasis*.[14] While discussing Jesus' promise in John 15: 26 to send the Holy Spirit to the disciples, Theodore explains what kind of aid he will give them:

> It was not the omnipresent divine nature of the Spirit that he was going to send to them; but he said this of the gift of the grace poured on them. He is also called the Paraclete, that is the 'Comforter', because he was well able to teach them what was necessary for the comfort of their souls in the numerous trials of this world. (*Hom. Cat.* 10.7 [257])

This statement makes clear that grace is not Jesus' giving the Holy Spirit himself to the disciples. Instead, grace is the gift of the Holy Spirit's aid (in the form of teaching and comfort), to the tasks God has ordained for the disciples.[15] Several modern interpreters have noticed that for Theodore, grace is the giving of gifts in this age that help people to progress to the second age, and perhaps most apt is Greer's conclusion that grace is 'the will of God that man should be given the life of the Second Age'.[16]

2.2.2. Grace as εὐδοκία

This idea of grace as divine aid or power that assists mankind, an idea gleaned from statements throughout Theodore's *Hom. Cat.*, comes into sharper focus in a long fragment from Book 7 of *De Incar*. This important discussion focuses primarily on the explanation of the christological union as one of grace or εὐδοκία, but there are several places in the passage where Theodore uses his general understanding of grace to explain the operation of grace in Christ's life. I will now consider the passage in order to show more clearly Theodore's foundational understanding of grace, and I will later return to the discussion to consider his christology.

As Theodore searches for an appropriate term to describe God's indwelling in the just generally and in Christ specifically,

[14] Cf. *De Incar.* 1.2 [291], where Theodore indicates that angels separate from sinners but come to the aid of the honourable. Cf. also *Hom. Cat.* 11.19 [321] and 16.44 [603–5], both of which assert that we will receive the benefits of the second age by grace, but which still place the emphasis on our striving to be worthy of those benefits.

[15] Cf. *De Incar.* 7 [296]. Dewart, *The Theology of Grace of Theodore*, 19–23, points out that grace consists of those gifts that the Holy Spirit gives, not the person of the Holy Spirit himself.

[16] Greer, *The Captain of our Salvation*, 195.

he rejects 'essence' (οὐσία) and 'activity' (ἐνέργεια) on the grounds that God is present with all creatures by his essence and his activity. If this were all that God meant in the scriptural promises to indwell his people, those promises would be trivial. Instead, Theodore argues that the indwelling must be by 'good pleasure' (εὐδοκία), which he defines as follows: '*Good pleasure* means that best and noblest will of God, which he exercises because he is pleased with those who strive to be dedicated to him, on account of their excellent standing in his sight' (*De Incar*. 7 [294]). Theodore cites several Old Testament passages in order to show that this is the biblical use of the word and then concludes that εὐδοκία is the means by which God distinguishes between those who are worthy of his pleasure and those who are not: 'He perfects his indwelling by good pleasure (τῇ εὐδοκίᾳ), not limiting his essence or his activity to these [whom he indwells] and remaining separate from the rest, but remaining present to all by his essence and separate from those who are unworthy by the disposition of grace (τῇ σχέσει τῆς διαθέσεως)' (*De Incar*. 7 [295]).[17] One should notice the similarity between these statements and those from *Hom. Cat*. in which Theodore describes the help that grace brings to a Christian. In those passages the believer receives grace (as power and divine aid) in conjunction with his efforts to do good works, and here a person receives εὐδοκία, as a special form of divine action in his life, when he pleases God. There is a definite connection between grace and εὐδοκία, and the latter is one of the main words by which Theodore expresses his idea of grace. For Theodore, grace is a special activity of God (distinct from his universal activity throughout creation) in the lives of those people who are worthy, those who strive to please him.

In addition to the concept of aid or power, another way

17 Scholars who have noted the centrality of this idea in Theodore's thought include Bethune-Baker, *Early History of Christian Doctrine*, 257–8; Sullivan, *The Christology of Theodore*, 245–6; Greer, *Theodore of Mopsuestia*, 56–7. Cf. Arnou, 'Nestorianisme et Néoplatonisme', 122–3, 129–31, who argues that Theodore's idea of union by will or good pleasure is strikingly similar to the description that the 3rd-cent. Neoplatonic philosopher Porphyry gives of the way the intelligibles dwell within corporeal objects. (See Porphyry's use of σχέσις, ῥοπή, and διάθεσις in *Sententiae* 3, 4, 27, 28.) Arnou points out that like Porphyry, Theodore believed that no greater kind of union could be possible without mixing deity and humanity.

Theodore expresses the action of divine grace in a person's life is through the idea of co-operation. While discussing Christ's sinlessness later in *De Incar.* 7, he draws an explicit parallel between Christ and us: just as we now have the firstfruits of the Spirit and receive his aid in avoiding sin, so also Christ received similar aid from the Spirit during his earthly life. Theodore insists that Christ pursued virtue by his own will and that he received co-operation from God in doing so. He writes that Christ 'had a great hatred for evil, and with indissoluble love he conjoined himself to the good and received the co-operation (συνέργειαν) of God the Logos in proportion to his own purpose. . . . On the one hand, he held fast to his way by his own will, while on the other this purpose was faithfully preserved in him by the co-operation of God the Logos' (*De Incar.* 7 [296]). What Theodore writes about Christ in these lines is clearly based on his understanding of the way divine grace operates in any person's life. His strong emphasis on free will makes him unwilling to assert that grace changes a person's nature or overrules his freedom. Instead, grace is God's co-operation (συνέργεια) with a person's good intentions; it is aid or power which he gives in proportion (ἀνάλογος) to that person's own desire to pursue the good. God's co-operative grace helps to preserve (διατηρεῖν) a person's good intentions without making those intentions any less his own.[18]

2.2.3. *Grace as God's Response to Foreknown Human Action*

From what I have asserted thus far, it may appear that in Theodore's view, human action is prior to God's grace and prompts God to respond by offering his help and co-operation. However, this is not accurate, at least not in a strictly chronological understanding of the word 'prior'. First of all, one should notice that the context for Theodore's co-operative understanding of grace is God's creation of mankind in the first *katastasis* (a good condition, although subject to mutability and mortality) and his offering people the possibility of aspiring to the second (an even higher, and in fact, perfect condition). God's ordering of the universe in this fashion and his provision of a means by which people can freely move towards the second age are acts of

[18] Cf. Greer, *Theodore of Mopsuestia*, 51; Dewart, *The Theology of Grace of Theodore*, 61.

grace or providence, and thus in a general sense, grace precedes all human action.

Second, one can argue that specific grace (co-operation and divine aid) is also chronologically prior to human action because God gives this grace on the basis of foreknowledge. Several times during his discussion of the Logos' indwelling of Christ, Theodore insists that the indwelling began from the assumed man's conception in Mary's womb,[19] and he explains that the basis for this indwelling from the beginning was God's foreknowledge of who Christ would be. Theodore writes that Christ had a greater than normal inclination towards noble things because of his union with the Logos, 'of which [union] he was also worthy according to the foreknowledge (*κατὰ πρόγνωσιν*) of God the Logos, who united him to himself from above' (*De Incar*. 7 [296]). Later, he writes similarly that the reason Christ could fulfil virtue more easily than other people was that 'God the Logos, according to his foreknowledge of the sort of person one will be (*ὁμοῖός τις ἔσται*), had united him [Christ] with himself at the moment of his conception and furnished him with a greater co-operation (*μείζονα συνέργειαν*) for everything that concerned him' (*De Incar*. 7 [298]). It is apparent that Christ's union with the Logos was a special case of a pattern that also holds true among people in general. God foreknows what sort of person one will be, that is, he foreknows how a person will use the grace and co-operation God intends to give him; and on the basis of this foreknowledge God gives his grace to the person. Clearly, the chronological priority lies with grace, but one can legitimately argue that in terms of logical priority, human action elicits God's grace.[20] Throughout *De Incar*. 7, Theodore stresses that God indwells those who are worthy and strive to please him. Divine grace does not diminish the significance of free human action, but rather works with it by strengthening and aiding our resolve to seek the good. Even though this grace is given prior to any action on the part of a person, it is still God's response to the action that he foreknows.[21]

[19] See *De Incar*. 7 [296–8].

[20] Cf. Greer, 'The Analogy of Grace', 94–5.

[21] Romanides, 'The Debate over Theodore's Christology', 168, argues that according to Theodore, only by linking grace to foreknown merit can one preserve both divine and human freedom.

In summary, Theodore's understanding of grace is based firmly on his idea of human progress from the first to the second age and on his strong belief in human free will. God provides the general context of grace by creating us and showing us the pathway to the second age, and he gives specific grace in the form of aid, power, and co-operation to those who he foreknows will use this grace well and thereby become pleasing to him.[22] Theodore believes that grace is some*thing* that God gives humanity; it is not God's giving *himself* to people.

2.3. CHRIST AS THE SUPREME EXAMPLE OF GRACE IN THEODORE'S THOUGHT

One can regard Theodore's christology as, to a large degree, an extension of his general understanding of grace. His emphasis on the human task of aspiring to the second *katastasis* and his view of grace as God's co-operation lead Theodore to a christology that stresses Christ's humanity and thus makes a clear distinction between the deity and the humanity (the assumed man). This distinction allows him to view the life of the assumed man as a life under the grace of the Logos: God knows that the man will use grace well, and in response to the man's foreseen virtue, God gives him co-operation and help. In this way, Christ is the supreme example of the interaction between God's grace and free human action.

2.3.1. Grace and Theodore's Divisive Christology

Like Diodore before him, Theodore distinguishes sharply between divine and human in Christ, and a large part of his reason for doing this is the desire to make clear that the Logos did not suffer or die. It is important to notice, though, that Theodore's concept of grace is what permits him to make such a distinction. Because he understands grace as God's giving us his aid, power, and co-operation, rather than as God's giving himself to us, his soteriology does not demand a direct personal

22 Greer, 'The Analogy of Grace', 88–92, points out that Origen first worked out this understanding of general providence and God's specific co-operative grace and that Gregory of Nyssa developed these ideas into a synergism in which God comes to the aid of human action. Theodore's understanding of grace follows this tradition very closely.

presence of God in the world. As a result, Theodore's concern for God's immutability rises to prominence and shapes the language he uses to describe Christ. During a discussion of the entrance of the Firstborn into the world in Heb. 1: 5, Theodore writes: 'Who is the one who is brought into the world and begins his reign, on account of which he receives for himself the angels' worship? For no one could be so insane as to say that the one brought in is God the Logos, who by his ineffable power made all things from nothing, giving them their existence' (*De Incar.* 12.5 [305]). Similarly, while commenting on Christ's death Theodore quotes Heb. 2: 9 and explains that the writer says Christ died apart from God[23] 'in order to indicate that in the trial of death the deity was separate from the sufferer—because it was impossible for deity to taste the trial of death—and yet in providential care the deity was not far from him, but being very near, deity accomplished what rightly befits the nature of the assumed' (*Hom. Cat.* 8.9 [199]). These two passages show the strength of Theodore's assumption that the Logos could not enter into the human experiences of Christ's life. Especially noteworthy is the fact that in the second citation, Theodore apparently equates the divine nature with the person of the Logos. He is either unaware of or does not accept Athanasius' distinction between the Logos' suffering as a man and his suffering in his own nature. For Theodore, the 'fact' that the divine nature cannot suffer means that the Logos must have been distinct from the man who did suffer and die.[24]

Because Theodore's idea of grace and salvation allows his concern for the immutability of God to determine his christology, he distinguishes sharply between the Logos and the assumed man on virtually every page of his christological writings. For example, Theodore interprets the Creed by arguing that the Nicene Fathers began with names appropriate to both natures and then made statements about one or the other (*Hom. Cat.* 3.6 [61]). He explains Phil. 2: 5–11 by insisting (as Nestorius will later do) that Paul begins with the name 'Christ'

[23] Theodore's text reads 'apart from God' (χωρὶς θεοῦ), rather than 'by the grace of God (χάριτι θεοῦ).

[24] Cf. *Hom. Cat.* 5.9 [111–13]. Many scholars have pointed out Theodore's emphasis on God's transcendence, e.g. Harnack, *History of Dogma*, iv. 166; Meyendorff, *Christ in Eastern Christian Thought*, 209–10.

in order to indicate both natures, and then he distinguishes between the form of God (the Logos) and the form of a servant (the assumed man) (*Hom. Cat.* 6.5–6 [139–41]). Even more striking is Theodore's discussion of Christ's second coming: he argues that only the divinity will come 'again', since only the divinity came from heaven at the incarnation. The man was created on earth and taken to heaven for the first time at the ascension, and he will come to earth for the first time at the 'second' advent (*Hom. Cat.* 7.14 [183–5]).[25]

2.3.2. The Assumed Man's Life under Grace

We have seen Theodore's emphasis on the way grace co-operates with free human nature, rather than overruling it, and his stress on the human role in attaining to the second age. Both of these emphases are present not only in his treatment of people in general, but also when he discusses the humanity of Christ. In *De Incar.* 2, he writes, 'The man Jesus is similar to all other men, differing from natural men in nothing except that he [the Logos] has given him grace, for the grace that has been given does not change the nature' (*De Incar.* 2 [291]). And in Book 15 Theodore asserts that if Christ had not had a human soul and the Logos had been the one who vanquished the passions of the flesh, none of Christ's accomplishments would have brought any gain to us; they would have been simply an ostentatious divine show (*De Incar.* 15.3 [311]). Jesus' free human obedience was not obstructed by divine grace or his conjunction with the Logos, and in fact, if it had been, then his life could not have been salvific for us. In making these points, Theodore treats the humanity of Jesus as if it were an independent man by calling that humanity 'the man Jesus', and in fact, his understanding of grace and the human aspect of salvation virtually necessitates such a view of the assumed man.[26]

Theodore's emphasis on the assumed man as an independent subject is so strong that even in passages where he discusses the

[25] Among the many other passages that draw a sharp distinction between the Logos and the assumed man, see e.g. *De Incar.* 2 [292], 8 [299], 10.1 [301], 10.3 [302], 11 [302], 12.1 [303]; *Hom. Cat.* 3.7 [61–3], 6.3 [135], 6.4 [137].

[26] McNamara, 'Theodore and the Nestorian Heresy', 269; Greer, *Theodore of Mopsuestia*, 52–3; Norris, *Manhood and Christ*, 198–200; and others argue that Theodore views the assumed man as an independent subject of reference.

Logos, he seems to accentuate the man. During a discussion of salvation, Theodore writes that when the human condition was hopeless, 'our Lord God willed in his grace to rectify our circumstances. This is the reason why he assumed from us a man; and he was a scrupulous keeper of the divine laws. And because he was free of any sin, he was evidently exempt from the sentence of death' (*Hom. Cat.* 12.9 [335]). He then explains that after the man submitted to an unjust death, he was released from the penalty of death and became immortal. Theodore concludes, 'The man assumed from us had had such free access [to God] that he became an ambassador on behalf of the whole race, so that the rest of humanity might become partners with him in this special transformation' (*Hom. Cat.* 12.9 [337]). Although Theodore has begun by discussing what God has done for our salvation, the assumed man so thoroughly dominates his understanding of Christ that he moves in mid-sentence from a discussion of the Logos to a consideration of the man's work. The subject of the clause 'he assumed from us a man' is God the Logos, but throughout the rest of the passage, the subject becomes the assumed man. It is the man who submits to an unjust death, the man who achieves immortality, and the man who becomes the ambassador for humanity.

Because of his emphasis on the independence of Christ's humanity, Theodore sees the role of the Logos largely in terms of his co-operation with the actions of the assumed man. We have already seen several passages from *De Incar.* 7 that indicate that the assumed man received co-operation from the Logos as he pursued virtue, and another passage from the same section is especially illustrative. Commenting on Luke 2: 52, Theodore explains that Christ 'increased in grace by pursuing the virtue that follows from understanding and knowledge. Because of this, the grace that was his from God received assistance (προσθήκην)' (*De Incar.* 7 [297]). Here Theodore again emphasizes the assumed man, who is obviously fully human since he needs to increase in wisdom and grace, just as any other person does. The grace which he receives from God consists of assistance (προσθήκη[27]) to help him in his own efforts to gain virtue as his

[27] The basic use of προσθήκη is to indicate an appendage, something added. In its secondary sense of 'assistance', it connotes something given as a supplement to a person's own efforts. See LSJ 1514.

knowledge increases. Thus God's role in the assumed man's life parallels his action in any other person's life: he gives grace in the sense of assistance to the pursuit of virtue.[28]

One should not take this to mean that Theodore denigrates the Logos' role in the assumed man's life, as if he were 'merely' helping him. Rather, the Logos' co-operative action by grace is necessary, and there are passages in which Theodore ascribes the initiative to him. For example, during a discussion of the atonement he argues that Satan's power over people was due to the presence of sin in us, and so victory over Satan hinged on Christ's sinlessness. Theodore asserts that in order to ensure Christ's sinlessness, by which alone victory over the devil could be secured, 'the grace of God kept that man whom God put on for us free from sin' (*Hom. Cat.* 5.18 [125]).[29] Nevertheless, even when the initiative lies with the Logos, Theodore's understanding of the action of grace in the assumed man's life is a co-operative one in which God works with the man's free moral action. And as we have already seen, God gives this co-operation on the basis of his foreknowledge of how the assumed man will use grace, just as he does with other people.[30]

Because of the striking similarities between the operation of grace in the lives of people in general and in the assumed man's life, it is hardly surprising that Theodore sees that man as our leader on a journey that we also travel. He argues that Christ's life was a passage from the first *katastasis* to the second: his fulfilment of the law of Moses acquitted us of the debt of the law-giver, his baptism gave us a model of the grace of our baptism, his obedience was a perfect model of the life of the gospel, and his crucifixion and resurrection destroyed the ultimate enemy (death) and showed us the new, immortal life (*Hom. Cat.* 6.2 [133]). Theodore often repeats the idea that through this life, the assumed man became the first to be worthy of the second age and opened the way for us to reach this *katastasis* as well. During a discussion of the difference between the Logos and the assumed man, Theodore quotes Heb. 2: 10 and writes, 'You see how he

[28] Cf. McNamara, 'Theodore and the Nestorian Heresy', 175, who argues that the assumed man's merits are his own, even though he acquires them with the help of the Logos.

[29] Cf. *Hom. Cat.* 7.1 [161].

[30] See *De Incar.* 7 [296–8], cited above. Cf. Jugie, *Nestorius et la controverse nestorienne*, 146; Grillmeier, *Christ in Christian Tradition*, 437.

has clearly said that God the Logos *has perfected the assumed man* (τὸν ἀναληφθέντα ἄνθρωπον) *through sufferings*, and he [the assumed man] is the one whom he has called the *pioneer* (ἀρχηγὸν) *of salvation*, since he was the one who first became worthy of it and who established the opportunity for others' (*De Incar.* 12.2 [304]). Here he takes the biblical word ἀρχηγός to mean 'pioneer' or 'trail blazer', one who first crosses the divide between the two ages and thereby smoothes other people's passage. During a similar discussion in *Hom. Cat.* he writes that we are now waiting for the second age: 'Because we are waiting to enjoy these benefits in which Christ our Lord became our firstfruits—he whom God the Word put on, and who through the close conjunction that he had with him became worthy of so much honour and gave to us also the hope of partnership with him' (*Hom. Cat.* 7.9 [175]). In these passages, the words 'pioneer' and 'firstfruits' are essentially equivalent: both connote a person who has gone before us and in partnership with whom we can travel the same road he has walked. In both cases, Theodore specifically states that this pioneer/firstfruits is the assumed man, not the deity or Christ's composite *prosopon*.[31]

This idea of Christ the man as the trailblazer who opens the path of salvation to mankind is the central aspect of Theodore's theology, since it is here that his charitology, soteriology, and christology converge. His emphasis on salvation as the human action of attaining to the second age with the help of divine grace leads him to give prominence to the assumed man in his christology and to the actions of each Christian in soteriology. Because of his notion that grace co-operates with human nature without changing it, Theodore insists that the Logos would not have given the assumed man union with himself apart from any action on the man's part, and he asserts that God would not give us the benefits of the second age apart from our action. In both cases, Theodore's concern is with free human action which comes in the context of general providence and which elicits divine co-operative grace. As a result, one can regard Christ as a man

[31] Many interpreters have noted the importance of this idea that the assumed man is the pattern for our journey to the second age: e.g. Florovsky, *The Byzantine Fathers of the Fifth Century*, 209; Gross, *La Divinisation du chrétien*, 268–70; Norris, *Manhood and Christ*, 194–5; Dewart, *The Theology of Grace of Theodore*, 103.

whose life constitutes the greatest example of the interaction between God's grace and human action: the Logos indwells him by εὐδοκία or grace in a way that is chronologically prior to any action on the man's part but logically dependent on his efforts to progress from mortality to immortality by virtue. As Greer concludes, 'The union in Christ is the supreme instance of the co-operative operation of God's grace and man's freedom of choice properly exercised.'[32]

2.4. CHRIST AS A UNIQUE CASE OF GRACE IN THEODORE'S THOUGHT

As insightful as Theodore's depiction of Christ's solidarity with the rest of humanity is, this alone cannot constitute an adequate christology. If this were all Theodore wrote about the person of Christ, he would be unable to answer the charge levelled against him that he makes Christ nothing more than a man in whom God dwells, just as God dwells in the just generally. I will now turn to Theodore's concept of Christ's uniqueness and the role that his understanding of grace plays in that concept.

2.4.1. The Difference between Christ and Christians

Theodore is well aware of the charge that his christology makes the indwelling of the Logos in Christ little different from God's indwelling in the righteous generally, and during his long discussion of indwelling in *De Incar.* 7, he attempts to answer this objection. He writes that no one could be insane enough to think that God's indwelling in Christ was the same as that in the righteous, and he argues that in the case of Christ, God indwelt him 'as in a son'. Theodore explains:

> What does it mean to say 'as in a son (ὡς ἐν υἱῷ)'? It means that having indwelt him, he united the one assumed as a whole (ὅλον) to himself and prepared (παρασκεύασεν) him to share with himself in all the honour in which he, the indweller who is Son by nature, participates, so as to be counted one *prosopon* (συντελεῖν εἰς ἓν πρόσωπον) in virtue of the union with him and to share with him all his dominion, and in this way to accomplish everything through him, so that even the examination and judgement of everything shall be fulfilled through him and his advent. (*De Incar.* 7 [296])

[32] Greer, *Theodore of Mopsuestia*, 56.

In this passage Theodore enumerates three ways in which God's indwelling of Christ is unique, each of which calls for a brief comment. First, the Logos has united the assumed man to himself as a whole (ὅλον), rather than merely partially. Theodore does not explain what he means by this ambiguous assertion, and I will shortly look at other passages that help shed light on the distinction between complete and partial indwelling. Second, the Logos has prepared the assumed man to share in all the honour that he, as Son of God by nature, possesses. Here it is significant that Theodore does not write simply that the Logos shared his honour with the assumed man. Instead, the fact that he prepared (παρασκεύασεν) the man for such honour seems to imply that the man still had the responsibility to attain to the honour of the Logos, and God helped him to attain such a status by equipping him for it. Third, through the sharing of honour, the Logos has counted the assumed man and himself as one *prosopon*. Here we see one of the hallmarks of Theodore's (and later Nestorius') christology: God uses the assumed man to accomplish his purposes, and in turn the man shares in the honour of God the Son. That the Logos and the man both use the other's *prosopon* in a co-operative fashion implies that they can be considered a single *prosopon* (συντελεῖν εἰς ἓν πρόσωπον).

What then does Theodore mean when he distinguishes between complete and partial indwelling? In a later passage, Theodore writes of Christ:

> God the Logos recognized his virtue, and on account of his foreknowledge immediately delighted to indwell him from above at the moment of his conception, and he united him to himself by a disposition of his will, supplying him with a certain greater grace (μειζονά τινα τὴν χάριν), even as the grace given to him was distributed to all other people.
>
> (*De Incar.* 14.2 [308])

Here the difference between Christ and other people seems to be one of degree: the Logos foreknows his virtue and on the basis of this foreknowledge unites the assumed man to himself by giving him greater grace (that is, greater aid and co-operation) than he gives others. However, one should not regard this as a purely quantitative difference. Abramowski points out that in Theodore's thought, the assumed man is never the mere man that we are; whereas our nature is not in a position to enter into connection with the divine nature, his is. The assumed man alone is connected to the Logos by being worshipped and honoured jointly with him.[33]

A passage from *De Incar.* 2 helps to illumine what Theodore means by this idea that the Logos shares his honour with the assumed man. During a discussion I have already cited, he insists that the nature of the man Jesus is the same as that of all other people; the grace that God the Logos gives him does not change his nature. Immediately after this, he adds, 'But after the destruction of death, *God gave him the name above all names* [Phil. 2: 9]. The one who gave is God; the one to whom he gave is the man Jesus Christ, the firstfruits of the resurrected ones' (*De Incar.* 2 [292]). Here Theodore makes clear that the assumed man shares the Logos' honour not from the moment the indwelling begins, but only after his resurrection, after he has passed from the first to the second *katastasis* and become immortal.[34] This helps to clarify Theodore's statement that the Logos prepares the assumed man to share his honour: it is still necessary for him to attain to the second age by his obedience, and the union (which consists of grace and honour) does not change this fact. Theodore's emphasis is on the redemptive actions of the assumed man with the help of the Logos, not on God's direct action. This is why he can argue that the Logos accomplishes all things through the assumed man.

From this discussion it should be clear that Theodore's understanding of grace helps to determine his picture of both Christ's similarity to other people and his uniqueness. He is similar to us in that he, as the assumed man, is our leader in progressing to the second age through free human obedience. Yet he is unique in that he has received grace and indwelling in a complete sense: he has been fully united with God the Logos, he has received such divine co-operation and power that God can be said to have accomplished all things through him, and after his resurrection from the dead, he has received honour equal to that of God the Logos. He is both the supreme example of grace and a unique case of grace. This raises another question that is important in

[33] Abramowski, 'Zur Theologie Theodors', 293. Cf. Dewart, 'The Notion of "Person"', 206, who argues that for Theodore, the distinction between full and partial possession of co-operative grace is a distinction in kind, not merely a distinction of degree.

[34] Cf. *De Incar.* 1.1 [291], *Hom. Cat.* 7.10 [175–7].

helping to understand why Theodore's (and Nestorius') christology provoked such a strong reaction from Alexandria and Rome, that of how Christ mediates grace and divine assistance to us. Is he God, the source of grace, who mediates this grace to people through his humanity? Or is he the mediator because he, the man, has received grace from God? The answer to this question depends on another issue, that of whether Theodore understands the one *prosopon* in Christ as the *prosopon* of the Logos, the *prosopon* of the assumed man, or some sort of composite *prosopon*.

2.4.2. *The Personal Subject of Christ*

Some modern scholars (although definitely a minority) believe that in Theodore's thought, Christ's one *prosopon* (and thus his acting personal subject) is God the Logos. Galtier argues that the Logos is the *prosopon* of union, since he unites the man to himself and uses him as an instrument, and he suggests that Theodore's 'conjunction' (*συνάφεια*) is the same concept as Cyril's hypostatic union.[35] On the other hand, most commentators assert that for Theodore, the one *prosopon* is not the Logos, but an external mode of expression brought about by the Logos' giving his *prosopon* to the man.[36] In the light of Theodore's persistent stress on the independent assumed man, he does not give the impression that he sees Christ's humanity as subsisting in the *prosopon* of the Logos. In fact, it appears that in most passages, the opposite is the case: the personal subject in Christ is the man, not the Logos or a composite *prosopon*. When Theodore defends himself against the charge that Christ is a mere man, he writes about the one *prosopon* that is conveyed by the names 'Christ', 'Lord', etc. and which indicates both natures.[37] But when he is free to express his thought about Christ without this constraint, he almost invariably uses the word 'Christ' to refer to the man, not to the Logos at all.[38] One can conclude that the *prosopon* of union is

[35] Galtier, *Théodore de Mopsueste*, 176, 339–40. Cf. Sellers, *Two Ancient Christologies*, 162–3; McKenzie, 'Annotations on the Christology of Theodore', 373.

[36] Cf. Sullivan, *The Christology of Theodore*, 260–1; Kelly, *Early Christian Doctrines*, 307–9; Grillmeier, *Christ in Christian Tradition*, 433–4.

[37] e.g. *Hom. Cat.* 3.6 [61] and 6.5–6 [139–41], both cited above.

[38] e.g. *De Incar.* 2 [291], 7 [297], 12.2 [304], 15.3 [311]; *Hom. Cat.* 6.2 [133], 7.9 [175], 12.9 [335], all cited above.

primarily a grammatical subject, a semantic idiom referring to the corporate unity formed by the Logos' gracious co-operation with the assumed man. Theodore makes this clear in Book 5 of *De Incar.*, when he explains how one can say that Christ is a single person. He writes:

Let the character of the natures remain without confusion, and let the person [= *prosopon*] be acknowledged as undivided: the former by virtue of the characteristic property of the nature, since the one assumed is distinct from the one who assumes him, and the latter by virtue of the personal union, since the nature of both the one who has assumed and that of the one who has been assumed are contemplated in single name. (*De Incar.* 5 [292–3)

Here the personal union (*adunatio personae*) consists of the fact that the Logos and the assumed man share the same name (*adpellatio*). Names such as 'Son', 'Christ', and 'Lord' apply to the assumed man as well as to the Logos, even though Theodore sees the two as distinct subjects within the unity of Christ. But in spite of his insistence on the *prosopon* of union as a semantic subject expressing a corporate unity, Theodore sees the genuine personal subject in Christ as the assumed man himself, who is united to the Logos by receiving greater grace than other men and sharing uniquely in the honour of the Logos' sonship.

Therefore, Theodore's picture of Christ is that of a uniquely graced man, a man who has received such grace, co-operation, and assistance from God the Logos that he can be considered one *prosopon* with him and can share in his honour. This man was united to the Logos by virtue of the latter's foreknowledge of his virtue, and with the assistance of divine grace, he has become the first to be transformed from mortality into incorruption. Since he has been the unique recipient of God's grace, he has also become the mediator of that grace to us, as we seek to travel from the first to the second *katastasis*. In several passages Theodore indicates that since Christ has received grace, he can thus pass it on to us. He writes: 'He [Christ] is *the firstborn of all creatures* [Col. 1: 15] because all creation was renewed and transformed in the renewal he gave it by grace as a result of the renewal he himself underwent first when he was transferred to new life and was exalted above all creatures' (*Hom. Cat.* 3.9 [65]). Here grace is connected with Christ's giving us new life, and he is able to give this because he himself received it when he was exalted above all other creatures after his resurrection. Similarly, Theodore argues that the Eucharist is able to give us immortality through the anointing of the Holy Spirit, although bread does not possess this capacity itself. He continues, 'It [the bread] does not effect this by its own nature but on account of the Spirit dwelling in it, as the Lord's body also, whose figure it is, received immortality by the power of the Spirit, and although not possessing it by nature at all, gave it [this immortality] to others also' (*Hom. Cat.* 15.12 [479–81]). These two statements indicate that the grace of the second age is something that Christ himself has received, and because he has received it at his resurrection, he can give this grace to us.[39] Christ is the unique human recipient of grace who can then give this grace to other people.[40]

2.5. CONCLUSIONS ON THEODORE'S CONCEPT OF GRACE AND CHRISTOLOGY

From this consideration of grace and christology in Theodore, it should be apparent not only what he is saying, but also what he is not saying. For Theodore, grace does not consist of God's giving himself to humanity directly. Mankind does not participate by grace in God's own character or his divine life, and Theodore's writings contain essentially no evidence of an idea of deification. Furthermore, Theodore does not place much emphasis on grace as God's giving his fellowship to humanity. It is true that believers are sons of God by grace and can call God our Father,[41] and occasionally Theodore indicates that Christians have fellowship with God through the assumed man,[42] but such passages do not represent the dominant thrust of his thought.

Instead, Theodore's focus is on the movement from a lower to a higher *human* existence, not from a human to a *divine* existence or from a state of alienation from God to one of fellowship with him. For Theodore, the immortality and corruption that will characterize the second age are not so much qualities of divine life that we will share, as they are characteristics of a perfected human life, products of free human obedience to God. As a

[39] Cf. *De Incar.* 10.3 [302]; *Hom. Cat.* 5.18 [125–7], 16.12 [553].
[40] Cf. Dewart, *The Theology of Grace of Theodore*, 93.
[41] e.g. *Hom. Cat.* 5.1 [99–101], 9.18 [243–5].
[42] e.g. ibid. 9.17 [241–3].

result, he focuses on our partnership with the assumed man who has ascended to the second age, not on our association with God through the assumed man. While commenting on the Creed, Theodore asserts, 'He who was assumed for our salvation took on himself all the usual features of human beings, and he became worthy of special distinction and became the source of benefits to us through our partnership with him' (*Hom. Cat.* 6.7 [143]). Here the assumed man is the one who has ascended to the second age (the one who 'became worthy of special distinction'), and our association is primarily with him, not with God the Logos.[43]

Because Theodore understands grace as some*thing* (power or aid) that God gives people or as his co-operative action in people's lives without violating human free will, he is able to sustain a view of mediation in which Christ gives us the grace that he has himself received. If he had understood grace more in terms of God's giving mankind his divine life, or even his fellowship, it would have been more difficult for him to sustain a christology that placed so much emphasis on the assumed man as the primary subject in Christ. Had that been the case, it would have been much harder for his concept of God's transcendence to dominate his thought and to lead him to such a divisive christology. Theodore's understanding of grace is what allows his christology to take the shape it does, and in fact, his idea of grace even constitutes his christological picture of Christ as the uniquely graced man, the supreme recipient of divine grace.

As we shall see, this idea that Christ gives us grace because he has first received it himself was one of the major concepts that provoked Cyril's and Cassian's vehement responses. It was the idea of grace and the soteriological emphases, rather than the more technical questions of whether one sufficiently explained that Christ was one person and whether one began with his unity or duality, that prompted the christological controversy. Before I turn to Cyril, though, I will look briefly at Nestorius in order to show that his christology reflected Theodore's understanding of grace.

[43] Cf. ibid. 2.18 [51–3], 7.10 [175–7]. Scholars who note this include de Vries, 'Der "Nestorianismus" Theodors', 108; Greer, *Theodore of Mopsuestia*, 71–2; Dewart, *The Theology of Grace of Theodore*, 148–9.

2.6. NESTORIUS AND THE EXTENSION OF THEODORE'S THOUGHT

We have seen that modern commentators regard Nestorius' thought as essentially an extension of Theodore's, but of course, the topics to which Nestorius devotes the bulk of his attention are quite different. Most of his extant works deal with the distinction between Christ's divine and human natures and their union in the common *prosopon*. Since these are his major emphases, I will first look at these ideas and will then turn to the little that Nestorius does write about grace.

2.6.1. *God's Transcendence and a Divisive Christology*

Like his teacher, Nestorius begins from the assumption that the divine nature is radically transcendent and incompatible with human nature, and this leads him to insist that the Logos did not participate in the human events of Christ's life. While discussing the Nicene Creed, Nestorius rather condescendingly states: 'Examine what was said more closely, and you will discover that the divine chorus of the fathers did not say that the coessential deity (τὴν ὁμοούσιον θεότητα) is passible or that the deity that is coeternal with the Father has recently been born, or that the one who has raised up the destroyed temple has [himself] risen' (*Ep.* 5 [174–5]). Similarly, in his first sermon against the title *Theotokos*, Nestorius declares: 'What was formed in the womb was not in itself God. What was created by the Spirit was not in itself God. What was buried in the tomb was not in itself God. If that were the case, we should evidently be worshippers of a man and worshippers of the dead' (*Ser.* 9 [262]). Here he indicates that if God had actually undergone conception, birth, death, and burial, that would have implied that God was changed into a man and was no longer God, so therefore we would have been guilty of worshipping a man. Early in *Lib. Her.*, Nestorius argues that those who assert a single nature after the union are Arians, and he explains: 'Here they are depriving God the Word of his integrity by all the human features of the nature they ascribe to him as a result of the unity of a natural hypostasis that would lead its life and and suffer naturally in all human aspects' (*Lib. Her.* 1.2 [88]). Nestorius is scandalized by others' apparent attribution of human sufferings to the Logos, and he believes that a hypostatic union must necessarily mean that the Logos himself suffered.[44] Clearly, the desire to demonstrate the transcendence of the Logos and his separation from suffering is one of the major ideas driving Nestorius' christology.[45]

As with Theodore, so also with Nestorius, the belief that the Logos did not undergo Christ's human sufferings leads to a sharp distinction between deity and humanity in Christ. He insists that the seed of Abraham was not the one who said, 'Before Abraham was, I am' (John 8: 58) or 'The one who has seen me has seen the Father' (John 14: 9). Instead, the seed of Abraham was the one who said, 'The Spirit of the Lord is upon me, because he has anointed me to preach good news to the poor' (Luke 4: 18). Nestorius concludes bitterly, 'It is the humanity, not the deity, that is anointed, you heretic!' (*Ser.* 5 [234–5]). Elsewhere he makes a similar distinction between the natures by arguing, 'The Holy Spirit did not create God the Logos, for *what is born of her is of the Holy Spirit* [Matt. 1: 20]. But he formed from the virgin a temple for God the Logos, a temple in which he might dwell. And the incarnate God did not die, but he raised up the one in whom he was incarnate' (*Ser.* 9 [252]). In these passages, as in all of Nestorius' christological writings, the distinction between deity and humanity is so strong that they appear to be not merely different natures, but different subjects. The Logos speaks and acts in some of the events of Christ's life, and the assumed man speaks and undergoes suffering in others.[46]

This stress on the Logos' transcendence and on the consequent distinction between the natures leads Nestorius to distrust the common title *Theotokos*. His arguments against the term are of a strictly rational character, for he insists, 'The one who was born must be consubstantial with the bearer,' and 'No one gives birth to one older than herself' (*Ep.* 1 [167–8]). To Nestorius, the title *Theotokos* is frankly absurd, but he is willing to accept it as long as one balances it with *Anthropotokos*. He

[44] Among the many passages in which Nestorius stresses the Logos' impassibility, see *Ep.* 1 [166], 3 [171], 5 [178–9]; *Ser.* 5 [234], 14 [286–7]; *Lib. Her.* 1.3 [133], 1.3 [144–5].

[45] Cf. Abramowski, *Untersuchungen zum Liber Heraclidis*, 229; Hallman, 'The Seed of Fire', 390.

[46] Cf. *Ser.* 3 [227–8], 8 [248], 11 [277–8]; *Lib. Her.* 2.1 [195].

explains that one should 'call the holy virgin the bearer of God and man, for she is not the bearer of God as if God the Word had assumed the beginning of his existence from her—for if it had been so, the virgin would have been the Creator himself!' (*Ep.* 9 [191]).[47] But Nestorius' preferred term is *Christotokos*. He writes to John of Antioch, 'We have called her the bearer of Christ, so that this title might clearly signify both [realities], that is, God and man' (*Ep.* 7 [185]).[48] Nestorius favours this term because it implies that the one born of Mary is the *prosopon* of union, the one who includes both deity and humanity, although Mary herself actually produced only his humanity. This term helps to guard against the nonsensical conclusion that Christ's eternal deity came into existence in the virgin's womb.

From these citations it is clear that Nestorius' thought is guided by his understanding of the Logos' impassibility and transcendence. When he adopts a christology that makes the Logos and the assumed man into virtually independent subjects, it is because his primary concern is to assert that the Logos did not undergo birth, suffering, or death. Nestorius' concern is the same as Theodore's has been previously.

2.6.2. *The Indwelling of the Logos in the Assumed Man*

Another way in which Nestorius follows Theodore closely is that he places great emphasis on the assumed man. He insists that neither of Christ's natures needed the other; both were complete in themselves (*Lib. Her.* 2.1 [265–6]). He sometimes uses the word 'Christ' to refer to the assumed man conceived of separately from the Logos, thus showing the degree to which he sees him as an independent subject. Nestorius asserts, 'Just as Israel is called "son" and Moses is called a "god", so likewise is Christ [i.e. the assumed man] to be called "God", although he is neither by nature "God" nor by nature "Son of God"' (*Lib. Her.* 2.1 [182]). Even more strikingly, Nestorius (like Diodore before him) claims that the reason there are not two sons is that the Logos, the true Son, has conjoined the man to himself by sharing the dignity of his sonship with him. He continues, 'On account of this, God the Logos is also called "Christ", since he has a continual conjunction (συνάφειαν) with the Christ' (*Ser.* 10 [275]).

[47] Cf. *Ser.* 18 [303]. [48] Cf. *Ep.* 5 [177], 6 [181–2].

Clearly, for Nestorius the Christ is the assumed man, and only when one is speaking in an improper sense can one call the Logos 'Christ' at all. It is the assumed man who dominates Nestorius' christology.

This stress on the assumed man leads Nestorius to follow Theodore in explaining the union as an indwelling of the Logos. A passage in which Nestorius discusses John 1: 14 is illustrative: '*The Logos became flesh*, that is, assumed flesh (ἀνέλαβε σάρκα), *and dwelt among us*, that is, put on our nature (ἐνεδύσατο φύσιν) and lived among us, *and we beheld his glory*, that is the Son's. He did not say, "We beheld the birth of the Logos"' (*Ser*. 14 [287]). Here Nestorius takes the dwelling of the Logos among us to mean that he dwelt in our nature by assuming a man to himself, which is exactly the way Theodore has explained the same biblical text in *De Incar*. 9.1–2 [300]. Similarly, just after arguing that the Logos was not born from Mary, Nestorius continues, 'Since God is within the one who was assumed, the one who was assumed, after being conjoined to the one who assumed him, is called "God" (συγχρηματίζει θεός) because of the one who assumed him' (*Ser*. 9 [262]).[49] Elsewhere, Nestorius indicates that this indwelling began at the assumed man's conception by writing, 'What was consubstantial with us was filled with inseparable divinity as he was born from the virgin' (*Ep*. 9 [192]).

Not only does Nestorius describe the christological union as an assumption of the man and as an indwelling, but he also follows Theodore in arguing that the union is one of good pleasure and the sharing of honour. I have not been able to find the actual expression 'union according to good pleasure' (ἕνωσις κατ' εὐδοκίαν) in Nestorius' writings,[50] but he seems to have used the phrase, since Cyril explicitly rejects the description of the union as being 'merely according to will or good pleasure' (κατὰ θέλησιν μόνην ἢ εὐδοκίαν) in his second letter to Nestorius (*Ep*. 4 [1.1.1.26–7]). It is unlikely that Cyril would have rebutted a Theodorean formula in a letter to Nestorius in 430,[51] and thus

[49] Cf. *Lib. Her*. 1.3 [127].

[50] McGuckin, *St. Cyril of Alexandria*, 162, argues that Nestorius made 'conjunction by good pleasure' his major technical term for describing the manner of the incarnation. But in support of this contention he cites *Lib. Her*. 1.1.58 [52], a passage that is from the disputed dialogue and that describes the union as one of love, without using the word εὐδοκία itself.

[51] Parvis, 'The *Commentary on Hebrews*', 417–18, shows that Cyril was

it seems probable that he saw the phrase in Nestorius' own writings. Furthermore, Prestige suggests that in *Lib. Her.*, 'voluntary union' is equivalent to Theodore's ἕνωσις κατ' εὐδοκίαν and may even be a translation of that Greek phrase.[52] But even if Nestorius did not actually use the phrase itself, he certainly saw the union in a way similar to Theodore, since he speaks repeatedly of the Logos' sharing his honour with the assumed man. He writes, 'Therefore, we preserve the unconfused conjunction (ἀσύγχυτον συνάφειαν) of the natures. We confess God in a man; we worship the man who is venerated together with almighty God by virtue of the divine conjunction (τῇ θείᾳ συναφείᾳ)' (*Ser.* 8 [249]). And in a famous passage from his first sermon against the title *Theotokos*, he asserts: 'I adore the one who is borne because of the one who bears him, and I worship the one who appears because of the one who is hidden. God is undivided (ἀχώριστος) from the one who appears, and therefore I do not divide the honour of what is not divided. I divide the natures, but I unite the worship (χωρίζω τὰς φύσεις, ἀλλ' ἑνῶ τὴν προσκύνησιν)' (*Ser.* 9 [262]).[53] Nestorius, like Theodore, sees the assumed man as the recipient of the Logos' honour in such a way that the two can be worshipped and adored together as a single Son.

2.6.3. *The* Prosopon *of Union and the Single Subject in Christ*

Nestorius devotes much attention to the idea of prosopic union, and in *Lib. Her.* he explains the incarnation as an exchange of *prosopa* whereby the Logos and the assumed man each use the other's *prosopon*.[54] This highly technical language raises two important questions: Is the *prosopon* of union the Logos, the man, or a composite? Also, is the *prosopon* of union really the personal centre of Christ's being? In his second letter to Celestine, Nestorius complains that his opponents 'dare to pour

already collecting materials for his battle against Theodore by 432, and perhaps as early as 428. However, it seems unlikely that he would have turned his attention to Theodore before Ephesus, so one can assume that even if Cyril did possess a Theodorean florilegium at this point, he would still have concentrated on Nestorius' terminology, not Theodore's.

52 Prestige, *Fathers and Heretics*, 292.

53 Cf. *Ep.* 3 [171], 9 [191]; *Lib. Her.* 2.1 [276].

54 e.g. *Lib. Her.* 1.3 [127], 1.3 [137], 1.3 [147], 2.1 [167], 2.1 [195], 2.1 [233], etc.

out bodily passions onto the deity of the Only-Begotten, and they devise to translate the immutability of the deity into the nature of a body, and by a change resulting from mixing, they confuse the two natures which should be adored whole and unconfused, united through a conjunction in the one person of the Only-Begotten' (*Ep.* 3 [171]). Here the expression 'conjunction in the one person of the Only-Begotten' could give the impression that Nestorius sees the union as taking place in the person of the Logos, and some scholars argue that this is, in fact, what Nestorius means.[55] However, it is important to remember that for Nestorius, the term 'Only-Begotten' does not denote the simple Logos, as the word does when used by other writers. Rather, Nestorius uses this word, like the titles 'Son', 'Lord', and 'Christ', to refer to both the man and the Logos.[56] While interpreting the Creed, he quotes the assertion of faith in the Lord Jesus Christ, the only-begotten Son of God, and he explains: 'Observe how they first of all establish, as foundations, the titles "Lord", "Jesus", "Christ", "Only-Begotten", and "Son", which are common to the deity and the humanity. Then they build on them the teaching about his becoming man, his passion, and his resurrection' (*Ep.* 5 [175]). Here, as elsewhere, Nestorius indicates that the single *prosopon* of Christ is a semantic entity, a way of referring to the co-operative unity between the Logos and the assumed man by using titles that apply to both.[57] One cannot conclude that he sees the single personal subject in Christ as being the Logos.[58]

In fact, not only does Nestorius refuse to say that the personal subject of Christ is the Logos, but he also indicates that this issue is the central difference between Cyril and himself. In *Lib. Her.* he interprets the Creed in the same way he has done previously and then adds:

I said and affirmed that the unity is in Christ's one *prosopon*, and I indicated by every possible means that God the Word was made man and is

[55] e.g. Bethune-Baker, *Nestorius and his Teaching*, 98; Abramowski, *Untersuchungen zum Liber Heraclidis*, 186.

[56] McGuckin, *St. Cyril of Alexandria*, 152, notes this.

[57] Cf. *Ep.* 11 [196]; *Ser.* 9 [254], 10 [269]; *Lib. Her.* 2.1 [185], 2.1 [207].

[58] Grillmeier, *Christ in Christian Tradition*, 453, argues that if Nestorius' statements at Ephesus are really ontological, then the *prosopon* of union is merely an additive subject, the sum of the properties of both natures, not a real personal subject at all. Cf. Kelly, *Ancient Christian Doctrines*, 316.

also God the Word in the humanity in which Christ was made man. And this is why, when the fathers taught us what Christ—about whom they were in dispute—is, they established first those elements Christ is from. But you, on the contrary, leave them [the two natures] out of account as superfluous and work to effect a dissolution [of them], because you intend God the Word to be the *prosopon of union* in the two natures. (*Lib. Her*. 1.3 [127])

This important passage shows that the issue in dispute between Nestorius and Cyril was not whether to describe Christ as having one nature or two, since Nestorius admits that Cyril as well sees two realities in Christ. The central issue was whether the personal subject of Christ was the Logos. Nestorius correctly understands that Cyril affirms this, but even at the end of his life, Nestorius himself does not do so. Since the *prosopon* of union is largely a grammatical subject, and since Nestorius places a great deal of emphasis on the independence of the assumed man in his portrayal of Christ, it seems that if he has a concept of the personal subject of Christ at all, he sees that personal subject as the man himself, the one in whom the Logos dwells.

2.6.4. *Grace and Christology in Nestorius' Thought*

It should be clear that Nestorius' christology follows the same pattern as Theodore's. In addition, what little he does write about grace gives warrant for assuming that the soteriological concerns behind his picture of Christ are also those of Theodore. These concerns surface most clearly in the first sermon against the title *Theotokos*, which I have already cited several times. Part of the reason for the distinction Nestorius makes in that sermon between the natures of Christ is that he sees the assumed man as the one who accomplishes our redemption. He points out that only a man could repay Adam's debt: 'It was necessary for the one who dissolved the debt to come from the same race as the one who had once contracted it. The debt came from a woman, and the remission came from a woman' (*Ser*. 9 [256]). Slightly later, Nestorius adopts the voice of humanity pleading with God for forgiveness:

You have been angry at me on account of Adam's transgression. I beseech you on his behalf to be favourable, if indeed you have conjoined to yourself an Adam who is without sin. So be it that on account of the former [Adam] you have handed me over to corruption. On account of the latter [the Adam without sin], make me partake of incorruption. Both of them have my nature. As I shared in the death of the former, so I shall become a participant in the immortal life of the latter.

(*Ser.* 9 [257])

One should note here that Nestorius places the same stress on the two ages as Theodore does. He sees mankind as currently partaking in Adam's mortality and corruption (the first age) and as participating in incorruption in the future (the second age). Notice also that the assumed man is the 'Adam who is without sin' who is united to the Logos, and this man, not the Logos himself, is the agent of redemption. It is the assumed man's incorruption and immortality that Christians will receive in the future, not the incorruption of God the Logos himself. Still later in the sermon, Nestorius argues that the reason Christ's intercession on our behalf is effective is that he possesses our nature:

Our nature, having been put on by Christ like a garment, intervenes on our behalf, being entirely free from all sin and contending by appeal to its blameless origin, just as the one who was formed earlier [Adam] brought punishment upon his race on account of his sin. This was the opportunity that belonged to the assumed man, as a man to dissolve by means of the flesh that corruption that arose by means of the flesh.

(*Ser.* 9 [258–9])

Here we see that 'our nature' is equivalent to 'the assumed man': it is the man who has the opportunity to undo by his sinlessness the corruption that has come upon us through Adam's sin. In this passage, as throughout the sermon, it is the assumed man who is the agent of redemption, the one who leads us to the age of incorruption.[59]

In *Lib. Her.* Nestorius also emphasizes the role of the assumed man in redemption by arguing that we associate with that man in his triumph. The man has taken part in our death so that we can participate in the name above all names, a name that he has been given by the grace of the Logos after his resurrection (*Lib. Her.* 1.3 [151]). It is important to note that what the assumed man receives from the Logos, he passes on to us. For Nestorius, as for Theodore, Christ is the mediator of grace because he has received it at his resurrection. Similarly, Nestorius later writes of the assumed man: 'He preserves obedience without sin because

[59] Cf. Prestige, *Fathers and Heretics*, 304; Greer, *The Captain of our Salvation*, 311.

of his supreme obedience, and because of this he was delivered from death for the salvation of all the world' (*Lib. Her.* 1.3 [161]). Here the man's obedience results in his own deliverance from death, and Nestorius links this deliverance to our salvation, our deliverance from corruption. He does not state whether this link consists primarily of our following the assumed man's obedience and thus obtaining deliverance from death or of the man's giving us this deliverance that he has won by his own resurrection.[60] But in spite of this ambiguity regarding the way Nestorius sees redemption as being effected, it is clear that the one who brings it about is the assumed man.

Nestorius gives little indication of whether he understands grace specifically as divine aid in the process of attaining to the second age and whether he views Christ as the supreme example of the interaction of grace and human freedom. Nevertheless, one should not assume that his silence about these issues results from a lack of concern for them. It is more likely, as Greer argues, that the reason Nestorius devoted so much attention to technical christological issues was that he had been forced to do battle on Alexandrian terms. The broader concerns of his thought (which would have helped one to understand his christology) have been lost.[61] It is very likely that if we could recover these broader concerns, we would find them to resemble those of Theodore. The similarity of Nestorius' starting point to that of Theodore, the congruence between what he does write about salvation and Theodore's idea of the two ages, and the consistency of his technical christology with Theodore's all suggest that Nestorius was operating from the same basic understanding of grace. In fact, the evidence we do have is sufficient that Turner can conclude confidently of Nestorius: 'If Christ was to be our "athlete" and the redemption which he brought was to speak to our condition, his victory must be his own with the assistance of the grace of God which is also available to us, and not an act of God the Logos.'[62] This assessment of Nestorius could easily pass verbatim as a summary of Theodore's thought.

60 Most scholars see Nestorius as emphasizing the former of these, the role of the assumed man in leading us to victory over death and to the second age: e.g. Bethune-Baker, *Nestorius and his Teaching*, 139; Loofs, *Nestorius and His Place*, 93–4; McGuckin, *St. Cyril of Alexandria*, 167.

61 Greer, *The Captain of our Salvation*, 313.

62 Turner, *Jesus the Christ*, 39.

Therefore, we have good reason to think that the christology that Nestorius brought to Constantinople in 428 was, at least in its general form, Theodore's christology of the uniquely graced man, the greatest recipient of grace, and thus the one who could mediate that grace to humanity. This understanding of grace and salvation did not require a direct personal presence of God in the world, and thus it allowed Nestorius' concern for the impassibility of the Logos to lead him, like Theodore, to a divisive christology. With this background in mind, I will now turn to Egypt, where a very different understanding of grace was maturing at the beginning of the fifth century.

3
Grace as the Sharing of Divine Communion in Cyril's Early Writings

The concept of grace that lies at the heart of Cyril of Alexandria's christology stands in marked contrast to that of Theodore and Nestorius. Rather than viewing grace as God's giving power, assistance, and co-operation to help people progress towards the second *katastasis*, Cyril understands it primarily as God's giving himself to humanity, and a dominant (perhaps *the* dominant) theme of his thought is the idea that we become gods and sons of God by grace. Ps. 82: 6 (81: 6 in LXX) and 2 Pet. 1: 4 loom large in his writings,[1] and Cyril sees salvation as deification. However, to say that human beings become gods and partake of the divine nature raises the urgent question of what it means for God to give us himself. In this chapter and the next, I will examine this question and its implications for Cyril's christology.

I will begin by looking at the structure of Cyril's soteriology, that is, his understanding of salvation largely as a restoration to the condition in which humanity was originally created. I will then consider various aspects of divine life that Cyril believes God shares with us as he gives himself to us. After discussing these relatively clear aspects of Cyril's thought, I will spend most of this chapter examining what he means by divine sonship, which is the heart of his idea of grace and the primary gift that God gives us in salvation. In doing this, I will use those writings that predate the outbreak of the Nestorian controversy, and then in Ch. 4 I will turn to Cyril's writings from the controversy itself, in order to demonstrate the close connection between his idea of

[1] e.g. *Trin. Dial.* 7 [246.166], where Cyril refers directly to both these biblical texts as he discusses the sense in which Christians can be said to be gods. Cf. *Com. Johan.* 1.9 [1.133]; *Trin. Dial.* 3 [237.82].

grace as God's giving himself to humanity and his understanding of Christ's unity.[2]

3.1. SALVATION AS A RESTORATION TO HUMANITY'S ORIGINAL CONDITION

We saw in sect. 1.3.1 that the writings of Irenaeus and Origen show a tension between the idea of salvation as a return to the original created condition (a three-act salvation scheme) and as an elevation to a completely new condition (a two-act scheme). In Athanasius there is little such tension; he regards salvation

[2] Scholars agree that all Cyril's exegetical and anti-Arian writings that survive more or less intact predate the controversy, although they do not agree on the order in which these books were written. Jouassard, 'L'Activité littéraire de Cyrille', 170, argues that Cyril wrote all the OT commentaries prior to 423, *Thes.* and *Trin. Dial.* between 423 and 425, and *Com. Johan.* beginning in 425. Charlier, 'Le "Thesaurus" de Cyrille', 64, believes the three anti-Arian writings were the earliest of Cyril's works and were followed by the exegetical writings. Liébaert, *La Doctrine christologique de Cyrille*, 16, concludes that one simply cannot be certain of the order of these early writings. For the purposes of this study, the sequence of Cyril's early writings is of no consequence, since I will not attempt to delineate a progression in his thought from one period of his career to another. The only chronological question that is of importance for my portrayal is that of which writings came before the Nestorian controversy and which came during and after that controversy. On this question, the only work about which there is dispute is *De Incar. Vnigen.* Many scholars (e.g. Pusey, *Cyrilli De recta fide*, p. vii; Mahé, 'Cyrille', 2490) regard *De Incar. Vnigen.* as a second edition of *De Fide Theod.*, addressed to the general public rather than to Theodosius alone. However, de Durand, *Cyrille: Deux dialogues christologiques*, 44–5, argues that the few differences between the two works can be explained better with the assumption that *De Incar. Vnigen.* was written earlier. For example, there are several places where *De Incar. Vnigen.* has ἄνθρωπος when *De Fide Theod.* has σάρξ or ἀνθρωπότης (cf. *De Incar. Vnigen.* [220.18] and *De Fide Theod.* 16 [1.1.1.52.15]; also *De Incar. Vnigen.* [226.16] and *De Fide Theod.* 18 [1.1.1.53.25]), variations that seem to represent Cyril's desire in the latter work to avoid writing anything that could imply that the humanity of Christ is an independent man. Furthermore, de Durand points out (52–3) that in *Ep.* 2 [1.1.1.24–5], Cyril claims that he has written a book on the Trinity in which there is a discourse on the incarnation consistent with what he is teaching now. This reference could be to the sixth dialogue of *Trin. Dial.* (as Pusey, *Cyrilli De recta fide*, pp. viii–ix, avers), but de Durand argues that it is more likely to be to *De Incar. Vnigen.* itself, which would then be a supplement to *Trin. Dial.* and would date from *c.*425. Following de Durand, I will include *De Incar. Vnigen.* in my discussion of Cyril's early writings, although if one were to place this work later, it would not affect my argument.

as essentially a restoration to the created condition, and the only major difference between the two states is that at creation Adam possessed incorruption in an unstable way, but in Christ believers receive incorruption in a way that is stable and cannot be lost.[3] In his general understanding of salvation, Cyril follows in the footsteps of his Alexandrian predecessor.

One of Cyril's clearest discussions of the idea that salvation is a return to the original condition comes as he comments on John 17: 18–19. He explains Jesus' prayer by asserting, 'From the Father he sought for us the holiness (*ἁγιασμὸν*) that is in and through the Spirit, and he desires what was in us by the gift of God at the first age of the world and the beginning of creation to be rekindled to life (*ἀναζωπυρεῖσθαι*) in us again' (*Com. Johan.* 11.10 [2.719]). He explains that at creation, God gave life to Adam by breathing his Spirit into him, and he continues: 'He desires, therefore, the nature of man to be renewed (*ἀνανεοῦσθαι*) and moulded anew (*ἀναπλάττεσθαί*), as it were, into its original likeness, by communion with the Spirit, in order that, by putting on that original grace and being re-shaped (*ἀνακομισάμενοι*) into conformity with him, we may be found able to prevail over the sin that reigns in this world' (*Com. Johan.* 11.10 [2.720]). There are two things in this passage that one should note. First, Cyril makes clear that holiness (*ἁγιασμός*) is not a natural characteristic of humanity, but nevertheless, it was man's possession at creation, since God breathed the Holy Spirit into Adam when he formed him. People are not holy in and of ourselves, but God gave us holiness at creation as a gift. Cyril refers to this initial participation in the Spirit as humanity's 'original likeness' and 'original grace': God gave himself to us at creation through his Spirit, thus fashioning our initial image after his own image. Second, Christ's desire for us is that we return to that initial condition of holiness. Cyril uses the word 'again' (*πάλιν*) and four verbs beginning with the prefix *ἀνα-* in order to show that salvation is a return to the participation in the Holy Spirit that he gave us previously. Holiness is *again re*kindled (*ἀναζωπυρέομαι*) to life in us; our nature is *re*newed (*ἀνανέομαι*) and *re*-formed (*ἀναπλάττομαι*) into its prior image; we are *re*-shaped (*ἀνακομίζομαι*) into conformity with God.

[3] e.g. *De Incar. Ver.* 3–5 [140–6], 7 [150]; *Con. Arian.* 2.68 [292c–3a].

Later, Cyril discusses Jesus' breathing on his disciples and commanding them to receive the Holy Spirit (John 20: 22–3): 'Just as at the beginning, man was formed and came into being, so likewise is he renewed (ἀνακαινίζεται); and as he was then formed in the image of his Creator, so likewise now, by participation in the Spirit, is he transformed into the likeness of his Maker' (*Com. Johan.* 12.1 [3.135]). Here again, Cyril draws an unmistakable parallel between our original formation in the image of God and our transformation into that impress. Both the forming and the re-forming take place through God's giving us participation in his Spirit.[4] Cyril's discussions of John 17: 18–19 and 20: 22–3 are illustrative of his consistent pattern for interpreting creation and redemption. At creation, God did not simply call people to participation in himself; he gave such participation through the gift of the Holy Spirit. Salvation restores human nature to this original participation.[5]

However, to say that salvation is a return to the original created condition does not mean that the two states are completely identical. Like Athanasius,[6] Cyril stresses the instability of Adam's participation in the Spirit and the fact that mankind lost that participation through the fall. When Christ restores this participation to the human race through redemption, we possess the Holy Spirit in a stable, secure way. As Cyril explains the outpouring of the Spirit on humanity (Joel 2: 28–9), he expresses this idea transparently by contrasting Christ's reception of the Spirit with Adam's:

As I said, when the Only-Begotten, *being rich, became poor* [2 Cor. 8: 9]

[4] Boulnois, 'Le Souffle et l'Esprit', 3–30, points out that most early Christian writers understood Gen. 2: 7 to refer to God's giving Adam a human soul, although a few joined Cyril in interpreting the passage to refer to God's giving the Holy Spirit himself to Adam. Boulnois comments that Cyril refers to this passage in at least 17 places and 9 times links it to Jesus' breathing the Holy Spirit into the disciples in John 20: 22. Clearly, he sees a close similarity between the created and redeemed states.

[5] Among the many other examples of Cyril's three-act understanding of salvation, see *Ep. Pasch.* 2.8 [372.230], 8.6 [392.110], 10.1 [392.192]; *Thes.* 32 [561b–d]; *Trin. Dial.* 7 [246.206]; *Com. Johan.* 1.9 [1.133], 2.1 [1.184], 9.1 [2.485–6], 11.10 [2.726]. Among writings during and after the Nestorian controversy, cf. *Con. Nes.* 4.3 [1.1.6.83]; *Schol.* 1 [1.5.219–20/1.5.184]; *De Dog. Sol.* 2 [190–2], 3 [194]; *Con. Theo.* 1.3 [3.512].

[6] See *Con. Arian.* 2.68 [292c–3a].

and received his own Spirit (τὸ ἴδιον Πνεῦμα) with us as man, as if from the outside (ὡς ἐπακτὸν), *he remained on him*. For such the blessed John the evangelist said [John 1: 32]. This happened in order that he might also dwell permanently in us, as he had already remained in the one who was the second firstfruits of our race, that is, Christ. For on account of this he is even named the second Adam, through whom we have mounted up to an incomparably better condition (τὸ ἀσυγκρίτως ἄμεινον) and we gain a better birth (ἀναγέννησιν εὖ μάλα) from above through the Spirit, whom we do not possess as we did at first, that is to say according to the flesh, leading to corruption and sin.

(*Com. Joel* 2 [1.338])

Here Cyril establishes a close connection between the permanence of Christ's possession of the Spirit and the permanence of our own reception of him. Even though Christ receives the Spirit 'as if from the outside' (ὡς ἐπακτόν), he possesses him in a stable way because he is the Only-Begotten and so the Spirit is his own Spirit. But because he receives the Spirit as man, he secures the possession of the Spirit for our human nature as well as his, and so the Holy Spirit remains in us in a stable way. Since redemption gives humanity participation in the Holy Spirit in Christ (who is God as well as the second Adam), our redeemed condition is permanent and stable, unlike Adam's unstable condition. Cyril can thus refer to this new condition as 'incomparably better' and as a 'better birth'.

In a similar passage from Cyril's festal letter for 428, he writes:

Therefore, since our condition had been made wretched, it was necessary for God the Father to send the Son himself, in order to transform our condition into one incomparably better (τὸ ἀσυγκρίτως ἄμεινον) than that of old and to rescue us who were on the earth, evidently by freeing us from sin and by destroying both sin's own root and that death which had sprung from it, and by delivering us from the tyranny of the devil over us. (*Ep. Pasch.* 16.6 [765b–c])

On the basis of the expression 'incomparably better position' (τὸ ἀσυγκρίτως ἄμεινον) in this passage and the previous one, Janssens argues that for Cyril, our condition is far superior to that of Adam, since we possess a stability he did not have.[7] However, Burghardt replies that the contrast Cyril draws is between the fallen condition and the saved condition, not

[7] Janssens, 'Notre filiation divine', 257. Cf. Wilken, *Judaism and the Early Christian Mind*, 117–18; Boulnois, 'Le Souffle et l'Esprit', 35.

between Adam's original state and the redeemed condition.[8] Burghardt is certainly right in the case of this passage, but the text quoted in the previous paragraph uses the same expression to show that the saved condition is far better than Adam's created condition because that state was unstable and led to sin and corruption.

One should not allow this disagreement about the degree of difference between our redeemed condition and Adam's original state to obscure the main thrust of Cyril's thought. What is the same about the two states is that humanity receives participation in the Holy Spirit as grace, and from this gift flow holiness, incorruption, and immortality. What is different is that in Adam's case, the gift was unstable and could be lost; in the case of humanity redeemed in Christ, the gift is stable. Because of this stability, one can say that the saved condition is better than Adam's original condition, but nevertheless, there is a great similarity between humanity before the fall and humanity in the second Adam. In fact, both Janssens and Burghardt agree on this,[9] and this is the consensus of virtually all scholars.[10] For Cyril, salvation is a return to the original condition, but the redeemed person possesses this state in a permanent, stable way.[11]

Just as Theodore's vision of the two *katastases* provides the structure for his understanding of grace, so also Cyril's adherence to what I call a three-act salvation scheme helps to establish the main lines of his thought. To assert that God has given humanity participation in the Holy Spirit at creation and has restored that participation at redemption is consistent with

[8] Burghardt, *The Image of God in Man*, 115 n.

[9] Janssens, 'Notre filiation divine', 259; Burghardt, *The Image of God in Man*, 65–71, 165.

[10] e.g. Gross, *La Divinisation du chrétien*, 282; du Manoir, *Dogme et spiritualité*, 175–7; Phan, *Grace and the Human Condition*, 139–50.

[11] I should note that there are a few dissenting voices. Dratsellas, 'Man in his Original State', 545–55, sees Cyril as emphasizing not just the instability of Adam's created condition, but also the incompleteness of it. He argues that Adam was created with the potential for perfection but still needed to perfect himself with the assistance of grace. Nevertheless, he still sees Cyril as emphasizing Adam's possession of holiness and immortality at creation and his loss of these qualities with the fall. (See, 'Man in his Original State', 541.) McGuckin, *St. Cyril of Alexandria*, 224–5, offers a somewhat similar portrayal.

an understanding of grace as God's giving us himself. The idea that God gives us himself through Christ and the Holy Spirit virtually demands a strongly unitive christology, in which the personal subject of Christ is the Logos himself. I will now turn to the way in which Cyril develops the specific emphases of his doctrine of grace as he works within his three-act soteriological framework.

3.2. GRACE AS GOD'S GIVING HIMSELF TO HUMANITY

At the beginning of the twentieth century, Weigl commented of Cyril, 'There is no other Church father for whom teaching on grace is tied to christology (soteriology) to such a degree and for whom it bears such an explicitly christological colouring.'[12] More recently, Wickham has stated the connection between grace and christology in Cyril's thought even more poignantly by writing that Christ 'is, in a word, divine grace, the "beyond in our midst"'.[13] These statements point to the importance in Cyril's thought of God's giving himself to humanity through Christ. Christ does not simply give us grace (conceived of as something other than himself); he *constitutes* the grace that he gives us. God the Logos incarnate is both the giver and the gift. Several passages from *Com. Johan.* make this aspect of Cyril's soteriology apparent.

While discussing John 1: 14, Cyril writes:

> He descended into bondage, not thereby giving anything to himself, but graciously giving himself to us (ἡμῖν ἑαυτὸν χαριζόμενος), so that we *through his poverty might become rich* [2 Cor. 8: 9], and by soaring up through likeness to him into his own proper and remarkable good, we might be made gods and children of God (θεοί τε καὶ Θεοῦ τέκνα) through faith. For he who is by nature Son and God (ὁ κατὰ φύσιν Υἱός καὶ Θεός) *dwelt among us*, and as a result, in his Spirit we cry, *Abba, Father* [Rom. 8: 15]. (*Com. Johan.* 1.9 [1.141–2])

Here I should note the strength of Cyril's emphasis on the Logos' gracing us with himself. Not only does he write this directly (ἡμῖν ἑαυτὸν χαριζόμενος), but he also asserts that the

[12] Weigl, *Die Heilslehre des Cyrill*, 127. Cf. Janssens, 'Notre filiation divine', 234.

[13] Wickham, 'Symbols of the Incarnation in Cyril', 44.

results of the Logos' gracious action are that we are raised up to his 'own proper good' (ἴδιον ἀγαθόν), become 'gods and sons of God', and are able to call God 'Abba, Father'. Later, Cyril contrasts Christ with the prophets by asserting:

> For grace was given by measure through the Spirit to the holy prophets, but in our Saviour Christ *all the fullness of deity has been pleased to dwell bodily*, as Paul says [Col. 2: 9]. Therefore *we have all* also *received of his fullness*, as John affirmed [John 1: 16]. How then will the Giver be on a par with the recipients, or how will the fullness of deity (τὸ τῆς θεότητος πλήρωμα) be reckoned in the portion of the minister?
>
> (*Com. Johan.* 2.3 [1.250])

Here Cyril virtually equates grace with the fullness of deity. The prophets and Christians receive a measure of this grace; that is, we receive *of* Christ's fullness. While Cyril's point in this passage is to demonstrate the uniqueness of Christ, his argument for doing so also makes clear that he equates grace and Christ. He is the fullness of deity, and he gives of himself to those who believe.[14] Similarly, as Cyril comments on John 14: 20, he argues that the purpose of the incarnation was to enable people to partake anew of God: 'It was not otherwise possible for man to escape death, since he was of a nature that was perishing, unless he recovered that ancient grace (τὴν ἀρχαίαν χάριν) and partook again of God (μετέσχε πάλιν τοῦ Θεοῦ) who holds all things together in being and preserves them in life through the Son in the Spirit' (*Com. Johan.* 9.1 [2.485–6]). Here it is clear that the grace God originally gave mankind and the grace he gives through the incarnation both constitute participation in himself.

Elsewhere, Cyril discusses Christians' anointing with the Holy Spirit (2 Cor. 1: 21–2) and their being formed to Christ (Gal. 4: 19). He writes, 'But if we are formed to Christ, we richly receive the divine in ourselves as a sort of likeness (εἰκονισμόν), but he is the image and the exact likeness of God the Father, and he is not like us who are called to likeness according to participation in holiness (κατὰ μέθεξιν ἁγιασμοῦ), but rather he is the image by nature and essentially (φύσει καὶ οὐσιωδῶς)' (*Com. 2 Cor.* 1.2 [3.326]). In this passage as well, it is apparent that Cyril sees salvation as our receiving God himself, not simply some gift from God. He is careful to make a distinction between Christ

[14] Cf. *Com. Johan.* 2.3 [1.253].

(the exact, natural, and essential image of God) and us (who are called to likeness with him by participation in his natural holiness). But since we receive God 'as a sort of likeness' (εἰκονισμόν), there is a sense in which God gives himself to us in grace.

Cyril's close identification of grace and Christ's person leads directly to his recurring insistence that Christ cannot have received grace from without. He uses the Apostle Paul's standard greeting 'grace and peace to you from God our Father and the Lord Jesus Christ' to argue that the Son distributes grace equally with the Father, and he declares that Christ could not have done so if he had himself received grace from the Father. He asks rhetorically, 'How could one who [merely] received grace upon himself be the co-giver (συνδοτὴρ) of grace along with the Father?' (*Trin. Dial*. 4 [237.254]). Similarly, while commenting on Jesus' statement in John 6: 44 that he will raise believers up on the last day, Cyril asserts: 'The power of making alive and of leading one who is mastered by death to return to new life will rightly belong only to the nature of God and will not be ascribed to any created thing. For making alive is a property of the Living, and not of one who receives (δανειζομένου) that grace from another' (*Com. Johan*. 4.1 [1.506]). By using the participle δανειζόμενος, Cyril indicates that if one receives life from another, that life is not really his own; it is merely borrowed.[15] No creatures possess life in their own natures; only God does. Thus only God has the power to bestow the grace of life on creatures.[16]

Another passage from *Com. Johan*. clarifies Cyril's idea further. Commenting on John 8: 34, he contrasts Abraham, who was once a slave to sin, with Christ, who is able to set people free from sin:

> The Lord was hinting that even the blessed Abraham himself, who had once been in bondage to sin and was set free only through faith in Christ, was not capable of passing this spiritual nobility on to others,

[15] LSJ 368, indicates that the basic meaning of δανείζω is 'to lend', and Lampe, 333, also lists 'to bestow' as a possibility. In the middle voice, the verb means 'to borrow' or 'to have lent to one'.

[16] Here Cyril follows Athanasius, who argues that if the Son were divine only by participation, he would not be able to give us life or deify us. Athanasius concludes: 'It is not possible for one who possesses something merely by participation to impart of that participation to others, since what he has is not his own, but the Giver's. And the grace he has received is barely sufficient for himself' (*De Syn*. 51 [784b]). Cf. *Con. Arian*. 1.39–40 [92–6].

since one cannot be master of the power of freeing others if he did not put away the bondage of sin by himself and if he was not himself the bestower of freedom, but received it from another.

(*Com. Johan.* 5.5 [2.65])

These comments again reflect Cyril's cardinal belief that one is not able pass on to others a personal condition that he has received from another. Abraham was set free from sin and received spiritual nobility not by himself but through another, that is, through Christ. As a result, even though he is now free, Abraham cannot free others from sin. To use terminology from the passage quoted in the previous paragraph, Abraham's freedom is borrowed, bestowed on him by another, and so he cannot give this freedom to anyone else. Only Christ, the Son of God who naturally possesses freedom and life, can give these gifts to others.[17]

It should now be apparent that even when writing of gifts that could conceivably be seen as separate from God's giving us himself, Cyril makes no such separation. For him, life consists of participation in God's life. Holiness and righteousness are participation in God's holiness. Freedom from sin is participation in God, the one who has never been a slave to sin. If one were to conceive of these characteristics as separable qualities, one could imagine that a person who receives these could then pass them on to another or help another obtain them. As we have seen, this is essentially the way Theodore and Nestorius understand grace. But for Cyril, these gifts are inseparable from the person of the giver, God himself. The way God gives us life and holiness is by giving us Christ, therefore causing us to share in the qualities that Christ possesses. Since Christ's giving of himself to us constitutes God's giving us participation in himself, Christ must be God by nature, not merely by a grace borrowed from another.

At this point I should acknowledge that Cyril's understanding of grace is not limited to the idea that God gives us himself.

[17] Cf. *Ep. Pasch.* 8.4 [392.90–2]; *Thes.* 12 [189b–c]; *Trin. Dial.* 3 [237.80]; *Com. Johan.* 1.9 [1.142–3], 2.1 [1.177], in which Cyril affirms that the Son did not receive glory, grace, or the dignity of deity from without. There are also numerous passages in which Cyril makes the related affirmation that Christ did not receive his sonship by grace or from without, but holds it by nature. I will examine several of these passages in sect. 3.3.2.

There are a number of passages in *Com. Johan.* in which he portrays grace as power, divine assistance, or co-operation. During his discussion of Jesus' healings in John 4: 46–5: 18, he equates grace with Christ's power to heal or with the gift of healing itself. Cyril has the man by the pool honour Christ as 'the one who has such great power and grace as to drive away my disease' (*Com. Johan.* 2.5 [1.310]). While commenting on John 7: 38, Cyril writes that the believer will enjoy God's richest gifts (*χαρίσματα*): 'For through the Spirit he will be so full of the gifts that he will not only enrich his own mind, but will even be able to overflow into others' hearts, like the river gushing forth the God-given good upon his neighbour also' (*Com. Johan.* 5.1 [1.688]). Shortly thereafter, he concludes, 'Then it is very evident that the Saviour says that *out of the inner being* of the one who believes will come forth the grace which through the Spirit gives instruction and eloquence' (*Com. Johan.* 5.1 [1.689]). Here Cyril sees grace as those gifts which the Holy Spirit gives, and he also believes that one Christian can give these *χαρίσματα* to another. While discussing Jesus' statement that Judas was a son of perdition (John 17: 12), Cyril emphasizes the need for Christians to work out their salvation, but he insists that their own effort is not sufficient: 'This alone will not avail to save the soul of a man, for it stands in urgent need of assistance and grace from above, to make what is difficult to achieve easy for it, and to make the steep and thorny path of righteousness smooth' (*Com. Johan.* 11.9 [2.703]). Here Cyril's emphasis falls on our action in salvation, and grace recedes to somewhat of a secondary status. It is God's co-operation with our own efforts to be virtuous, and this co-operative grace makes what would have been difficult for us easy.

If one were to read these passages in isolation, Cyril's understanding of grace would look very much like that of Theodore. Grace seems to consist of the gifts and co-operation that the Holy Spirit gives in order to help us work out our salvation, and it even appears that those who have received such gifts can pass them on to others, in the form of instruction about virtuous living. However, passages such as these are very rare in Cyril's writings, and what I have written above should make clear that they are far from representing the main aspect of Cyril's doctrine of grace. His primary idea is that in Christ and through the Holy Spirit, God gives us himself, making us holy and incorruptible by participation in his own nature. This action of God in giving us himself impels us to live in a way that reflects who he is (and who we have become by participation), and God then gives us aid and co-operation in that task.[18] As Burghardt helpfully explains, Christians receive both ontological holiness (through participation in the Holy Spirit) and dynamic holiness (through a life of imitation of Christ). He writes: 'The ontological is a prelude to the dynamic. In imaging Christ we are transformed to a new life, a holy life.'[19] For Cyril, these gifts of power and aid in the task of holy living are more the result of grace than its essence.

From this discussion the main lines of Cyril's understanding of grace have emerged: God the Son gives us himself, so that we partake of the divine nature. This is the gift humanity received at creation and lost with the fall, and this is the primary gift that we receive anew through redemption. I will now turn to the question of which specific aspects of divine life God shares with us when he gives us himself.

3.3. GOD'S GIFT OF HIMSELF: INCORRUPTION, HOLINESS, AND SONSHIP

In Cyril's thought, the most obvious way God gives himself to humanity is by sharing his incorruption (and consequent immortality) and his holiness. As we have seen, Theodore also understands salvation as the gift of incorruption and holiness, although he links these qualities to the assumed man's achievement of the second age. Salvation is thus a perfect human condition, not a condition of sharing in God's own life. In contrast, Cyril follows Athanasius[20] in viewing incorruption and holiness as the result of human participation in the Logos.

[18] Some scholars, such as Gross, *La Divinisation du chrétien*, 294, and Phan, *Grace and the Human Condition*, 151, see in Cyril an emphasis on both uncreated grace (the presence of the Holy Spirit himself in our lives) and created grace (a form that the Spirit implants in us to form us to Christ and sanctify us), although Gross admits that Cyril is not very clear about what created grace is or how it operates. It seems better to regard the passages I have cited here as referring to the continuing results of our participation in God himself, rather than to some separate created grace.

[19] Burghardt, *The Image of God in Man*, 163.

[20] e.g. *De Incar. Ver.* 5 [144–6].

3.3.1. Sharing in Divine Incorruption and Holiness

One could produce many examples of Cyril's stress on incorruption, but two will suffice to make this point clear. During a discussion of the Eucharist on the basis of John 6: 51, Cyril writes that Christ made his flesh a ransom for the flesh of the world, so that in him death might die and the fallen nature of man might rise. He explains:

> For since the life-giving Word of God dwelt in the flesh, he transformed it into his own proper good (τὸ ἴδιον ἀγαθὸν), that is life, and by the unspeakable character of this union, coming wholly together with it, rendered it life-giving (ζωοποιὸν), as he himself is by nature. Therefore the body of Christ gives life to all who partake of it. For it casts out death when it comes to be in those who are dying, and it removes corruption (τὴν φθορὰν) since in itself it is fully the Word who abolishes corruption. (*Com. Johan.* 4.2 [1.520])

Here we see that the efficacy of Christ's death, and thus of the Eucharist as well, depends on the union between the Logos and his flesh. The Son gives his own life to his flesh, and therefore he renders that flesh capable of driving death and corruption away from us. Thus incorruption is not merely a condition of perfect human life; it is a participation in the Logos' own life, which comes to people through his flesh. Later, commenting on Jesus' high priestly prayer in John 17, Cyril writes: 'He came among us and became man, not for his own sake, but rather he prepared the way, through himself and in himself (δι' ἑαυτοῦ τε καὶ ἐν ἑαυτῷ), for human nature to escape death and return to its original incorruption (τὴν ἀπ' ἀρχῆς ἀφθαρσίαν)' (*Com. Johan.* 11.10 [2.726]). In this passage he makes clear that overcoming corruption is not simply something that takes place through Christ; it is also something that is accomplished in Christ (δι' ἑαυτοῦ τε καὶ ἐν ἑαυτῷ). God originally gave mankind incorruption when he breathed his Spirit into Adam, and Christ restores us to this incorruption by giving himself to us and causing us to dwell in him.[21]

21 Cf. the emphasis on God's sharing his own incorruption with humanity in *Ep. Pasch.* 2.8 [372.230]; *Com. Johan.* 2.prooem. [1.170], 2.1 [1.185], 9.1 [2.482]. Among Cyril's later writings with the same accent, cf. *Ep. Pasch.* 17.4 [785d]; *Ep.* 1 [1.1.1.22]; *Con. Nes.* 1.1 [1.1.6.17], 3.6 [1.1.6.75], 5.1 [1.1.6.95]; *De Fide Aug.* [1.1.5.30]; *Expl. 12 Cap.* 6 [1.1.5.17]; *De Dog. Sol.* 6 [200–4]; *Ep.* 55 [1.1.4.60]; *Con. Theo.* 1.3 [3.512].

As we have already seen, Cyril understands the original created condition not merely in terms of human sharing in God's incorruption, but also as our sharing in his holiness, and this holiness is likewise a major part of what God gives us anew in salvation.[22] In his festal letter for the year 416, Cyril asserts that God delights in internal worship, not external, because 'each of those who believe in Christ is made fully a temple of the Spirit, in order that, as I said, he might receive the source of holiness' (*Ep. Pasch.* 4.5 [372.262]). Clearly, ἁγιασμός is not simply a human state of holiness; it is the result of possessing the person of the Holy Spirit, the source of holiness. In a similar passage from *De Ador.*, Cyril contrasts Christ with Aaron by writing: 'But now, since we are among those who have been made holy in Christ, the great and true high priest, to whom we have clung by the Spirit, we have been shown to be sharers and partakers of his own nature (μέτοχοι τῆς οἰκείας αὐτοῦ φύσεως)' (*De Ador.*12 [785a]). Here he directly links Christians' holiness with their being partakers of the divine nature, and he argues that such participation takes place in Christ.[23]

3.3.2. Sharing in Divine Sonship

Many commentators have noted Cyril's emphasis on sharing in divine incorruption and holiness,[24] but scholars are also quick to point out that these are not all that God gives us in salvation. Rather, Cyril's primary emphasis is on the gift of divine sonship.[25] Since Cyril sees grace as Christ, a person, then to say that he gives us himself in grace can hardly mean only that he gives us

[22] *Com. Johan.* 11.10 [2.720], discussed in sect. 3.1.

[23] Cf. the stress on holiness as participation in the Holy Spirit in *Trin. Dial.* 6 [246.34]; *Com. Johan.* 11.10 [2.720], 11.11 [2.731]; *Com. 2 Cor.* 1.2 [3.326]. Among passages in Cyril's later writings with the same accent, cf. *Con. Nes.* 3.6 [1.1.6.75]; *Ep.* 17 [1.1.1.37]; *Schol.* 1 [1.5.219–20/1.5.184]; *De Dog. Sol.* 2 [188–90], 3 [194].

[24] For Cyril's emphasis on salvation as incorruption, see Florovsky, *The Byzantine Fathers of the Fifth Century*, 282; Dratsellas, 'Questions of the Soteriological Teaching', 407; Meunier, *Le Christ de Cyrille*, 76–7, 111. For the stress on holiness, see Mahé, 'La Sanctification d'après Cyrille', 35–6; Dhôtel, 'La "Sanctification" du Christ', 526; and especially Burghardt, *The Image of God in Man*, 83.

[25] e.g. Mahé, 'La Sanctification d'après Cyrille', 38–9; de Durand, *Cyrille: Deux dialogues christologiques*, 93; Meunier, *Le Christ de Cyrille*, 111.

some 'physical' and moral qualities that he possesses. Instead, one would expect a person to give us something personal, and sonship is a crucial part of Cyril's idea of salvation.

The idea that God gives people divine sonship through Christ permeates all Cyril's writings. We have seen that he insists on the natural deity of the Son, since only one who is divine by nature can give God to us. Likewise, Cyril also insists that Christ must be Son by nature, since only then can he make us adopted sons of God. In *Trin. Dial.* he argues that the Only-Begotten is not a mere creature, nor is his sonship merely by grace: 'The title "Son" was not given to the Only-Begotten as something added from the outside (ἐπακτὸν), but the name pertains to him in his very being, in just the same way as the title "Father" pertains to God the Father' (*Trin. Dial.* 1 [231.214]). Similarly, commenting on John 1: 1 Cyril writes:

> If God the Word who shone forth from God the Father is truly Son, then our opponents must necessarily confess, even against their will, that he is of the essence of the Father; for this is what true sonship means. Then how is such a one inferior to the Father, if he is indeed the fruit of his essence, which in no way receives an inferior within itself?
> (*Com. Johan.* 1.3 [1.37])

Shortly after this, he asks poignantly, 'How is he Son at all, if he is not so by nature?' (*Com. Johan.* 1.3 [1.38]). In these passages, Cyril indicates that there is only one kind of genuine sonship, namely, that which comes from natural generation. If the Son were not truly begotten from the substance of the Father, then one could not justly call him Son, and further, one could not use the word 'Father' either. Strictly speaking, God is not a father to created beings; he is a lord and master. If he is to be a true father at all, then the Son must be his natural Son, not merely an exalted created being.[26] Cyril's insistence on this, in opposition first to Arian thought and later to Nestorius' christology, grows out of his understanding of grace. Only one who is truly the Son of God can graciously give us divine sonship.

In his stress on grace as the gift of divine sonship, just as in his emphasis on incorruption and holiness through participation in

26 Cf. Cyril's emphasis on Christ's natural sonship in *Thes.* 32 [525b]; *Trin. Dial.* 4 [237.226]; *Com. Johan.* 2.1 [1.190], 2.1 [1.207]. In sect. 4.2.1 I will consider passages from his later writings that convey the same idea.

God, Cyril adheres closely to the lines that Athanasius has laid down.[27] But his portrayal of the relation between grace and sonship goes beyond that of his master, both in the degree of emphasis he places on this idea and the specificity that he gives to it. Athanasius has stressed that there is a difference between Christ's natural sonship and our sonship by grace, but he has not attempted to explain exactly what it means to become sons of God. But this question assumes important dimensions for two reasons. First, if one insists that the only kind of true sonship is natural sonship, then it is unclear how we can be called sons of God at all. Second, if one sees salvation as deification (as Athanasius and Cyril do) and ties deification closely to sonship, not just to incorruption, then one is in danger of blurring the line between God and his creation unless one can state explicitly what our divine sonship does and does not include. I will now turn to the question of what Cyril means by divine sonship, and in doing so, I hope to show something of the precision and depth with which he explains God's gift of himself to humanity.

3.4. CHRIST'S SONSHIP AND OURS

Consideration of what sonship can mean discloses four possibilities. First, the actual generative relationship of a son to his father. Second, identity of substance. Third, the status of being a son, the prerogatives and rights (and perhaps even characteristics) that one possesses as a result of being a son. Finally, the intimate personal relationship, the warm communion that (at least in ideal cases) characterizes a son's relationship to his father. Throughout his writings Cyril makes it quite clear that by our sonship to God he does not mean the first or second of these possibilities. It is also apparent that he does mean the third; we gain the status of sons by grace. Some commentators argue that this is all Cyril means by our sonship, but I will suggest that he also intends the fourth: we share by grace in intimate communion with the Father.

[27] For Athanasius' insistence that only if Christ is Son by nature can he make us sons by grace, see *Con. Arian.* 1.27–40 [68–96], 2.61 [276–7].

3.4.1. Not the Substance of God or the Natural Relation of Son to Father

Cyril often repeats that our divine sonship does not obscure the Creator–creature distinction, and the primary way he does this is by insisting on the difference between Christ's sonship and that of believers.[28] We receive sonship by adoption and grace from the outside, but Christ is Son by nature and in truth. Cyril argues:

> The concept of sonship means this when applied to one who is so naturally, but the matter is otherwise with those who are sons by adoption (κατὰ θέσιν). For since Christ is not a son in this manner, he is therefore truly (ἀληθῶς) a Son, so that on account of this he might be distinguished from us, who are sons by adoption. For there would be sonship neither by adoption nor by likeness to God if he did not remain the true Son, to whose likeness our sonship is called and formed by a certain skill and grace. (*Thes.* 32 [525b])

Here he draws a very sharp line between Christ, the true Son, and Christians, who are sons by adoption, by being formed to his likeness through grace. Furthermore, Cyril argues that our adopted sonship depends on Christ's natural sonship. He must be genuinely begotten from the Father, since otherwise he could not adopt us into God's family.

Cyril makes this point even more forcefully in *Com. Johan.* 1.9, which is perhaps his most extended discussion of the difference between Christ's sonship and ours. Cyril comments on John 1: 9 by explaining the sense in which we can be called gods:

> Shall we then abandon what we are by nature and mount up to the divine and unutterable essence, and shall we depose (ἐκβάλλοντες) the Word of God from his very sonship and sit in place of him (ἀντ' ἐκείνου) with the Father and make the grace of him who honours us a pretext for impiety? May it never be! Rather, the Son will remain unchangeably in that condition in which he is, but we, adopted into sonship and gods by grace (θετοὶ εἰς υἱότητα καὶ θεοὶ κατὰ χάριν), shall not be ignorant of what we are. (*Com. Johan.* 1.9 [1.110–11])

28 Among the many interpreters who have noted this emphasis in Cyril, see Janssens, 'Notre filiation divine', 271–2; Abramowski, 'Zur Theologie Theodors', 281; Boulnois, *Le Paradoxe trinitaire chez Cyrille*, 376–9.

In this passage, he argues that true sonship cannot be shared. If we were to become true sons of the Father, that would require that we *displace* the Logos as genuine Son. Cyril angrily dismisses this thought, since there can be only one true Son of God. Instead, he argues that even when we are called sons and gods by grace, we remain aware of what we actually are, that is, creatures. There is no question of our aspiring to the substance of God; Cyril recognizes that this is impossible and that it would be blasphemous even to consider it.[29]

3.4.2. The Status of Adopted Sons

However, even as Cyril stresses that Christians do not become true sons of God, he makes clear that they do gain the status of sons through adoption and grace. In *Trin. Dial.* 2, Cyril writes:

> Everyone will confess that we were created, but that one came forth from the essence of God the Father. We are also conformed to him, and since we receive, in place of the rank of generative birth, the grace of his kindness, we are ranked as God's children and gain a dignity (ἀξίωμα) that is external and added from without. We are adopted sons, having been formed to the true Son and having been called to the glory of the one who is Son by nature. (*Trin. Dial.* 2 [231.288–90])

Here again there is a strong contrast between our sonship and Christ's, and what is especially noteworthy in this passage is the way Cyril uses the word ἀξίωμα. This word is often associated with human merit, in the sense that people gain a certain worth or value through their actions. However, Cyril uses it to refer to the dignity of sonship, the status of being a son of God. He shows here that this dignity is not something we earn; God gives it to us through adoption. It does not inhere in us, as it does in Christ, but it is given to us from the outside when we become sons of God. Similarly, while commenting on John 14: 20, Cyril writes that the Only-Begotten became man 'in order *to condemn sin in the flesh* [Rom. 8: 3], and by his own death to slay death, and to make us sons of God, regenerating in the Spirit those who are on earth into supernatural dignity (τὸ ὑπὲρ φύσιν ἀξίωμα)' (*Com. Johan.* 9.1 [2.482]). These words show that the sonship that

[29] Cf. later passages from *Com. Johan.* 1.9 in which Cyril continues to accent this distinction: 1.133, 1.134, 1.142–3. Cf. also *Thes.* 12 [189b–c], 32 [561b–d]; *Trin. Dial.* 4 [237.186]; *Com. Johan.* 11.11 [2.732].

Christ's incarnation and work secure for us is a condition of dignity that is beyond our nature (ὑπὲρ φύσιν); it is something akin to the status that Christ himself enjoys before the Father. Even though we cannot become sons of God by natural generation from his substance, we can and do receive the dignity of being called God's children.[30]

3.4.3. *The Intimate Communion of Son and Father*

There are scholars who see the status of divine sonship as the primary aspect of adoption in Cyril's thought. For instance, Burghardt summarizes Cyril's understanding of the believers' position as follows: 'Brothers of the Son, we are at the same time sons of the Father. Conformed to the Son, we participate in His relationship to the Father; our divine sonship is, in the realm of grace, an imitation of the real, substantial generation of the Son by the Father.'[31] One should note here the equation of our relationship to the Father and our imitation of the generation of the Son by the Father. Burghardt reads Cyril as saying that just as Christ is the natural offspring of the Father, so also (in a way at once similar and distinct) we are images of the natural Son and thus stand in a relation to the Father that is similar to Christ's relationship to him. In other words, it is the status of sonship or the fact of being declared sons of God that Burghardt has in mind. As we have seen, this is a significant part of Cyril's understanding of divine sonship, but what Burghardt omits is the idea of our communion or intimacy with the Father. To stand in a natural or adopted relation to God as a child to a father is not necessarily to share with him in a relationship of warm fellowship and love. In contrast to the impression Burghardt gives, however, Cyril's portrayal of sonship does include a strong sense that we share in precisely that communion and intimacy with God, as children to our Father.

[30] For other uses of ἀξίωμα in this sense, cf. *Com. Johan.* 2.1 [1.190], 2.5 [1.316], 5.5 [2.70]. LSJ 172 and Lampe, 167–8, both list 'worth', 'value', and 'position', 'rank', 'dignity' as possible translations for ἀξίωμα. Cf. also *Com. Johan.* 1.9 [1.135], 5.5. [2.65], where Cyril uses the word εὐγένεια to refer to the nobility of sonship, thus conveying the idea of status in much the same way as he does through his use of ἀξίωμα. LSJ 708 and Lampe, 561, render εὐγένεια as 'nobility' or 'excellence'.

[31] Burghardt, *The Image of God in Man*, 112–13.

Two passages from *Com. Johan.* illustrate the importance Cyril attaches to God's gift of fellowship with himself. Commenting on John 14: 11, Cyril underlines the difference between Christ's communion with the Father and ours: 'We obtain for ourselves the grace of communion (τὴν τῆς κοινωνίας χάριν) with them. But shall we therefore say that the Son is in the Father in a manner similar to this, and that he possesses only a non-essential and artificially added communion with the one who begat him?' (*Com. Johan.* 9.1 [2.453]). To say that we receive the grace of κοινωνία with the Father and Son is to say that in our case, such intimacy is non-essential (σχετική) and artificial (ἐπιτετηδευμένη), but Christ's fellowship is of a different order than this because he was begotten naturally from the Father, not merely adopted. Although Cyril's primary aim in this passage is to safeguard the distinction between Christ and us, his statement also reveals his conviction that Christians do share κοινωνία with the Trinity. Later, as he discusses John 15: 9–10, Cyril paraphrases Christ as saying that he will give us as much love as he has received from the Father. He continues: 'I have presented you, who are men and who have for this reason received the nature of slaves, as gods and sons of God. Through my grace I have given you dignities surpassing your nature. I have made you sharers in [the communion of] my kingdom (κοινωνοὺς τῆς ἐμῆς βασιλείας), have presented you *conformed to the body of* my *glory* [Phil. 3: 21], and have honoured you with incorruption and life' (*Com. Johan.* 10.2 [2.571]). This passage provides an excellent summary of the aspects of divine sonship examined in the preceding paragraphs. Even though we remain human and slaves by nature, God has by grace given us incorruption and life, dignity surpassing that which we naturally possessed, and especially the communion that characterizes God's kingdom. One could read κοινωνοὺς τῆς ἐμῆς βασιλείας εἰσεδεξάμην as implying merely that we become participants in the kingdom itself, but the prior statement that Jesus gives us as much love as the Father has shown him makes it clear that Cyril has in mind fellowship and intimacy with the God who rules. His point concerns Christians' personal interaction with God, not merely a quasi-legal status as members of the kingdom.

We have seen that when he discusses the way God gives

humanity sonship by grace, Cyril is very careful to distinguish our sonship from that of Christ. We do not share in the substance of God or in the natural, generative relation Christ has with the Father. Instead, Christ gives us the dignity or status of sonship and gives us intimate communion with himself. However, this last idea requires further explanation. Cyril rarely states explicitly what he means by this fellowship, but one can gain a great deal of insight into his intent by examining an important terminological distinction that he introduces as he combats Arianism: the distinction between the idea of the word *ἴδιος* and the concept of *οἰκειότης*. I will now turn to this issue in order to show more fully what Cyril intends by saying that we become sons of God, and therefore to illuminate more clearly the heart of his understanding of grace.

3.5. ἴδιος, οἰκειότης, AND CYRIL'S UNDERSTANDING OF DIVINE SONSHIP

In classical and patristic Greek as a whole, the *ἴδιος* and *οἰκεῖος* word groups have considerable overlap in usage; both can refer to a close belonging in a wide variety of situations. During the fourth century, the adjective *ἴδιος* began to be used in a much more specific way in Alexandrian circles, and Cyril follows his predecessors in the technical use of this word.[32] I will argue that in addition to adopting this specific use of *ἴδιος*, Cyril also develops a much more precise use of the noun *οἰκειότης*, and that the difference in the way he uses these two words has much to do with his understanding of grace and christology. In order to demonstrate this, I will need first to consider the general use of the two word groups, then the use of *ἴδιος* in Athanasius' and Cyril's writings, and finally the use of *οἰκειότης* and the more concrete expression *οἰκειότης φυσική* in Cyril's early writings.

3.5.1. The General Use of ἴδιος, οἰκειότης, and Related Forms

The basic idea of *ἴδιος* is 'one's own' or 'pertaining to oneself', in contrast to *ἀλλότριος* ('another's'). The word can refer to *things*

[32] Louth, 'The Use of the Term *ἴδιος*', 202, points out that the Alexandrian use of *ἴδιος* was different from the Cappadocian use of the word and that it was the latter that eventually gained pre-eminence in Greek theology. I will examine Louth's essay in sect. 3.5.2.

that are properly one's own (possessions, interests, peculiar properties, characteristics) or to *people* who belong properly to one (servants, relatives, disciples, friends, compatriots). As a result, the noun *ἰδιότης* refers either to the specific character, peculiar nature, or distinctive property of someone or something, or to the relationship, the state of belonging to someone. The verb *ἰδιοποιέω* can be used to mean 'to appropriate', 'to make one's own', or 'to claim as one's own'. The adjective *οἰκεῖος* means basically 'belonging to the house' or 'proper', 'suitable', and it can be used of things that are one's own (possessions) or of people who are one's own (friends, relatives, servants, countrymen). The noun *οἰκειότης* can refer to a relation or similarity of ideas, to the proper sense of words, or to kinship, friendship, or intimacy between personal beings. The verbs *οἰκειόω* and *οἰκειοποιέω* can both refer either to appropriating something to oneself or to making another person one's own relative or friend.[33]

Therefore, both these word groups are very general; they refer to a close sort of belonging, whether an impersonal relation (as in an association of two ideas), a possessive relation (as in the way an object or characteristic belongs to a person), or a personal relationship (as in a friendship or family relationship). In the New Testament, *ἴδιος* is used in all three of these ways,[34] but the passages that are noteworthy are the ones in which the word is used of personal relationships involving God. In John 5: 18, the Jews seek to kill Jesus not merely because he has broken the Sabbath, but also because he called God his own father (*πατέρα ἴδιον*), thus making himself equal to God. Similarly, in Rom. 8: 32 Paul writes that God did not spare his own Son (*τοῦ ἰδίου υἱοῦ*) but gave himself up for us all. In both these verses the word *ἴδιος* refers to a uniquely close relationship between Jesus and the Father, one the Jews understood to imply that he was equal to God. However, in John 10: 3, 4, and 12, Jesus refers to his disciples as his own sheep (*τὰ ἴδια πρόβατα*), indicating an intimate, but not unique, relationship.[35] The three occurrences of *οἰκεῖος* all refer to personal relationships. Galatians 6: 10

[33] This general survey of the use of these words comes from LSJ 818, 1202; Lampe, 664–6, 937–8; and BAGD 369–70, 556. Cf. Michel, '*οἶκος, κτλ.*', 134–5.

[34] In the NT, *ἴδιος* is used *c.*114 times and *οἰκεῖος* 3 times. No other forms of the words occur.

[35] Cf. John 13: 1.

describes Christians as the household of faith (τοὺς οἰκείους τῆς πίστεως), and Eph. 2: 19 states that believers are not strangers but fellow citizens with the saints and members of God's household (οἰκεῖοι τοῦ θεοῦ). 1 Timothy 5: 8 uses both words to refer to the members of one's household. These passages show that the New Testament displays the same non-specific use of these two words that Greek literature in general does. Both words refer to the relationship between people or between God and Christians, and ἴδιος is also used to refer to the relationship between the Father and the Son.

3.5.2. ἴδιος in Athanasius and Cyril

In a short but important paper published in 1989, Louth argues that the Alexandrian theologians, especially Athanasius and Cyril, used the word ἴδιος to indicate intimacy and inseparability. He points out that in Athanasius the word refers to the relation between the Son and the Father and to the relation between the Logos and his flesh. In the first case, Athanasius is making a distinction between the Son, who is of the Father's essence, and all created things, which are created out of nothing. In the second case, Athanasius insists that if the flesh were not the Logos' own body, then his death would not avail to save people from corruption and to give us participation in God in a more stable way than Adam possessed. Louth points out that both the intimacy between the Father and the Son and the intimacy of divine and human in Christ are necessary for salvation, so Athanasius' two uses of ἴδιος go together.[36]

Louth's work shows that by the time of Athanasius, the Alexandrian use of ἴδιος had become much more specific than the general usage I have sketched above, and a brief look at some of the passages where the word occurs will confirm Louth's conclusions. Athanasius insists that the Son is eternal and is the Father's own (ἴδιον) (*Con. Arian.* 1.11 [36a]). He calls God a

[36] Louth, 'The Use of the Term ἴδιος', 198–200. I should point out that Boulnois, *Le Paradoxe trinitaire chez Cyrille*, 322, and Russell, *Cyril of Alexandria*, 26–7, argue that Athanasius and Cyril do sometimes use the word ἴδιος in a way more like the Cappadocians' usage, to refer to those properties that belong uniquely to one or another person of the Trinity. Be that as it may, it will become clear from my discussion that Louth has correctly grasped the primary way in which Athanasius and Cyril use the word, and in fact Boulnois and Russell concur on this point.

fountain and insists that life and wisdom (that is, the Logos) are proper (ἴδια) to this fountain (*Con. Arian.* 1.19 [52a]). He insists that the Son is not a work of God (which could be temporal) but the proper offspring (ἴδιον γέννημα), who must be eternal (*Con. Arian.* 1.29 [73a]).[37] Finally, Athanasius distinguishes between the Son's relation to the Father and ours by saying that he is in the Father as his proper Word and radiance (ὡς Λόγος ἴδιος καὶ ἀπαύγασμα αὐτοῦ), but we are united to God only by participation in the Holy Spirit (*Con. Arian.* 3.24 [373b]).

In none of these passages does Athanasius use the word ἴδιος to refer to an intimacy of communion between Father and Son. Rather, he uses the word to indicate a unity of substance. The Logos is the Father's own Son (ἴδιος υἱός) because he is from the Father's substance, not because he shares close communion with the Father (even though that is also true). Louth comments that Athanasius does not develop the New Testament idea that believers are Christ's own sheep (ἴδια πρόβατα),[38] but he does not give a reason for this. The most plausible reason, I suggest, is that the Arian crisis led Athanasius to use the word much more specifically than the New Testament did. He made a general word for intimacy (of either relationship or substance) into a specific technical term for substantial unity. It would do no good for Athanasius to insist that the Son was the Father's own if one could construe ownness as the sort of intimacy that two people can have with each other or that God has with Christians. Although there is biblical precedent for using ἴδιος to refer to a relationship between personal beings, and even though the Father and the Son do have that kind of intimacy, this is not what Athanasius is referring to when he calls the Logos the Father's ἴδιος υἱός. What he has in mind is a much closer kind of belonging, but also a less personal one: the closeness and inseparability that come from being of the same substance. Only this specific use of the word ἴδιος will serve satisfactorily in the battle against Arianism, and this is the use that Athanasius adopts.

Athanasius' christological use of ἴδιος directly parallels his trinitarian use of the word. He writes that the Logos took a body from the virgin 'and made it his own (ἰδιοποιεῖται) as an

37 In fact, in this chapter Athanasius uses forms of ἴδιος 5 times to indicate an offspring who is of the same substance as his parent.

38 Louth, 'The Use of the Term ἴδιος', 200.

instrument, in which to be known and dwell' (*De Incar. Ver.* 8 [152]). He asserts that even though the Logos was immortal, he 'took to himself a body that could die in order to offer it as his own (*ὡς ἴδιον*) on behalf of all' (*De Incar. Ver.* 20 [184]). Discussing Christ's *kenosis* in Phil. 2, Athanasius writes that he yielded his own body (*τὸ ἴδιον ἑαυτοῦ σῶμα*) to death (*Con. Arian.* 1.44 [104a]).[39] This emphasis that the flesh that died on the cross was the Logos' own flesh, not another's, is central to Athanasian soteriology. As Louth points out, if the flesh were another's, then the death would be merely that of a man for humanity, not that of the Logos for us. In such a case, we would not possess incorruption in a stable way but only in a way analogous to Adam's condition before the fall.[40] However, it was only after the word *ἴδιος* had gained its specific Alexandrian sense during the Arian controversy that it could be applied usefully to christology. If the word could have indicated a close relationship between two separate people (as it could have in its earlier, more general usage), then it could not have safeguarded the Athanasian emphasis that the crucifixion brought about the death of the Logos' own flesh.

Louth argues that Cyril uses the word *ἴδιος* in much the same way, except that he employs it to refer to three relations, that between the Father and the Son, that between the Logos and his flesh, and that between the Logos and the eucharistic bread. Louth concludes that using the same word to describe all three relations underlines 'their reality, closeness, and intensity. We have to do with what is unequivocally divine in the Son, the Incarnation, in the Eucharist: and this contact with the divine is our salvation.'[41]

As we saw with Athanasius, so also in the case of Cyril, *ἴδιος* refers to the unity of substance between the persons of the Trinity, not to the personal fellowship between them. He calls Christ 'the heir of the identity (*ἰδιότητος*) of the one who begat him' (*Com. Johan.* 2.1 [1.190]), referring to the identity between the Son and the Father. Cyril explains Jesus' statement that God

[39] Cf. *De Incar. Ver.* 18 [176] and *Con. Arian.* 1.45 [104c], where Athanasius uses the equivalent expression *οὐχ ἑτέρου* to refer to the relation between the Logos and his flesh.

[40] Louth, 'The Use of the Term *ἴδιος*', 200. Cf. *Con. Arian.* 2.68 [292c–3a].

[41] Louth, 'The Use of the Term *ἴδιος*', 201.

is his own Father (ἴδιον πατέρα) to mean that the Logos is of the essence of God the Father (*Com.Johan.* 2.1 [1.207]).[42] Cyril also insists that the Holy Spirit is the Son's own, and here as well it is apparent that he has in mind an intimacy of substance, not of personal communion. He writes: 'For the Spirit is the Son's own (ἴδιον), and not supplied from without as the things of God come to us from without, but exists in him naturally even as in the Father, and through him proceeds to the saints, apportioned by the Father as is fitting for each' (*Com.Johan.* 5.2 [1.692]). Here the fact that Cyril describes the Spirit as existing naturally (ἐνυπάρχει φυσικῶς) in the Son and the Father indicates that his focus is on the identity of nature or substance between the Son and the Holy Spirit, not on their personal communion.[43]

When he applies the word ἴδιος to christology, Cyril again follows closely in Athanasius' footsteps. He writes that Christ's body was 'his own, and not another's garment' (*Glaph. Lev.* 4.4 [576b]), and insists, 'We understand the Word to be one with his own flesh' (*Com.Johan.* 12.1 [3.155]). Cyril asserts that when the Logos died according to the flesh, he was offering his own life as the equivalent for the life of all (*Com. Johan.* 9.prooem. [2.378]).[44] Cyril calls the flesh the Logos' own proper good (τὸ ἴδιον ἀγαθόν) (*Com.Johan.* 5.5 [2.70]). In fact, Cyril insists on this close substantial unity between the Logos and his flesh even when he distinguishes deity from humanity in the Saviour's person. Commenting on John 1: 14, he writes, 'He is also God by nature in flesh and with flesh, possessing it as his own (ὡς ἰδίαν), and recognized as being other than it, and worshipped in it and with it' (*Com.Johan.* 1.9 [1.140]). Even though one can recognize the difference between the flesh and deity, the incarnate Logos is nevertheless a single divine entity and is worshipped as such.

In a helpful analysis of Cyril's use of the word ἴδιος, Siddals points out that he sees Christ's humanity not just as the human constitution, but also in the sense of human experience. Humanity is something the Logos adds to himself, making it his own so that the entire range of human experience can become his own as well. Siddals argues that Cyril uses the Aristotelian

42 Cf. *Trin. Dial.* 3 [237.80–2]; *Com.Johan.* 2.1 [1.184].

43 Cf. *Com. Is.* 1.5 [70.237d]; *Com.Joel* 2 [1.337–8]; *Trin. Dial.* 6 [246.38].

44 Cf. *Com.Johan.* 12.prooem. [3.61].

logical categories of natural qualities and accidents to explain the incarnation. Deity is the natural quality of the Logos (he is God by nature), but he adds humanity to himself as a set of accidents according to the economy of the incarnation. However, she points out, the Logos adds humanity to himself in such a way that it becomes an inseparable property, and this is what Cyril means by saying that the flesh is the Logos' own.[45] An important passage from Cyril's *De Incar. Vnigen.* illustrates Siddals's point. While discussing how the Logos can be both Only-Begotten and firstborn, Cyril writes, 'For just as the quality of being Only-Begotten has become a property of the humanity (*ἴδιον τῆς ἀνθρωπότητος*) in Christ on account of its union with the Logos through an arrangement of the economy, so also the quality of being among many brothers and of being firstborn has become a property of the Logos (*ἴδιον τοῦ Λόγου*) on account of his union with flesh' (*De Incar. Vnigen.* [256]).[46] This sentence comes in the context of an illuminating discussion of how salvation passes from Christ to us, and I will return to it in sect. 3.6. For now, it is sufficient to note the way Cyril uses the word *ἴδιος* to accentuate the single subject of Christ. The Logos adds the qualities of humanity (in this case, the fact of being first-born among many brothers) in such a way that they become genuinely his own. Nevertheless, even when he is considered in his humanity, he still possesses the qualities of deity (the fact of being Only-Begotten), since he is a single entity. This is the sense in which Cyril understands the flesh to be the Logos' own.

Just as he uses *ἴδιος* to show that the humanity of Christ is the Logos' own, so also Cyril insists that the Eucharist is the Logos' own flesh. During his extended discussion of John 6, Cyril writes the same thing about the Eucharist that he writes about the humanity of Christ: it is the Logos' own proper good (*ἴδιον ἀγαθόν*) (*Com. Johan.* 4.2 [1.520]). He speaks of the Logos' 'own flesh' (*ἰδία σάρξ*) when discussing Jesus' statement that whoever eats his flesh and drinks his blood will have eternal life (*Com. Johan.* 4.2 [1.532–3]), and he also makes the equivalent

45 Siddals, 'Logic and Christology in Cyril', 67–9. Gebremedhin, *Life-Giving Blessing*, 37, seems to be expressing the same idea with less philosophical precision when he writes that according to Cyril, the Logos' *ἰδία φύσις* is his deity, but his *ἰδία σάρξ* is a property of the union.

46 Cf. *De Fide Theod.* 30 [1.1.1.61–2], where the wording is identical.

statement: 'For it is understood as the body of none other (οὐχ ἑτέρου τινὸς), but of him who is by nature life' (*Com. Johan.* 3.6 [1.475]).[47]

It should be clear that in Athanasius, and especially in Cyril, ἴδιος and its related forms indicate a special kind of close relation. Although the word's more general Greek usage can extend to a relationship between two people considered separately, Cyril does not use it this way in theologically significant contexts. Instead, he uses ἴδιος as a way of indicating a mysterious substantial unity such that the one in question remains a single entity. The Father, Son, and Spirit are different divine persons, but they are also of the same substance and are therefore a single being, a single God. When Cyril (like Athanasius) refers to the Logos as the Father's own Son or the Holy Spirit as the Logos' own Spirit, his emphasis is on this identity of substance, not on the personal intimacy and communion which the Father, Son, and Spirit (considered as different persons) have with each other. Similarly, when Cyril refers to Christ's humanity as the Logos' own flesh, his stress is on the fact that Christ is a single entity, a single divine person who has added humanity to what he already was without changing or becoming two subjects.

This Alexandrian use of ἴδιος helps to undergird the idea of grace that I have traced in Cyril's writings. In order for God to grace us with himself through Christ, the Son must be of the same substance as the Father, and Christ must be a single entity who is, in fact, this same divine Son consubstantial with the Father. Otherwise, grace would constitute God's giving us another, not himself. However, this specific use of ἴδιος, forged during the Arian crisis, addresses only the question of what sort of Christ is *able* to give us himself in grace. It does not deal with the issue that I raised at the end of the previous section, the question of what aspect of Christ's divine sonship he *actually* gives us. Therefore, with Cyril's use of ἴδιος as background, I will now turn to the way he develops a specific use of the word οἰκειότης.

[47] Among the many scholars who have noted Cyril's emphasis on the Eucharist as the Logos' own flesh, see H. Chadwick, 'Eucharist and Christology', 155; Gebremedhin, *Life-Giving Blessing*, 111; Welch, *Christology and Eucharist*, 36.

3.5.3. *οἰκειότης in Cyril's Early Writings*

The *οἰκεῖος* word-group is not very prominent in Athanasius' writings. He uses the adjective less than one-tenth as often as he uses *ἴδιος* (*c*.63 times vs. *c*.682), and he uses the noun *οἰκειότης* only 6 times.[48] Furthermore, Athanasius still employs the noun in a very general sense. It appears in *Vit. Anton.* 5 [400.142] in reference to family relationships between people, and he uses it in *Con. Arian.* 1.46 [108b] and twice in *Ex. Pss.* 17.45 [121b] in reference to people's communion with God. On the other hand, Athanasius uses the word twice to refer to the relation between the Father and the Son, and here the word is clearly a synonym for *ἰδιότης*. He writes that the Son and the Father 'are one in sameness (*τῇ ἰδιότητι*) and oneness (*οἰκειότητι*) of nature, and in the identity (*τῇ ταὐτότητι*) of the one Godhead' (*Con. Arian.* 3.4 [328c–329a]). Later, Athanasius insists that there is only one God and adds, 'The Son is that One's own (*ἴδιος*) and is inseparable according to the sameness (*ἰδιότητα*) and identity (*οἰκειότητα*) of his essence' (*Con. Arian.* 3.16 [357a]). Thus Athanasius has retained the rather general use of the word *οἰκειότης*; it can refer either to a relationship between two persons conceived of separately or to an identity of nature or substance in which only one entity is in view. This ambiguity in the standard use of this word helps to explain why he uses it so rarely. Unlike *ἴδιος* (in the newer, Alexandrian sense), the word *οἰκειότης* does not unequivocally imply the unity of substance between the Father and the Son, and therefore it is of little use in the battle against Arianism.[49]

However, when we come to Cyril, the situation is completely different. He uses various forms from the *οἰκεῖος* group *c*.1,023 times in his early writings (more than one-third as often as he uses words from the *ἴδιος* group), including using *οἰκειότης*

[48] For a statistical survey of Athanasius' use of words in the two groups, see Table 1.

[49] Athanasius also uses other forms from the same group in this non-specific way. In his writings, *οἰκεῖος* can refer to a similarity between ideas (*Con. Arian.* 3.28 [384a]), to what is appropriate to say in a given instance (*Con. Arian.* 2.56 [265c]), or to family relationships (*Vit. Anton.* 36 [896b]). The verbs *οἰκειόω* and *οἰκειοποέω* can refer both to the appropriation of something as one's own (*Ex. Pss.* 44 [205a–b]) and to God's act of making people his own (*Ex. Pss.* 99 [242c]).

itself *c.*228 times.[50] The noun appears frequently in all Cyril's exegetical and anti-Arian writings that survive intact[51] except for *Thes.* and *De Incar. Vnigen.*, in which it does not occur at all. The absence of *οἰκειότης* from *Thes.* is noteworthy in light of Liébaert's contention that in this work Cyril has relied heavily on Athanasius' *Con. Arian.* and a certain *Contra Eunomium*, perhaps by Didymus.[52] It may be that in *Thes.* Cyril has adhered not only to the thought, but even to the vocabulary of his sources, so he does not use a word that is of little significance for Athanasius. In contrast, when Cyril writes on his own, *οἰκειότης* assumes considerable importance. In addition to using the noun often, Cyril also uses it very specifically. I have been unable to locate a single passage in his early writings in which Cyril uses *οἰκειότης* to refer to an association of ideas or to the possession of a thing by a person. By my count, he uses the word 10 times in reference to relationships between people, 206 times in reference to a relationship between God (or Christ) and people, and 12 times to refer to the relationship between the persons of the Trinity.[53]

Cyril's use of the word to refer to relationships between people is not of great theological significance; he sometimes indicates family/blood relationships in general (*οἰκειότης ἐξ αἵματος*),[54] marriage,[55] parent–child relationships,[56] or even the spiritual kinship between Abraham and believers.[57] Of much greater

[50] For a statistical summary of the occurrence of words from the two groups in Cyril's early writings, see Table 2.

[51] e.g. *c.*23 occurrences in *De Ador.*, *c.*29 in *Com. Proph. Min.*, *c.*61 in *Com. Is.*, *c.*49 in *Com. Johan.*

[52] Liébaert, *La doctrine christologique de Cyrille*, 19–60.

[53] For a complete list of the passages where Cyril uses the word *οἰκειότης* to refer to each kind of relationship, see Table 4. One should regard these categories as general guides. In some passages, there is a bit of ambiguity, since he might use the word to refer to more than one of the three types of relationships I have listed. Be that as it may, the major point is clear. Cyril uses the word only of personal relationships, and in the vast majority of cases, he has our relationship with God in view.

[54] e.g. *De Ador.* 16 [1045d]; *Com. Os.* 5 [1.184]; *Com. Is.* 3.4 [781d].

[55] e.g. *Glaph. Gen.* 4 [184a], although here marriage is a symbol of the spiritual relationship between Christians and Christ, so this passage could be assigned to the category of relationships between God and people.

[56] e.g. *Trin. Dial.*1 [231.156].

[57] e.g. *Com. Johan.* 6.prooem. [2.131].

consequence are the many passages in which Cyril describes Christians' relationship to God as one of *οἰκειότης*.[58] Especially common are the phrases 'communion with God' (*ἡ πρὸς θεὸν οἰκειότης*) and its equivalent 'communion with him' (*ἡ πρὸς αὐτὸν οἰκειότης*—where the context shows that *αὐτόν* refers to God),[59] and also the phrase 'spiritual communion' (*οἰκειότης πνευματική*—where again the context shows that the phrase refers to our relationship with God).[60] An illustrative passage from Cyril's *Com. Is.* will help to clarify what he means by this relationship. Commenting on Isa. 8: 18, he writes that although God has turned his face away from Israel, he will turn back to his people through the Messiah:

> He immediately introduces the face of his Emmanuel, who graciously gives communion (*χαριζομένου τὴν οἰκειότητα*) to those who have based their hope on him. For the Son has given us his own Spirit (*τὸ ἴδιον πνεῦμα*), and we have become his friends (*οἰκείοι*). And *in him we cry out, 'Abba, Father'* [Rom. 8: 15]. Therefore he names us children of the Father, since we have new birth through the Spirit, in order that we might be called brothers of the one who is truly the Son by nature.
>
> (*Com. Is.* 1.5 [237d–40a])

Here one can see that our entering into a relationship of *οἰκειότης* with God depends on the substantial unity of all three trinitarian persons, since we receive this communion when we receive the Son's own Spirit (*ἴδιον πνεῦμα*). Possessing *οἰκειότης* with God means being children of the Father, by virtue of the fact that we are brothers of the true Son. Cyril makes clear that we enter this relationship by grace rather than by nature (notice the word *χαρίζομαι*), and he also shows that he intends more than the status of sonship by indicating that we can call God 'Abba, Father'. *Οἰκειότης* involves more than the mere dignity of sonship; it also includes the intimacy of fellowship with God that the word 'Abba' conveys.

58 Liébaert, *La Doctrine christologique de Cyrille*, 220, notes Cyril's use of *οἰκειότης* to indicate the union between people and God, but he does not discuss what Cyril intends to convey by the word, except to say that it is a synonym for *συνάφεια*.

59 e.g. *Com. Os.* 5 [1.204]; *Com. Johan.* 11.8 [2.690]; *Trin. Dial.* 1 [231.154]; *Com. Rom.* [3.223].

60 e.g. *De Ador.* 2 [237b]; *Glaph. Gen.* 4 [184a]; *Com. Amos.* 1 [1.395]; *Com. Johan.* 3.5 [1.449].

Cyril's most revealing treatment of *οἰκειότης* comes in the passage from *Com. Johan.* that deals with John 10, where Jesus discusses his relationship with his sheep/disciples. Commenting on Christ's statement that he knows his own and they know him, just as he and the Father know each other, Cyril writes, 'For I think that in these words he does not mean by "knowledge" simply "acquaintance", but rather he employs this word to signify "communion" (*οἰκειότητος*), either by kinship and nature, or as it were in the participation of grace and honour' (*Com. Johan.* 6.1 [2.231]). Here Cyril shows that *οἰκειότης* has to do with a relational kind of knowledge, with that intimate understanding of another person that comes from a deep friendship. He also indicates that Christ has the same kind of intimacy with believers as he does with the Father. With the Father he has *οἰκειότης* by kinship and nature, whereas Christians have it with him through participation of grace and honour, but in both cases the intimacy of communion is the same. Shortly after this, Cyril paraphrases Jesus' words as follows: 'I will enter into communion (*προσοικειωθήσομαι*) with my sheep, and my sheep will be brought into communion (*οἰκειωθήσεται*) with me, according to the manner in which the Father is intimate (*οἰκεῖός*) with me, and again I also am intimate (*οἰκεῖός*) with the Father' (*Com. Johan.* 6.1 [2.232]). In this sentence Cyril uses the verb and adjective forms rather than the noun, but again he indicates that Christ's sheep have intimacy with him in the same way that he does with the Father. Then Cyril goes on to indicate that this is what it means for people to be partakers of the divine nature:

> For the Word of God is a divine nature even when in the flesh, and although he is by nature God, we are his kindred because of his taking the same flesh as ours. Therefore the manner of the communion (*οἰκειότητος*) is similar. For just as he is closely related (*ᾠκείωται*) to the Father, and through the identity (*ταυτότητα*) of their nature the Father is closely related (*ᾠκείωται*) to him, so also are we to him and he to us, in so far as he was made man. And through him as through a mediator we are conjoined (*συναπτόμεθα*) to the Father. (*Com. Johan.* 6.1 [2.232]).

Here it emerges that for Cyril the concepts of grace, deification, and the sharing of divine communion are virtually one and the same. As God, the Son shares by nature in fellowship with the Father; as man, he shares in our humanity. Thus he can be the mediator through whom God gives us himself by sharing with us the communion he has within himself.

Cyril's discussion of John 10 is extremely important, since this is the chapter in which Jesus refers to Christians as his own sheep (ἴδια πρόβατα). Although Cyril's exegesis of verses 1–30 spans 44 pages in Pusey's edition, he never uses the word ἴδιος to refer to the relationship between God and people except when he is actually quoting the phrase ἴδια πρόβατα from the biblical text.[61] He uses ἴδιος to refer to the Son's relation to the Father,[62] but when writing of Christians' relationship to God he invariably changes Christ's words from forms of ἴδιος to forms of οἰκεῖος, οἰκεόω, and οἰκειότης.[63] Cyril's consistency in making this distinction, even when discussing this passage of Scripture, shows that for him, the ἴδιος and οἰκεῖος word-groups are no longer synonymous. The former does not describe a personal relationship at all, but rather it indicates an identity of substance such that the subject can be conceived of as one entity. The latter, particularly in the noun form, describes a relationship characterized by warm fellowship between two personal beings conceived of as distinct from each other.

3.5.4. οἰκειότης φυσική in Cyril's Early Writings

Cyril's comments on John 10 show that he uses οἰκειότης not merely to indicate that believers have *some sort* of communion with God, but to indicate that we share in *the same* οἰκειότης that the persons of the Trinity have with one another. In fact, this is the primary aspect of God's being that he grants us when he gives himself to us in grace. Cyril demonstrates even more clearly that this relationship within the Godhead is the primary content of οἰκειότης through a very pointed expression, οἰκειότης φυσική, which he uses seven times in *Trin. Dial.* and *Com. Johan.* to refer to the relationship within the Trinity. In most of these passages,

[61] I should point out that this is one of the sections of the commentary that has not completely survived. However, the three occurrences of the word ἴδιος in John 10 come in vv. 4, 3, and 12, on which we do have Cyril's comments intact. Book 7, which survives only in fragments, begins with John 10: 18.

[62] e.g. *Com. Johan.* 6.1 [2.232], 6.1 [2.245].

[63] In fact, the various forms of the οἰκεῖος word-group appear 26 times in this section and οἰκειότης itself 13 times, 9 of which are from the discussion of John 10: 15 [2.230–4].

Cyril uses this expression as a way of insisting on the difference between the Son and the saints, and thus on the identity between the Son and the Father. He argues that the Arians 'cut the Son off from his relation to and natural communion (οἰκειότητος φυσικῆς) with God the Father' (*Trin. Dial.* 1 [231.152]). Cyril insists on the equality between the Son and the Father and asks rhetorically, 'In that case, certainly the communion (οἰκειότης) between the Begotten One and the Begetter must be not merely tenuous or illusory, but natural (φυσική), must it not? For one who is born is surely of the same essence as the one who bore him. Therefore, how could the One begotten of God lack the fact of being truly God?' (*Trin. Dial.* 3 [237.12]). Elsewhere he compares the relationship between the Son and the Holy Spirit to that between a lily and its fragrance. Quoting Jesus' statement that the Spirit will take what is his and announce it to the disciples (John 16: 14), Cyril explains, 'He has indicated clearly the substantial and natural communion (τὴν οὐσιώδη καὶ φυσικὴν οἰκειότητα), according to which his Spirit is one with him.' Then after discussing the lily-fragrance analogy, he adds, 'This indicates natural communion (τὴν φυσικὴν οἰκειότητα), and certainly not a communion of participation, as if of something separate, and you will recognize that this [natural communion] is the case with the Son and the Spirit' (*Trin. Dial.* 6 [246.28]). Similarly, commenting on John 1: 32–3, Cyril argues for the full deity of the Spirit by insisting that although he descends on Jesus as a dove, he preserves 'natural communion and likeness to the Son' (*Com. Johan.* 2.1 [1.189]). As he criticizes an unnamed heretic for attempting to divide Christ, Cyril asserts that that person's purpose is 'to cut him [Christ] off altogether from that natural and essential communion (τῆς φυσικῆς καὶ οὐσιώδους οἰκειότητος) which he has with his own Father, God' (*Com. Johan.* 9.1 [2.438]). Cyril emphasizes that the Son is a true and natural Son, not a servant, by asking whether Christ would call himself free (Matt. 17: 26) if he did not possess 'natural communion with the one who begat him' (*Com. Johan.* 9.1 [2.442]).[64]

In all these passages Cyril's obvious intent is to assert the

[64] In a closely related passage which does not contain the word φυσική, Cyril argues that blasphemers 'cast the Son out from deity by nature, and as we have said before, they assign to him nothing more than a precarious communion with God the Father' (*Com. Johan.* 9.1 [2.451]).

consubstantiality of the trinitarian persons. As a result, one might think that *οἰκειότης φυσική* is a synonym for *ἰδιότης φυσική*, which would weaken the case I have built for a clear distinction between *οἰκειότης* and *ἴδιος* in Cyril's thought and would lead one to question my translation of the phrase as 'natural communion' in these passages. However, these six passages[65] are certainly not sufficient to overthrow the weight of the evidence I have already surveyed, and there are two ways one could explain Cyril's use of this expression. First, one could argue that although Cyril uses *οἰκειότης* by itself to refer specifically to fellowship between personal beings, he can still use the expression *οἰκειότης φυσική* to refer to the substantial unity between the persons of the Trinity. Alternatively, one could argue that even in these passages, Cyril intends the expression to refer to the communion, the personal intimacy between Father, Son, and Spirit. In this case, *οἰκειότης φυσική* is not strictly equivalent to the fact that the persons of the Trinity are of the same substance, even though the expression comes in passages whose primary purpose is to make that affirmation. Rather, *οἰκειότης φυσική* is the result of the unity of substance. Because the Father, Son, and Spirit are consubstantial, they have warm, intimate fellowship with each other, and they have such communion naturally and essentially, not in any participatory sense. This, of course, is the interpretation reflected in my translations of the passages.

If one were to consider only these six passages, the first of the two explanations would be more plausible, and the translations I have offered would need to be revised. However, the second explanation is more consistent with the overall distinction Cyril makes between the two word-groups, and a consideration of the remaining passage will tip the balance towards that explanation. Commenting on John 1: 13, Cyril explains the difference between the way the Son is begotten of God and the way Christians are:

> When he had said that *authority was given to them* from him who is by nature Son to become *sons of God*, and had hereby first introduced that which is of adoption and grace, he can afterwards add without danger [of misunderstanding] that they *were begotten of God*, in order that he might show the greatness of the grace that was conferred on them,

[65] I wrote that Cyril uses this expression 7 times. I will discuss the remaining passage shortly.

gathering as it were into natural communion (*οἰκειότητα φυσικὴν*) those who were alien from God the Father, and raising up the slaves to the nobility (*εὐγένειαν*) of their Lord, on account of his warm love towards them. (*Com. Johan.* 1.9 [1.135]).

Here Cyril indicates not merely that Christians share *οἰκειότης* with God, but also that they share in his *οἰκειότης φυσική*. In the light of how emphatically Cyril distinguishes believers from Christ throughout all his writings, *οἰκειότης φυσική* cannot be the identity of substance that characterizes the trinitarian persons. Nothing could be more foreign to Cyril's thought than the idea that God would share his very substance with us in the sense that we lose our own personal identity and acquire God's. Rather, in this passage *οἰκειότης φυσική* must be the communion that the Father, Son, and Holy Spirit share as a result of their consubstantiality, and thus this is very likely what Cyril means by the phrase in the other six passages as well. Although we were foreign to God, his warm love for us has led him to raise us up to the intimacy of communion that characterizes his own intertrinitarian relationships, and the only difference is that we possess that fellowship by grace, whereas the Son has it naturally. The idea that Christians can possess *by grace* the *natural* communion of the Trinity is a striking one indeed. The concept is tantalizingly paradoxical, and only Cyril's careful distinction between *ἴδιος* and *οἰκειότης* prevents it from being self-contradictory. But this arresting language shows the depth of God's self-giving as he graciously shares his own fellowship with us.

It should now be apparent that Cyril's careful distinction between the idea of identity of substance (which implies a single entity, a single God) and the concept of intimacy of communion (between two persons understood as distinct) does more than simply help illuminate what he means by God's sharing of divine fellowship with humanity. It also lies very close to the heart of his understanding of grace. For Cyril, grace is God's giving himself to people through Christ. As we have seen, part of what it means to say that God gives us himself is that God shares with us the incorruption and holiness that characterize his nature. Furthermore, God gives us himself by giving us the status of sons, just as the true Son possesses sonship. However, Cyril sees divine sonship not merely in terms of status, but also in terms of the close intimacy and loving communion that Father and Son have with each other. This, Cyril argues, is primarily what it means to say that God gives us himself.

This understanding of grace is consistent with (and indeed virtually demands) the sort of language about the Trinity and the Saviour that Cyril uses. Only if the Logos is really the Father's own Son (*ἴδιος υἱός*) can the gift of the Son constitute God's giving us himself. If grace were God's giving people gifts such as aid, power, or co-operation (all of which could be understood as being separate from God himself), then God could use a creature to mediate these gifts to humanity. But God's giving us himself would not be possible if the Son could be construed as other than the very same being, the same God, as the Father. On the other hand, if one construed the Father and the Son *only* as a single entity, and not also as distinct persons, then there would be no *οἰκειότης*, no communion, between them. In this case God would have little of consequence to share with humanity when he gives us himself. Incorruption and holiness *are* qualities of God's nature, but they are not nearly as central as the love that flows from one person of the Trinity to the others and that is the very core of God's being. This, in Cyril's understanding, is the heart of God's character, and this loving fellowship is the heart of what God shares with us when he gives himself to us in grace. To be God is to be an eternal fellowship of three divine persons. The Christian shares by grace in that very communion, even as he remains a creature in his own nature. The distinction Cyril makes so carefully between *ἴδιος* and *οἰκειότης* is a tool he has developed and pressed into service to express this understanding of God's being and this concept of grace.

3.6. GRACE AS CHRIST'S SHARING *οἰκειότης* WITH HIS OWN HUMANITY

It remains now to consider how God shares this *οἰκειότης* with us. We have seen that according to Cyril, at creation God gave himself to Adam by giving him his Spirit. How then does God give himself anew to fallen mankind through Christ? I will not attempt to discuss Cyril's concept of the atonement, as important as the death and resurrection of Christ are in his thought,[66] but will limit myself to the way he sees salvation as being wrought within the person of Christ through the interplay between his deity and humanity.

In sect. 3.5.2, I cited an important passage from *De Incar. Vnigen.* in which Cyril indicates that the Logos assumes the properties that pertain to humanity, and I now quote that passage more fully. Cyril writes:

> The one who was the Only-Begotten as God, has as man become *firstborn* among us and *among many brothers* [Rom. 8: 29], according to the incarnational union, in order that we also in him and because of him might become sons of God naturally and by grace. First, we have become sons naturally in him and in him alone, but then also by participation and grace we have ourselves become sons through him in the Spirit. For just as the quality of being Only-Begotten has become a property (ἴδιον) of the humanity in Christ on account of its union with the Logos through an arrangement of the economy, so also the quality of being among many brothers and of being firstborn has become a property (ἴδιον) of the Logos on account of his union with flesh.
>
> (*De Incar. Vnigen.* [254–6])

One should note the precision with which Cyril explains the dynamics of salvation. As he emphasizes repeatedly elsewhere, there are two modes of sonship, natural (φυσικῶς) and by grace (κατὰ χάριν). But here Cyril indicates that humanity has sonship in both these ways, although he must make a subtle distinction between Christ's humanity and ours in order to argue this. Only Christ's humanity becomes a son of God naturally, because his humanity is the Logos' own, and the Logos is the natural Son of God. But through Christ and in the Spirit, each Christian gains sonship by participation and grace. Cyril explains this bold assertion by describing the way the Logos makes his humanity his own (the part of the passage that I discussed in sect. 3.5.2). God the Logos gives himself (primarily his οἰκειότης φυσική with the Father) to the concrete humanity that he makes his own at the incarnation, thereby bringing that humanity into natural sonship with God within the Logos' own person. But that humanity also represents our humanity (Christ is 'firstborn among many

[66] Several scholars have noted that Cyril places more emphasis than other patristic theologians on the death of Christ: e.g. Kelly, *Early Christian Doctrines*, 397; Blanchette, 'Cyril's Idea of the Redemption', 479; Wilken, *Judaism and the Early Christian Mind*, 199.

brothers as man'), and so what happens naturally *in Christ* takes place by grace *through Christ* in the life of each Christian.

This passage also helps to fortify my case for understanding sonship primarily as *οἰκειότης φυσική*, the communion that the Son naturally has with the Father. If sonship were largely a matter of status, then there would be little need to make the distinction that Cyril makes here between natural and adopted sonship; an adopted son usually has the same legal status as a natural one. On the other hand, if sonship were primarily a matter of consubstantiality with God the Father, then it would be unthinkable to say that even Christ's humanity has divine sonship naturally. In order for passages such as this one to be comprehensible, Cyril must mean by sonship something more than mere status but less than the possession of God's very substance.

Because of this emphasis on the way salvation is effected within the person of Christ, Cyril explains the incarnation and Jesus' human life in terms of the Logos' giving what he already is as God to himself as man, or to state it differently, the Logos' giving himself to his own humanity. Cyril expresses this in three ways: he writes that although the Logos is the natural Son, he becomes a son by adoption as one of us. He asserts that although the Holy Spirit is his own Spirit, he receives him from without as a man. And he declares that although the Logos is life by nature, he overcomes death and corruption as a man. One illustration of each of these should suffice.

In *Trin. Dial.* 3, Cyril discusses Christ's humiliation and exaltation (Phil. 2), and he insists that both movements are actions of God the Logos, who laid aside his glory and returned to that same glory. Cyril then explains Christ's reception of the name above all names: 'Therefore, it was then fitting to think that the name above all names should be given to the Son after he had assumed an appearance like ours, so that he, the true Son would be accounted a son of God like one of us and be adopted with us and on our account, in order that we also, on his account might as sons lay hold of a glory that surpasses our nature and be shown to be *partakers of* his *divine nature* [2 Pet. 1: 4]' (*Trin. Dial.* 3 [237.82]). Here we see a concise summary of Cyril's understanding of grace and salvation: The Logos, the true Son (*ὁ γνήσιος υἱός*), became an adopted son (*θετός*) on our account. The purpose of this was that we could become sons, and Cyril equates this adopted sonship with being partakers of the divine nature. Christ's adoption as a man could not have been for his own profit, for one who was the true Son could hardly consider it an advantage to become an adopted son. Rather, he gave his natural divine sonship to his humanity and became a *θετός* so that we too could become *θετοί*.[67]

While commenting on John 1: 32–3, Cyril explains that Adam received the gift of the Spirit but did not preserve this gift. In contrast, he writes of Christ:

> When the Word of God became man, he received the Spirit from the Father as one of us (not receiving anything for himself individually, for he was the giver of the Spirit); but in order that he who knew no sin might, by receiving the Spirit as man, preserve him to our nature, and might again inroot in us the grace which had left us.
>
> (*Com. Johan.* 2.1 [1.184])[68]

Here it is apparent that one person, the Logos incarnate, both gives and receives the Holy Spirit. Cyril makes clear that Christ did not need to receive the Spirit, nor did he (even considered in his humanity) gain anything by doing so. Instead, he received the Spirit so that the grace (that is, the person of the Spirit) would be rooted in us again. Also, as he discusses John 16: 33, Cyril ties humanity's conquest of death to the resurrection of Christ. He insists that 'as man, for us and for our sakes Christ became alive again, making his own resurrection the beginning of the conquest over death', and he asserts, 'Christ conquered as man for our sakes, therefore becoming the beginning and the gate and the way for the human race' (*Com. Johan.* 11.2 [2.657]).[69] In this passage, Cyril shows that what the Logos did as a man constituted our victory. His death was our death; his resurrection was our resurrection. What the Logos did was a human action, but it was a human action that we could not do ourselves. He died and rose as man on our account, so that in and through him we might conquer death and corruption.[70]

67 Cf. *Trin. Dial.*6 [246.22–4].

68 Cf. *Com. Johan.* 5.2 [1.692].

69 Cf. *Ep. Pasch.* 1.6 [372.184], 2.8 [372.232], where Cyril states that Christ offered himself as the firstfruits of all humanity. Cf. also *Trin. Dial.*1 [231.168], where he insists that Christ mediated as man.

70 Among Cyril's later works with the same emphasis on Christ's giving

Many scholars have noted Cyril's emphasis on the way the Logos effects salvation for humanity by giving his sonship, his Spirit, and his incorruption to his own humanity.[71] I should simply point out again that such an understanding grows out of Cyril's concept of grace. If grace consisted of God's giving us assistance or power to accomplish something ourselves or even of God's accomplishing something on our behalf, then such an idea of the Logos' giving himself to his own humanity would be unnecessary, and probably inconceivable. But since Cyril sees grace as God's gift of himself to humanity, the force of his thought moves him to the view that salvation is not simply something that is accomplished for people *by* Christ, but something that takes place *in* Christ. The Logos gives his own communion with the Father to his own humanity, in order to give this intimacy to all humanity as well.

3.7. THE CONNECTION BETWEEN GRACE AND CHRISTOLOGY IN CYRIL

One might think that Cyril's emphasis on the way the Logos gives himself to his humanity would lead to a divisive christology, but in fact, exactly the opposite is the case. If the humanity of Christ were conceived of as an independent subject, then the Logos' humanity would be not a natural son of God, but rather a son by grace. In that case, our union with Christ in his humanity would be of no benefit, since in Cyril's thought only a natural Son can give us sonship with God. Only if Christ is a single personal subject and if this subject is the incarnate Logos himself can he give us the *οἰκειότης* that he shares with the Father.

Therefore, Cyril's strongly unitive christology is directly related to his understanding of grace, and in fact, one might even say that christology is the primary way he writes about grace. One could adduce countless examples of Cyril's insistence on the unity of Christ's person from his early writings, and we have already seen several of these as I discussed the difference

himself to his own human nature for our sake, cf. *Schol.* 1 [1.5.219–20/1.5.184]; *Quod Vnus Christ.* [334, 430]; *Con. Theo.* 1.3 [3.512].

[71] e.g. Young, 'A Reconsideration of Alexandrian Christology', 113–14; Torrance, *Theology in Reconciliation*, 161–2; Hallman, 'The Seed of Fire', 374.

between Christ's sonship and ours. But rather than concentrating on the technical christology from the early period of Cyril's career, I will now turn to his later writings, in order to show the consistency of his mature christology with the concept of grace he has developed previously.

4
God's Own Son as the Source of Grace in Cyril's Later Writings

We have seen that Cyril's careful distinction between *ἴδιος* and *οἰκειότης* plays an important role in his portrayal of grace in his early writings. During and after the Nestorian controversy, however, Cyril virtually ceases using the word *οἰκειότης*.[1] One can account for this striking change by noting that his attention has shifted from more general soteriological concerns to the specific question of technical christology: the relation between Jesus' deity and humanity. In spite of this paucity of direct reference to divine *οἰκειότης*, Cyril's technical christology grows directly out of his conviction that God shares with humanity the intimate communion he has within himself. As a result, the christological notes that Cyril sounds so emphatically during the controversy are in complete harmony with the soteriological symphony he has conducted previously, and his theology of grace is a large part of what drives his expression of Christ's unified person.

In this chapter, I will examine the consistency of Cyril's broader early thought with his more narrowly christological thought in his later writings. I will do this by explaining his conviction that the word *οἰκειότης* is inadequate to describe the christological union, by probing the relation between grace and his insistence on the unity of Christ's person, by looking at the way Cyril uses the word *ἴδιος* to express that personal unity, and by considering the relation between Cyril's understanding of grace and two of his most famous slogans: the appellation *Theotokos* for Mary and the formula 'one incarnate nature of God the Logos' (*μία φύσις τοῦ θεοῦ λόγου σεσαρκωμένη*).

[1] For a statistical summary of the use of words in the *ἴδιος* and *οἰκεῖος* groups in Cyril's later writings, see Table 3.

4.1. THE INADEQUACY OF οἰκειότης AS A CHRISTOLOGICAL DESIGNATION

Because Cyril sees the word οἰκειότης as representing fellowship or intimacy between two different personal beings, and because he insists so strongly on the unity of Christ, he will certainly not tolerate the use of this word as a description of the christological union. In fact, a large part of what sparks Cyril's vehemence during the controversy is the very fact that Nestorius himself uses this word of the union. In this section, I will consider Nestorius' understanding of the union as οἰκειότης and will examine the response this provokes from Cyril.

4.1.1. Nestorius' Use of οἰκειότης

We have seen that in his second letter to Cyril, Nestorius argues that the New Testament and the Creed use titles common to both the Logos and the assumed man when discussing the birth, sufferings, and death of Christ. He cites a number of biblical passages in support of this contention and then concludes:

> The body therefore is the temple of the Son's deity, and a temple united to it by a complete and divine conjunction (συνάφειαν), so that the nature of deity is related (οἰκειοῦσθαι) to the things belonging to the body, and the body is acknowledged to be noble and worthy of the wonders related in the Gospels. To attribute also to him, in the name of this relation (οἰκειότητος), the properties (ἰδιότητας) of the flesh that has been conjoined with him—I mean birth and suffering and death—is, my brother, either the work of a mind that truly errs in the fashion of the Greeks or that of a mind diseased with the insane heresy of Arius and Apollinarius and the others. Those who are thus carried away with the idea of this relation (οἰκειότητος) are bound, because of the relation (οἰκειότητα), to make the divine Logos have a part (κοινωνὸν) in being fed with milk and participate to some degree in growth and stand in need of angelic assistance because of his fearfulness at the time of the passion. (1.1.1.31–2)[2]

Nestorius uses the verb οἰκειόω as a synonym for ἰδιοποιέω, to indicate that the Logos appropriates to himself the body taken from the virgin and makes it his own. This is traditional language, and Cyril could probably have agreed with it (at least

[2] In Loofs this is *Ep.* 5 [178–9].

to some degree), since he uses *οἰκειόω* in a similar way himself.[3] However, Nestorius immediately turns from the verb to the noun, and he uses *οἰκειότης* three times in this passage to indicate the relation between the Logos and the temple (the assumed man). In one sense, this is a perfectly logical move: if the verb can refer to the christological union, why cannot the noun form of the same word refer to the union? In fact, Siddals argues that Nestorius uses both *οἰκειότης* and *οἰκείωσις* to refer to the appropriation of the properties of each nature by the other because the relation between them is so close.[4] Nestorius is not necessarily implying here that the Logos and the assumed man are independent personal subjects, although much of what he writes moves very close to such a separation.

Regardless of what Nestorius intended, however, there is no other way Cyril could have read these words than as indicating a separation between the Logos and the man. As we have seen, for Cyril the noun *οἰκειότης* refers only to a personal relationship, specifically, to the relationship between the persons of the Trinity and to God's sharing that relationship with humanity. Even though Cyril can and does understand *οἰκειόω* and *οἰκείωσις* in the sense of appropriation,[5] he does not understand *οἰκειότης* this way. In the light of the great emphasis he has placed on this word in his early writings and the consistency of his use of it, one may say with virtual certainty that Cyril would have read Nestorius' assertion to mean that the christological union is merely a personal relationship between two personal entities conceived of separately. It is not the Logos' entrance into human existence while remaining a single entity.

It is also noteworthy that in this passage, Nestorius uses the expression 'the properties of the flesh which has been conjoined with him' (*τὰς τῆς συνημμένης σαρκὸς ἰδιότητας*) to refer to Christ's humanity. In fact, he often uses the verb *συνάπτω* ('to conjoin') and the noun *συνάφεια* ('conjunction') to describe the

[3] e.g. *Ep. Pasch.* 5.7 [372.324], where Cyril uses the verb to indicate that the Logos has appropriated the sufferings of his own body. Cf. *Glaph. Lev.* [561b]; *Com. Johan.* 2.4 [1.265]; *Com. Heb.* [3.379]; *Con. Nes.* 1.1 [1.1.6.18]; *Quod Vnus Christ.* [470].

[4] Siddals, 'Logic and Christology in Cyril', 108.

[5] On *οἰκειόω*, see n. 3. On *οἰκείωσις*, see *Apol. Cap. Or.* 49 [1.1.7.45]; *Ep.* 39 [1.1.4.19]; *Ep.* 50 [1.1.3.95]; *Quod Vnus Christ.* [448].

christological union, as Theodore has done before him,[6] and it seems that for Nestorius, *συνάφεια* and *οἰκειότης* are synonymous. Cyril also appears to see these words as synonyms, since he uses *συνάπτω* and *συνάφεια* to refer to our union with God, our sharing in divine communion.[7] However, precisely because he uses these words to refer to *our* union with God, Cyril insists that they cannot be used to describe the incarnation.[8] For Theodore and Nestorius, Christ is the supreme example of one who has received grace, one who has gained co-operation and aid from the Logos and has used these gifts to aspire to the second *katastasis*. Thus they quite naturally use the same words to describe the relation within Christ and the relationship between God and people. But Cyril's understanding of grace demands that he emphasize the *difference* between Christ and us, not simply the *similarity*. Christ is not primarily a human guide who shows us the way to the second age; he is God the Logos incarnate, accomplishing for us in his own person what we cannot do ourselves, namely, sharing divine fellowship with humanity so that we may become sons of God by grace. Therefore, Nestorius' description of the christological union as *συνάφεια* and *οἰκειότης* in this passage reveals the heart of the difference between his understanding of grace and Cyril's. Even if Nestorius does not mean to imply that the assumed man is a *separate* person from the Logos, he does intend us to see the personal subject of Christ as the assumed man, rather than as God who is personally present with us on earth. As a result, Nestorius and Cyril must part company here.[9]

[6] On Theodore, see *Hom. Cat.* 6.3 [135], 8.14 [207]; *De Incar.* 8 [299]. On Nestorius, see *Ep.* 3 [171]; *Ser.* 8 [248–9]; *Ser.* 10 [273–5]. Cf. Cyril's *Ep.* 55 [1.1.4.60], in which he summarizes Nestorius as saying that only the Logos is the true Son and that the one from the seed of David has been conjoined to him.

[7] On *συνάπτω*, see *Ep. Pasch.* 2.8 [372.230], 10.1 [392.192]; *De Ador.* 3 [297c]; *Glaph. Gen.* 6.4 [329a]; *Com. Is.* 4.1 [889a], 5.6 [1440d]. On *συνάφεια*, see *Trin. Dial.* 7 [246.166].

[8] McKinion, *Words, Imagery, and the Mystery of Christ*, 88, makes this point as well. I should note that Cyril himself has occasionally used *συνάπτω* to refer to the Logos' appropriation of human characteristics (e.g. *Com. Johan.* 1.9 [1.136]), but when confronted with the dangers inherent in Nestorius' use of this verb to describe the incarnation, he no longer does so.

[9] McKinion, *Words, Imagery, and the Mystery of Christ*, 103, offers a concurring opinion when he writes that Cyril sees Nestorius' view as merely the collective unity of two constitutents.

4.1.2. Cyril's Rejection of the Idea that the Union is One of οἰκειότης

Cyril's reaction to Nestorius is dramatic. If the latter is going to use *οἰκειότης* to describe the christological union, thus implying (in Cyril's eyes at least) that the union is nothing more than a close fellowship between God and the assumed man, then Cyril will stop using the word, even though it has been one of his favourites previously. In Cyril's extant writings from the time he receives Nestorius' second letter until the end of his life, *οἰκειότης* appears only eight times. In one passage[10] the word refers to the fellowship between Israel and angels, and in five others[11] Cyril uses *οἰκειότης* in his customary way to indicate the communion between people and God. The two other passages call for more attention.

During the debate over Cyril's tenth anathema (which condemns those who say that Christ offered sacrifice for his own sake), Theodoret insists that the high priest is the one from the seed of David, the one whom the Logos has assumed (*Apol. Anath. Thrdt.* 68 [1.1.6.137]), and Cyril argues that if this were the case, it would mean a denial of the mystery of the incarnation. He continues:

> And as the blessed David also said, *the Lord assumes* [or '*raises up*'—*ἀναλαμβάνων*] *the humble* [Ps. 147: 6 (146: 6 in LXX)], evidently according to disposition and spiritual communion (*οἰκειότητα τὴν πνευματικὴν*) which come to us by his will and grace and sanctification, just as we are ourselves *who are joined to the Lord are one spirit*, according to the Scripture [1 Cor. 6: 17]. But God's becoming a man and his coming to resemble us so as to share flesh and blood were not like this, for this would be simply the appropriation of a man [or 'the bringing of a man into close communion'—*οἰκειώσασθαι*] in a way no different from what could also be said of the prophets and apostles and all other holy people.
> (*Apol. Anath. Thrdt.* 72 [1.1.6.138])

This passage rehearses several of the key ideas that we have seen in Cyril's early writings. By grace and the holiness of the Spirit, God lifts people up to spiritual fellowship with himself. But the assumption of a person to God is what happens to *us*; it cannot be

[10] *Ep.* 41 [1.1.4.46.21].

[11] *De Fide Aug.* [1.1.5.30]; *De Fide Dom.* [1.1.5.97); *Ep. Pasch.* 23 [873c], 23 [877c], 28 [949d].

what has happened in the incarnation. Cyril argues that the appropriation of a man (*οἰκειώσασθαι ἄνθρωπον*) would make the incarnation no different from what God has done in the case of prophets, apostles, and saints. One should notice here that although Cyril does occasionally use the verb *οἰκειόω* to describe the incarnation, he refuses Theodoret the right to the expression *οἰκειώσασθαι ἄνθρωπον*. This phrase, according to Cyril, implies the appropriation of an independent man, which means that Christ is no longer a single person (the Logos enfleshed) but rather an *οἰκειότης* of two people. One may speak of the incarnation as the Logos' appropriating *humanity* into his own person, but not as his appropriating *a man* into fellowship with himself. Cyril thus makes clear that *οἰκειότης* is not an acceptable description of the christological union. As he uses the word, it refers to communion between two people, not to the relation of a single person to his own properties.[12]

The other passage in which Cyril uses the word *οἰκειότης* is somewhat problematic for the case I have presented. He explains Christ's passion by using the analogy of the two birds that are offered for the cleansing of a leper in Lev. 14. He explains that one bird is killed, and then the live bird is dipped in the blood of the dead one. Cyril continues: 'Why is this? The Word was alive even though his own flesh was dead, and the passion was said to be common to them because of the relation (*οἰκειότητά*) and the union (*ἕνωσιν*) he had with the flesh. And so he himself indeed was alive as God, but he made the body his own (*ἴδιον*), and thus accepted in himself by association (*κατ' οἰκείωσιν*) the sufferings of the body, while in his own nature (*ἰδίαν φύσιν*) he suffered nothing' (*Schol*. 34 [1.5.229]). This is the closest Cyril ever comes to using the word *οἰκειότης* as a description of the incarnation, but one should note that he does not write directly that the Logos shared communion with flesh through *οἰκειότης*; he writes that the Logos was united with the flesh and therefore shared in the passions of the flesh. Furthermore, it is clear that Cyril does not mean to imply any separation of the Logos and his flesh; he writes that the Logos himself (*ὁ αὐτός*) was alive as God, that he made his body his own (*ἴδιον*), and that he received the sufferings of his body by association (*κατ' οἰκείωσιν*). In this passage, Cyril

[12] Cf. *Ep*. 17 [1.1.1.36], where Cyril argues that *συνάφεια* is not an appropriate designation for the union.

appears to be using οἰκειότης in the sense of οἰκείωσις. The Logos appropriated the passions of his own body to himself when he made the body his own, so that the same one suffered in the flesh while remaining impassible in his own nature.

This passage from *Schol.* is the only potential exception to a remarkably consistent pattern of usage of οἰκειότης. Under the influence of a thought that concerns the Logos' relation to impersonal sufferings, in a context in which he uses both οἰκείωσις and ἴδιος (his normal words for expressing such an impersonal relation), Cyril seems to use οἰκειότης in the same impersonal way. Of course, the presence of one counter-example does not overthrow the evidence from *c.*235 occurrences of the word to refer to fellowship between personal beings, and it is possible that not even this passage is actually an exception to the pattern. Here οἰκειότης refers not to the christological union itself but to the Logos' participation in one aspect of human experience, namely suffering. So one could interpret the statement to mean that the Logos shared communion *with us* in our sufferings and death by suffering as one of us. If this is correct, then even here Cyril's use of the word is consistent with his general pattern.

Instead of the words συνάφεια and οἰκειότης, Cyril uses a variety of expressions to describe the christological union. Most are phrases that he has used often in his earlier writings, and he continues to enlist them to show the strength of the union. Among these are his insistence that Christ is 'one out of both [realities]' (εἷς ἐξ ἀμφοῖν or εἷς ἐκ δυοῖν),[13] that Christ is one in the same way that a human being, composed of body and soul, is one,[14] that the Logos became man while remaining what he was,[15] and that the Logos became man, rather than coming into a

[13] Among Cyril's writings before the controversy, see *Glaph. Gen.* 6.1 [297c]; *Glaph. Lev.* 4.4 [576b]; *Trin. Dial.* 1 [231.184]; *Com. Johan.* 3.5 [1.442], 4.2 [1.532–3]. Among his later writings, see *Ep. Pasch.* 17.2 [776]; *Ep.* 4 [1.1.1.27]; *Ep.* 40 [1.1.4.26].

[14] Among Cyril's early writings, see *Com. Johan.* 12.1 [3.155]. Among his later writings, see *Con. Nes.* 2.prooem [1.1.6.33], 3.6 [1.1.6.73]; *Ep.* 17 [1.1.1.38]; *Expl. 12 Cap.* 14 [1.1.5.20]; *Ep.* 45 [1.1.6.154].

[15] Among Cyril's early writings, see *Ep. Pasch.* 1.6 [372.182]; *Trin. Dial.* 1 [231.166]. Among his later writings, see *Ep. Pasch.* 17.4 [785d]; *Ep.* 4 [1.1.1.28]; *Ep.* 17 [1.1.1.35]; *Expl. 12 Cap.* 5 [1.1.5.17]; *Schol.* 5 [1.5.187], 12 [1.5.191].

man.[16] In addition, Cyril begins to use even stronger language to describe the christological union; he argues that it is a natural union (ἕνωσις φυσική)[17] or a union according nature (ἕνωσις κατὰ φύσιν),[18] and he introduces the expression 'union according to *hypostasis*' (ἕνωσις καθ' ὑπόστασιν).[19] Cyril uses these three phrases as synonyms (one could translate all of them as 'substantial union' or 'actual union') to convey the idea that there is a true union between humanity and the Logos, not merely a conjunction or fellowship between the Logos and a man.[20] The idea of conjunction describes our union with God; the union in Christ must be more than this.[21]

This sudden disappearance of *οἰκειότης* from Cyril's writings during the controversy can hardly be a coincidence, especially since he writes directly in *Apol. Anath. Thrdt.* that this word is not an acceptable way to refer to the christological union. Whereas previously he has written at length about grace as the sharing of divine communion, now Cyril's attention is focused more narrowly on the christological union itself. To continue using the word *οἰκειότης* might lead to confusion about the issue now at hand. However, although Cyril's writings during the controversy are more specifically focused, the idea of grace that has shaped his christology remains prominent in his mind, even if it does not surface as directly in his words. I will now demonstrate this by looking at the connection between Cyril's concept of grace and his portrayal of Christ's single personal subject.

16 Among Cyril's early writings, see *Ep. Pasch.* 11.8 [392.304]; *Trin. Dial.* 1 [231.166]; *Com. Johan.* 1.9 [1.140], 4.4 [1.577]. Among his later writings, see *Theot. Nol. Confit.* 14 [1.1.7.25]; *Ep.* 17 [1.1.1.36].

17 e.g. *Ep.* 17 [1.1.1.36].

18 e.g. ibid.

19 e.g. *Ep.* 4 [1.1.1.26]; *Ep.* 17 [1.1.1.36]; Anathema 2 [1.1.1.40].

20 Cf. *Con. Nes.* 2.prooem. [1.1.6.33], where he insists that the Only-Begotten has been made man *οὐ κατὰ συνάφειαν ἁπλῶς* but *καθ' ἕνωσιν ἀληθῆ*.

21 Several scholars have noted that Cyril's understanding of the way God gives us grace and divine sonship by adoption would be impossible without a substantial union of humanity to the Logos: e.g. Samuel, 'Some Facts about the Alexandrine Christology', 141; Torrance, *Theology in Reconciliation*, 171–2; Russell, *Cyril of Alexandria*, 45–6.

4.2. GRACE AND THE UNITY OF CHRIST'S PERSON

To a large degree, Cyril's insistence on the single subject of Christ is a direct result of his conviction that God the Logos gives himself to humanity through his incarnate life. This should become clear as I examine the primary ways in which Cyril attacks Nestorius' alleged separation of the Logos from the assumed man and defends his own understanding of Christ's person. After I consider these aspects of his thought, I will look at two of the modern disagreements that Cyril's christology has occasioned.

4.2.1. The Logos as the Single Subject of Christ

Many of the arguments that Cyril uses during the Nestorian controversy to show the unity of Christ's person are identical to the arguments he has used earlier to show that the Logos is of the same substance as the Father. He insists that Christ is the Son of God by nature; he did not receive deity, sonship, or grace from the outside.[22] Cyril argues that if Christ were not Son by nature, he would not be able to make us sons or to give us grace.[23] He sharply contrasts Christ's natural sonship with our sonship by grace.[24] Of the many passages in which Cyril continues these emphases, three are especially noteworthy. In the first, Cyril cites Nestorius' argument that Scripture sometimes calls people 'gods' and insists that Emmanuel is not God in the same way that people are. He writes to Nestorius: 'You have made [merely] equal to the sons by grace him on account of whom they have been enriched with the grace of sonship.' Shortly thereafter, Cyril continues:

If *he gives authority to them that received him to become children of God*, as John says [John 1: 12], and if it is true that his Spirit makes us also to be

[22] e.g. *Ep.* 4 [1.1.1.28]; *Con. Nes.* 3.1 [1.1.6.57]; *Expl. 12 Cap.* 25 [1.1.5.23]; *Quod Vnus Christ.* [334–6]; *Ep.* 55 [1.1.4.53]; *Ep. Pasch.* 28.4 [952b].

[23] e.g. *Schol.* 1 [1.5.219–20/1.5.184], 25 [1.5.203]; *Ep.* 46 [1.1.6.161]; *Quod Vnus Christ.* [382–4]; *Con. Theo.* 1 [3.512].

[24] e.g. *Theot. Nol. Confit.* 8 [1.1.7.22], 25 [1.1.7.30]; *Ep.* 1 [1.1.1.14, 18]; *Con. Nes.* 2.2 [1.1.6.37]; *Ep.* 14 [1.1.1.98]; *Ep. Pasch.* 24.3 [896b]; *Quod Vnus Christ.* [334].

sons of God, *for God sent forth the Spirit of his Son into our hearts crying, 'Abba, Father'* [Gal. 4: 6], no one who is accustomed to think correctly will endure this man's saying that he [Christ] too is son in such manner as was Israel. (*Con. Nes.* 2.4 [1.1.6.40])

One can see that here, as in his early writings, Cyril connects grace with our adoption as sons of God, and he insists that Christ must be Son in a greater way than this, or he could not be the one on whose account we gain our adoption.

The second noteworthy passage comes in Cyril's festal letter for the year 436. He discusses Jesus' trial, at which the crowd tells Pilate that Jesus has made himself out to be God's Son (John 19: 7). Cyril argues:

He did not [simply] *make himself out to be God's Son*, but he truly was so. For he possessed the quality of sonship not from the outside, nor as something added, but as being the Son by nature, for this is what we must believe. For we are sons of God by adoption as we are conformed to the Son who has been begotten of him [the Father] by nature. For if there were no true Son, who would remain to whom we could be conformed by adoption? Whose representation would we bear? Where indeed would the resemblance be, if we were to say that the original did not exist? (*Ep. Pasch.* 24.3 [896b])

Adoption is not a matter of divine fiat; it is a conformity that God gives us to the true Son. If there were no true Son, then there would be no one to whom we could become conformed, and therefore we could not become adopted sons.

The third passage comes in *Ep.* 55, where Cyril alludes to Phil. 2: 6–8 and argues that those who postulate two sons distort the meaning of the mystery:

He is not someone who after being empty attained fullness; instead he humbled himself from his divine heights and unspeakable glory. He is not a humble man who was exalted in glory, but rather he was free and took the form of a slave. He is not a slave who made a leap up to the glory of freedom; he who was in the Father's form, in equality with him, has been made in the likeness of men. He is not a man who has come to share the riches of God's likeness. (*Ep.* 55 [1.1.4.55])

One should notice that in this passage, as in the previous one, Cyril's understanding of grace lies directly behind his argument. Only if there is a genuine Son who has moved from his own wealth to our poverty can we become sons of God. God's downward movement, the Logos' *kenosis*, is the only thing that can bring grace to us and enable us to receive God himself and become his children. No elevation of a man to divine status would accomplish anything for us. The Nestorian understanding of Christ, Cyril argues, makes an abasement of the Logos to the human condition impossible by turning the incarnation into the assumption and uplifting of a man.

With this idea that our adopted sonship depends on Christ's natural sonship as his foundation, Cyril expends a great deal of ink during the controversy insisting that Christ is a single person. He does this primarily by arguing that one cannot divide the titles, actions, or experiences of Christ among two subjects. In his second letter to Nestorius, Cyril affirms that deity and humanity have been hypostatically united in Christ, and he writes:

> If we deny substantial union (*τὴν καθ' ὑπόστασιν ἕνωσιν*) as a crass impossibility, we fall into talk of two sons, for it will then be necessary for us to assert a distinction between the particular man honoured with the title 'Son' on the one hand, and the Word from God, natural possessor of both the name and the reality of sonship, on the other. Therefore the one Lord Jesus Christ must not be divided into two sons. (*Ep.* 4 [1.1.1.28])

In this important passage, Cyril shows that the primary issue driving his unitive christology is that of sonship. He does not deny the presence of separate divine and human realities in Christ, but he excludes any thought of a dual sonship. To deny an actual, substantial union (*ἕνωσις καθ' ὑπόστασιν*) between the Logos and his humanity is to introduce two different modes of sonship into the one Christ. If one were to do this, then the human son to whom we can be united by faith would no longer be the true Son of God, but only a son by grace. If this were the case, Cyril's entire soteriology would fall to the ground. The issue of Christ's natural sonship (and therefore the importance of his unity of person) is crucial precisely because our adopted sonship depends on his natural sonship. This is what lies behind Cyril's repeated emphasis that one cannot divide the titles of Christ among two subjects.[25]

[25] Cf. *Ep.* 1 [1.1.1.16]; *Con. Nes.* 2.prooem. [1.1.6.33]; *Ep.* 17 [1.1.1.38]; Anathemas 3, 4, 6, 7, and 8 [1.1.1.40–1]; *Expl. 12 Cap.* 9 [1.1.5.18]; *Schol.* 13 [1.5.222/1.5.194]; *Ep.* 44 [1.1.4.37]. For the same emphasis in Cyril's early

As he insists on the single person of Christ, Cyril also makes clear that this personal subject is the Logos himself, not a composite. While discussing the biblical statement that Jesus increased in grace (Luke 2: 52), Cyril affirms:

> For we believe that out of the very womb of the virgin, Emmanuel proceeded forth as man while [still] being God, while certainly remaining full of all the wisdom and grace that were naturally inherent in him. What sort of growth will he then admit of, since he is the one in whom are all the treasures of wisdom, who is the co-giver with God the Father of grace from above? How then is he said to advance? It is, I suppose, by God the Word's co-measuring with the increase and stature of his own body the manifestation of the most God-befitting goods that are in him. (*Con. Nes.* 3.4 [1.1.6.70])

This idea has received a good deal of criticism from some scholars, who see Cyril as making Christ's human growth and development into a mere bit of divine play-acting.[26] However, what Cyril writes here is consistent with his earlier emphasis on the way the Logos gives himself to his own humanity, in order to give himself to us as well. Cyril asserts very strongly that the one born of Mary is God the Logos, since this person whom she bore is full of all wisdom and grace and is even the co-giver of grace (along with God the Father). If Christ were a graced man, such giving of God's fullness to his own humanity would be impossible. His personal centre must be that of the Logos himself for this self-giving to take place.[27] Again, Cyril's christological concerns coincide with his conviction that grace is predominantly God's giving us himself by giving himself to his own humanity within the person of Christ.

4.2.2. Modern Discussions about Cyril's Emphasis on Christ's Unity

Almost all modern interpreters have noted Cyril's assertion that the subject of Christ is the Logos himself, rather than a

writings, cf. *Ep. Pasch.* 8.6 [392.102]; *Ep. Pasch.* 11.8 [392.304–6]; *Com. Johan.* 6.1 [2.200], 12.1 [3.152].

[26] e.g. Greer, *The Captain of our Salvation*, 340.

[27] Cf. *Ep.* 17 [1.1.1.38]; Anathema 12 [1.1.1.42]; *Expl. 12 Cap.* 8 [1.1.5.18], 14 [1.1.5.20], 31 [1.1.4.25]; *Ep.* 39 [1.1.4.19]; *Ep.* 44 [1.1.4.36]. Among passages in Cyril's early writings with the same emphasis, cf. *Ep. Pasch.* 1.6 [372.182], 11.8 [392.304–6]; *Com. Johan.* 1.9 [1.136], 6.1 [2.157–8, 200].

composite.[28] However, Cyril's insistence on this point leads to several problems in portraying the genuine humanity of Christ, and there have been disagreements among scholars about this aspect of his thought. Of these, I will briefly survey two that are relevant for my discussion, and I will offer suggestions about the way Cyril's understanding of grace throws light on these disagreements.

The first of these concerns the consistency of Cyril's thought about the christological union. Scholars concur that Cyril's primary concept of the incarnation is that of a *kenosis* of the Logos, a movement from one condition to another while remaining what he was, not that of combining two elements to make the person of Christ.[29] However, Cyril's frequent use of the expression 'one out of both' and of the body–soul analogy to describe the christological union appears to be at odds with his major emphasis. Norris argues that these concepts, which he calls a 'composition model' of the incarnation, are too corporeal to do justice to the dominant aspect of Cyril's thought, since he is actually concerned not with the physical act of combining substances, but with the more dynamic idea that the Logos extends what he is to embrace what he is not (or, to say it differently, the Logos appropriates humanity to his own person, without thereby changing in himself). Norris concludes that Cyril is rather clumsy in his use of the composition model because he is trying to explain his own logical and linguistic schema using analogies of a physical order that are ill suited to the task.[30]

On the other hand, Wickham points out that although Cyril often refers to the body–soul analogy in passing, he never explores it or states precisely its relation to the christological union. Wickham asserts that this and Cyril's many other images

[28] e.g. Jugie, 'La Terminologie christologique de Cyrille', 24–6; Richard, 'L'Introduction du mot "Hypostase" dans la théologie', 247; Jouassard, 'Une intuition fondamentale de Cyrille', 184–5; Gould, 'Cyril and the Formula of Reunion', 245–7.

[29] The very fact that Cyril lays so much stress on the Logos as the one subject of Christ rules out the possibility that he sees his person as such a composite. Scholars who have specifically noted that the *kenosis* idea is Cyril's dominant one include Norris, 'Christological Models in Cyril', 261, 265; Angstenberger, *Der reiche und der arme Christus*, 167–9; McKinion, *Words, Imagery, and the Mystery of Christ*, 145–6, 225.

[30] Norris, 'Christological Models in Cyril', 268. Cf. Greer, *The Captain of our Salvation*, 325.

of the incarnation (a burning coal, a lily and its fragrance, the gilded ark, etc.) are all designed to show only a single feature: the fact that Christ was God and remained God. The Logos moved from one mode of being to another while remaining what he was.[31] McKinion concurs with Wickham when he insists that Cyril's many images are not descriptions of the christological union, but illustrations of certain aspects of it.[32]

If Wickham and McKinion are correct, one may conclude that the composition analogies are not so much inconsistent with Cyril's primary conception as they are incomplete. There are no real analogies to the incarnation, nor (according to Cyril) is there any satisfactory way to explain it. He often writes that the incarnation is beyond our understanding,[33] and one of his criticisms of Theodore and Nestorius is that they remove the mystery from the incarnation.[34] Furthermore, when he does explain these analogies, Cyril makes clear that the one subject of Christ is the Logos, not a person constructed by the combination of two natures. He asks Nestorius: 'When the *hypostases* have been severed into two and are conceived of as existing separately and apart, as you say, how would there be a coalescence into one *prosopon*, unless one is spoken of as the property (*ἴδιον*) of the other, just as the body will be conceived of as the property (*ἴδιον*) of a man's soul, even though it is of a different nature?' (*Con. Nes.* 3.6 [1.1.6.73]). Here Cyril's explanation makes clear that in the body–soul analogy, the soul is a human being's locus of personality, and the body is a property of the soul. In the same way, the Logos is the personal centre of Christ, and he has added humanity to himself as a property. Similarly, Cyril writes to the Egyptian monks: 'Emmanuel is admittedly out of two realities, divinity and humanity. However, there is one Lord Jesus Christ and one true Son, God and man at the same time; not a deified man (*ἄνθρωπος θεοποιηθεὶς*) who is [merely] equal to those who are deified according to grace, but rather true God who has appeared in human form for our sakes' (*Ep.* 1 [1.1.1.18]). This

31 Wickham, 'Symbols of the Incarnation in Cyril', 45–9. Cf. Siddals, 'Logic and Christology in Cyril', 132–3, who also understands the body–soul analogy as indicative of the Logos' addition of human qualities to what he already was.

32 McKinion, *Words, Imagery, and the Mystery of Christ*, 46–7.

33 e.g. *Ep.* 4 [1.1.1.27]; *Con. Nes.* 2.prooem. [1.1.6.33]; *Expl. 12 Cap.* 5 [1.1.5.17].

34 e.g. *Con. Theo.* 2 [3.532].

passage shows that even when he uses expressions such as 'one out of both', Cyril still identifies the single subject of Christ as the Logos. Cyril's talk of two realities indicates that the Logos has genuinely added humanity to what he already was; it does not imply that deity and humanity in the abstract were combined to make a composite personal being.

Of course, we have already seen that Cyril's understanding of grace demands that the subject of Christ be the Logos. A composite person who came into existence at the incarnation could not have given God to us; only one who is God and Son by nature can give us divine οἰκειότης and make us adopted sons. This, coupled with the fact that Cyril specifically states how his use of the body–soul analogy and the expression 'one out of both' should be understood, implies that one should regard these analogies as incomplete, rather than actually inconsistent with Cyril's thought. When he uses these expressions, he is not (consciously or unconsciously) moving away from his dominant idea of the incarnation as an action of the Logos. Rather, he is using admittedly incomplete images to bolster the single point on which he consistently insists: that Christ is the Logos incarnate, not a mere graced man or a composite of deity and humanity. Neither when faced with the Nestorian model of Christ as a composite *prosopon*, nor even when using images that might imply such a composition, does he waver from his view of the person of Christ. To do so would jeopardize his understanding of grace and salvation.

A second disagreement (one that has assumed the proportions of an actual debate among modern scholars) concerns the question of what Cyril means by Christ's humanity. He writes so insistently about the Logos' movement from a divine mode of existence to a human one that a number of scholars believe he regards humanity as being a condition, not a concrete reality. Liébaert argues that Cyril sees flesh as the *thing* which Christ assumed but understands humanity as the *state* of the incarnate Logos. To be a spirit united to a human body is to be human, and since the incarnate Logos obviously meets this criterion, he is human.[35] Liébaert concludes that at least in the early part of his

[35] Liébaert, *La Doctrine christologique de Cyrille*, 158–78. Cf. Prestige, *Fathers and Heretics*, 332–3; Norris, 'Christological Models in Cyril', 266.

career, Cyril had no place in his thought for a human psychology of Christ.[36] In opposition to Liébaert, Diepen argues that even in his early writings, Cyril understood Christ's humanity to be a concrete reality, not simply a state of being an embodied spirit.[37] He insists that Cyril never understood the incarnation in Apollinarian terms.[38]

I should point out that scholars recognize that at all phases of his career, Cyril affirmed the *presence* of a human soul in Christ.[39] Liébaert and others argue simply that he attached no *significance* to that human soul until the time of the Nestorian controversy. In the light of Cyril's strong emphasis on the two states of the Logos and on the incarnation as something the Logos does, it is certainly attractive to see him as understanding humanity to be the state of an enfleshed spirit. It is true that this is part of what Cyril means; the Logos did assume our condition when he became man. However, what we have seen of Cyril's concept of grace shows that this cannot be his entire understanding of humanity, even in his early writings. I asserted in sect. 3.6 that the way the Logos gives grace to us is by giving himself (primarily his own communion with the Father) to his own humanity. If Cyril had seen humanity merely as the state of being an enfleshed spirit, this emphasis would not have been possible. The Logos could not give himself to a condition, a mere state. He could (and did) enter a condition; he could live in a condition; but he could not give οἰκειότης to a condition. If Cyril had understood God's gracious self-giving only in terms of granting us his life and incorruption, then it is conceivable that he could have seen Christ's humanity only as a condition of being a spirit

[36] Liébaert, *La Doctrine christologique de Cyrille*, 179. Grillmeier, *Christ in Christian Tradition*, 415–17, 474–6, concurs with this analysis, arguing that not until the Nestorian controversy did Cyril make the human soul a theological factor in his portrayal of Christ.

[37] Diepen, *Aux origines de l'anthropologie de Cyrille*, 46–7. Cf. du Manoir, *Dogme et spiritualité*, 129.

[38] Diepen, *Aux origines de l'anthropologie de Cyrille*, 47. Cf. Welch, 'Logos-Sarx?', 280–8, who argues that in his early writings, Cyril makes the human soul of Christ the locus of his victory over human suffering.

[39] e.g. *Ep. Pasch.* 8.6 [392.106]; *Glaph. Gen.* 6.1 [297c]; *Com. Johan.* 3.5 [1.442], 8 [2.318]; *Theot. Nol. Confit.* 9 [1.1.7.23]; *Expl. 12 Cap.* 5 [1.1.5.17]; *Res. Tib.* 7 [158]. Even Raven, *Apollinarianism*, 231, who labels Cyril an Apollinarian too clever to acknowledge his debt to his master, admits that Cyril *claims* to regard Christ as having a human soul.

enfleshed, since only the flesh was subject to corruption and needed to be made alive. But because he sees grace as the Logos' bringing his humanity directly into the natural communion (οἰκειότης φυσική) that he shares with the Father, then Christ's humanity must be a concrete reality that can participate in this communion. Cyril insists that the humanity of Christ is not a separate subject but subsists in the person of the Logos; but nevertheless, this humanity must be a genuine reality that represents the humanity of all people, not *merely* a state in which the Logos lives. Therefore, as attractive as it may be for Cyril to see Christ's humanity as a condition, his understanding of grace implies that he cannot limit himself to this understanding, even in his early writings.

One can conclude that although Cyril's controversial writings rarely spell out his understanding of grace as the sharing of divine οἰκειότης, that understanding directly informs what he writes about the unity of Christ's person. If he were not a single person, he would not possess the natural sonship that alone makes our salvation possible. If Christ's one personal subject were not the Logos himself, then the Logos would no longer be the instigator of all Christ's actions, and God could not give himself to us in grace. These concerns are completely consistent with and lie behind Cyril's insistence that one cannot divide the titles and actions of Christ among two subjects. Furthermore, Cyril's understanding of grace helps to clarify what he means by his so-called composition analogies of the incarnation and what he understands humanity to be. Christ's humanity is a genuine reality that the Logos has added to his own person in order to give us his own οἰκειότης.

4.3. ἴδιος AND THE IMMEDIACY OF DIVINE PERSONAL PRESENCE

In sect. 3.5.2, we saw that Cyril follows Athanasius in using ἴδιος to refer to a close relation of which the subject is a single entity, and that Cyril applies the word specifically to the relation between the persons of the Trinity (who are of the same substance), between the Logos and his humanity, and between the Logos and the eucharistic bread. In his controversial writings,

Cyril uses ἴδιος even more often than he has previously,[40] in order to insist that the flesh of Christ is the Logos' own, since only then can he save us.[41] However, what is most noteworthy about Cyril's use of the word ἴδιος in his later writings is not the frequency of its occurrence, but the way he uses it. The word does not merely convey the inseparable union between the Logos and his flesh. Rather, Cyril uses it to show the Logos' personal presence in precisely those human situations from which Nestorius tries so hard to shield him. I will give four examples of this pattern.

In his second letter to Nestorius, Cyril denies that a man was born and then the Logos descended onto him, and he argues instead that the Logos 'was united with flesh in her [Mary's] womb and so is said to have undergone birth according to the flesh, so as to appropriate the birth of his own flesh (ἰδίας σαρκὸς)' (*Ep.* 4 [1.1.1.27]). Here Cyril makes clear that it is the Logos himself who undergoes birth from Mary, although this birth obviously refers not to the origin of his divine substance, but to his flesh. Commenting on Acts 20: 28, Cyril writes:

> Do you hear the way the apostle clearly proclaims the deity of the crucified one? For he says that we are *to be shepherds of the church of God, which he purchased through his own blood* (τοῦ αἵματος τοῦ ἰδίου). Not that he suffered in the nature of his deity, but that the sufferings of his flesh are ascribed to him because the flesh is not that of some other man, but is the Logos' own (αὐτοῦ τοῦ λόγου ἰδίαν). Therefore, since the blood is said to be God's blood, then clearly he was God, clothed with flesh.
> (*Theot. Nol. Confit.* 22 [1.1.7.29])

The biblical phrase τοῦ αἵματος τοῦ ἰδίου is somewhat ambiguous; it could mean either 'the blood of his own [Messiah]' or 'his own blood'. Cyril does not hesitate to interpret the phrase as referring to God's own blood which the Logos shed on our behalf on the cross. Similarly, as he explains his twelfth anathema, Cyril insists that although the Logos is impassible, he still suffered in his flesh: 'Even though the Word of God the Father is so [i.e.

[40] Cyril uses the adjective ἴδιος *c.*200 times in *Con. Nes.* alone, *c.*84 times in *De Fide Dom.*, *c.*75 times in *Quod Vnus Christ.*, *c.*73 times in *De Fide Aug.* For a complete statistical summary of Cyril's use of this word, see Tables 2 and 3.

[41] e.g. *Ep. Pasch.* 17.2 [777b]; *Con. Nes.* 3.6 [1.1.6.73], 5.7 [1.1.6.106]; Anathema 11 [1.1.1.41–2]; *Expl. 12 Cap.* 8 [1.1.5.18]; *Ep.* 39 [1.1.4.19]; *Res. Tib.* 7 [158]; *Quod Vnus Christ.* [330, 466, 508].

impassible] essentially, he made his own (ἰδίαν ἐποιήσατο) the flesh that is capable of death, so that by means of what is accustomed to suffer he could assume sufferings for us and on our account, and thus liberate us all from death and corruption by acting as God to make his own body (τὸ ἴδιον σῶμα) alive, and by becoming *the firsfruits of those who have fallen asleep, and the firstborn from the dead* [1 Cor. 15: 20, Col. 1: 18]' (*Expl. 12 Cap.* 31 [1.1.5.25]). These two passages show Cyril's insistence on the Logos' genuine suffering for our sakes. Because the flesh was the Logos' own, the suffering of the flesh was the Logos' personal suffering. Finally, in *Quod Vnus Christ.* Cyril states that Christ makes us sons of God by giving us his own Father. He continues:

How will this be true, unless he has himself become flesh, that is, man, by making the human body his own (ἴδιον) by a union that cannot be torn apart, in order that the body may be conceived of as his and not another's? For in this way he will send the grace of sonship to us as well, and we too shall be born of the Spirit, since human nature first attained such birth in him. (*Quod Vnus Christ.* [336])

Here Cyril connects the Logos' making the body his own to humanity's receiving the grace of adoption. We could not call God 'Father' and share in his divine fellowship with the Son unless the Son made humanity his own.

In all four of these passages, Cyril insists on the Logos' direct personal presence in even the lowest of human situations. It was God the Logos who was born as a helpless baby; it was God the Logos who shed his blood and died on our behalf; it is through the Logos' own humanity that we become sons of God. These bold assertions do not mean that Cyril has abandoned his belief in the Logos' impassibility; he insists that the Logos suffers in his flesh, not in his own nature. But his understanding of grace as God's giving us himself demands that he affirm the Logos' personal presence in the lowest depths of human experience. Indeed, it is precisely in the depths that we need God's presence the most, and if God were not to meet us there, we would have no hope of grace, adoption, or salvation, as Cyril understands these. Cyril's use of ἴδιος in these and similar passages helps to underscore the implications of his understanding of the unity of Christ. Since the one subject of Christ is the Logos, and since the humanity of Christ is the Logos' own flesh, then he can and does take part in all aspects of human experience except personal sin.

While discussing Cyril's understanding of Christ's abasement in Phil. 2, Torrance writes:

> The emphasis was laid by Cyril upon the fact that the Son or Logos, *being God*, humbled himself to become one with us in our straitened and exiguous condition as finite creatures, even in our mean and ignominious existence, in order to take upon himself our lack of worth, our nothingness or emptiness, and fill it with his own worth and fulness in God.[42]

Of course, what Torrance means by the fullness of God[43] is what I am calling grace. Only if Christ is fully and unequivocally divine can God give us himself through Christ. And only if God the Logos has descended to the very depths of human experience can God meet us where we are, in order to fill us with his presence, with his grace, with himself. As Cyril sees it, the Theodorean/Nestorian Christ can do no more than point the way to God; he cannot bring God to humanity, since he is not God himself but merely a graced man. Cyril's understanding of grace demands that God's presence in our world be personal and direct, which in turn requires that God himself, the Logos, be the one personal subject in Christ. It is this that Cyril trumpets with staggering frequency as he repeats that the flesh is God the Logos' own flesh (*ἰδία σάρξ τοῦ θεοῦ λόγου*).

4.4. GRACE, *THEOTOKOS*, AND 'ONE INCARNATE NATURE OF GOD THE LOGOS'

Cyril is probably best known as the champion of the two great slogans that comprise the heading for this section. The first of these was destined to become universally recognized (at least until the Reformation) as a hallmark of orthodoxy, but the second was never to gain unequivocal acceptance and was to be regarded by some as the firstfruits of the Monophysite heresy. In

[42] Torrance, *Theology in Reconciliation*, 161. Cf. Frend, 'Popular Religion and Christological Controversy', 27–8; McGuckin, 'The Influence of the Isis Cult on Cyril', 298–9; McKinion, *Words, Imagery, and the Mystery of Christ*, 225.

[43] Cf. O'Keefe's discussion of the fullness of divine presence ('Impassible Suffering?', 45–6), cited in sect. 1.1.3.

spite of the different fates these two slogans would meet, in Cyril's thought they were closely connected both to each other and to his understanding of grace. This is the connection I will consider now.

4.4.1. Theotokos *and the Double Birth of the Logos*

It is Nestorius' attempt to mediate between opposing camps in Constantinople by proposing the title *Christotokos* that first arouses the suspicions of both Alexandria and Rome about his christology. After Cyril becomes aware of the debate to the north, he writes in his festal letter for 429 that Mary gave birth to 'the Logos who was from God the Father, made man and united to flesh', and thus he concludes that she 'is said to be the mother of God and the one who corporeally bore God who was manifested in flesh on our account' (*Ep. Pasch.* 17.3 [777c]). In *Theot. Nol. Confit.*, Cyril uses biblical argumentation to refute the idea that Christ is merely a man; his logic is that since Christ is God the Logos who has entered human existence through Mary, then Mary must be called the Mother of God. In his letter to the monks, he asks poignantly: 'If our Lord Jesus Christ is God, how is the virgin who gave birth to him not the bearer of God (θεοτόκος)?' (*Ep.* 1 [1.1.1.11]), and he goes on to argue that since anyone who has received the grace of the Holy Spirit can be called 'Christ' (i.e. 'anointed one'), the mother of any Christian could be called *Christotokos*, but only Mary can be called *Theotokos* (*Ep.* 1 [1.1.1.14]). From these passages it is clear that Cyril's point is to proclaim the uniqueness of the Son whom Mary bore: he is God the Logos himself in human form. In this way, Cyril safeguards the distinction between the way in which we become sons of God and the way Christ is Son of God.

As he explains his first anathema (which condemns those who do not call Mary *Theotokos*), Cyril writes:

> Certain people have denied his birth according to the flesh, that birth which took place from the holy virgin for the salvation of all. It was not a birth that called God into a beginning of existence but one intended to deliver us from death and corruption when he became like us. This is why our first anathema cries out against their evil faith and then confesses what is the right faith, saying that Emmanuel is truly God, and for this reason the holy virgin is the bearer of God (θεοτόκον).
>
> (*Expl. 12 Cap.* 6 [1.1.5.17])

Here we see that to Cyril, a denial of the title *Theotokos* constitutes a denial of the saving economy. The Logos did not receive the beginning of his divine existence from Mary, since he was eternally begotten from the Father, but he was born a second time 'for the salvation of all', in order to free us from death and corruption.[44] Similarly, in Cyril's first letter to Succensus, he explicitly refers to both the eternal and the temporal births of the Logos and insists that because the same person has been born twice, there is one Son both before and after the incarnation. The Logos was born of the virgin according to the flesh, since 'the flesh was his own (ἰδία γὰρ ἦν αὐτοῦ ἡ σάρξ).' In this context Cyril says that Mary can justly be called *Theotokos* (*Ep.* 45 [1.1.6.152]).

A number of scholars have pointed out that for Cyril (as for most of the fifth-century Church), the title *Theotokos* was not so much a statement about Mary as it was a way of demonstrating the true deity of Christ. The one whom Mary bore is God, and in fact, the Son (the *begotten* God, in contrast to the Father and the Spirit).[45] What is most relevant to my discussion is the fact that Cyril ties the title *Theotokos* so closely to the aspects of his thought that I have examined. The one whom Mary bore is the same Logos who was born eternally of the Father because the Logos took flesh from the virgin and made that flesh his own. He did this in order to free us from our slavery to corruption and death. Because of this, Cyril says that there is only one Son, an assertion that is directly linked to his idea that only the true Son can give us himself and make us sons by grace. For Cyril, the truth behind the title *Theotokos*, that the same Son was born twice, is crucial precisely because only this Son can share with us the communion he has with the Father. This truth, this concept of grace and salvation, will be in jeopardy if one denies Mary the title.

4.4.2. 'One Nature' and the Unity of Divine Sonship

In his controversial writings, Cyril uses the famous slogan (or to some, the *infamous* slogan) 'one incarnate nature of God the

[44] Cf. *Ep.* 4 [1.1.1.28].

[45] e.g. Bethune-Baker, *Early History of Christian Doctrine*, 262; Florovsky, *The Byzantine Fathers of the Fifth Century*, 218; Galtier, *L'Unité du Christ*, 69–75.

Logos' (μία φύσις τοῦ θεοῦ λόγου σεσαρκωμένη) at least nine times. Of these, two (*De Fide Dom.* [1.1.5.65] and *Apol. Cap. Or.* [1.1.7.48]) come in quotations of the Apollinarian writing (which Cyril attributes to Athanasius) in which he found the phrase, and one (*Con. Theo.* 1.11. [3.516]) occurs in a very short fragment preserved only in Syriac. These three occurrences give little indication of how Cyril intends the phrase to be understood. However, the six remaining occurrences of the phrase all come in discussions of the unity and diversity of Christ, and in each of these passages, Cyril makes clear that there are two unmixed realities in Christ. I will look briefly at three of these six passages.

In *Con. Nes.*, Cyril criticizes Nestorius for distributing the sayings of the Gospels among the Logos and the man considered separately. He argues that the Logos has truly been made man, so that 'he is conceived of as one and only, and everything said pertains to him, and all will be said of one *prosopon*. For the incarnate nature of the Word himself is after the union now conceived of as one.' He goes on to assert that although the things named can be understood as being different, Christ is one out of both, and there is a true union (*Con. Nes.* 2.prooem. [1.1.6.33]). Here we see that the idea of *physis* is essentially that of 'person' or 'subject'. Cyril's point is that everything the Gospels say about Christ must be applied to the same *prosopon*; one cannot divide the sayings among two subjects considered separately. In the light of Cyril's pronounced insistence that the subject of Christ is the Logos, his point here is that we must see the Logos as the one who undergoes all the actions and experiences of Christ. Thus the 'one nature' formula concerns the personal subject of Christ, the Logos; it is not a denial of the presence of different realities (deity and humanity) in Christ.[46]

While writing to Acacius of Melitene to explain why he signed the Reunion Formula, Cyril asserts:

> When we have the idea of the realities from which (τὰ ἐξ ὧν) is the one and unique Son and Lord Jesus Christ, we speak of two natures being united (δύο μὲν φύσεις ἡνῶσθαι); but after the union, the duality has been abolished and we believe the Son's nature to be one (μίαν εἶναι πιστεύομεν

[46] Cf. *Ep.* 44 [1.1.4.35]; *Ep.* 46 [1.1.6.160]; *Quod Vnus Christ.* [378]. Russell, *Cyril of Alexandria*, 26, points out that in Cyril's trinitarian thought he distinguishes *physis* from *hypostasis*, but in his christological thought he identifies the two words.

τὴν τοῦ υἱοῦ φύσιν), since he is one [Son], yet become man and incarnate. Though we affirm that the Word is God on becoming incarnate and made man, any suspicion of change is to be repudiated entirely because he remained what he was, and we are to acknowledge the union as totally free from merger. (*Ep*. 40 [1.1.4.26])

In spite of Cyril's terminological imprecision, his idea is quite apparent. When he speaks of two natures, he is referring to deity and humanity, and again, Cyril repudiates any thought that these have changed or become confused through the union. But when he speaks of one nature after the union, he is referring to a single sonship; and he makes this connection between Christ's single nature and his single sonship explicit by writing *μίαν εἶναι πιστεύομεν τὴν τοῦ υἱοῦ φύσιν ὡς ἑνός*. In this phrase, the word *ἑνός*, which might be ambiguous in isolation (one what?), is clarified by the preceding phrase *τοῦ υἱοῦ*. This single sonship is that of the Logos who is the sole subject of Christ. This suggests that the 'one nature' formula functions in Cyril's thought in a way analogous to his use of *ἴδιος*. Both are means of pointing to the fact that when considered in personal terms, Christ is a single entity, the Father's natural Son.

In a very similar passage from his first letter to Succensus, Cyril writes:

After the union we do not divide the natures (*φύσεις*) from each other and do not sever the one and indivisible into two sons but say 'one Son' and, as the fathers have put it, 'one incarnate nature of the Word'. Thus, inasmuch as the question of the manner of the Only-Begotten's becoming man appears for purely mental consideration by the mind's eye, our view is that there are two united natures but one Christ, Son and Lord, the Word of God become man and incarnate.

(*Ep*. 45 [1.1.6.153–4])

Here again one can see that Cyril moves from using the word *physis* to describe the two elements of Christ to using it as a description of the one person of Christ, and again, the idea that drives his terminological change is that of the Logos' single sonship. Of course, Nestorius can also speak of a single sonship, but in his case, the concept concerns the status of sonship, the honour and worship due to the Logos naturally and given to the man by grace. For him, the word 'sonship' does not concern the intimate communion between Father and Son, but for Cyril, sonship is primarily a matter of such fellowship.

Virtually all scholars recognize that Cyril's use of the 'one nature' slogan does not constitute a rejection of Christ's true humanity or a belief that the humanity has been absorbed into his deity and lost. Rather, interpreters acknowledge that in this formula, he uses the word *physis* in the sense that Chalcedon will later give to *hypostasis*: Christ is a single personal subject, the Logos-made-man.[47] To this consensus I will simply add that the reason Cyril is so insistent on the unity of person is that he is concerned to portray Christ's single sonship, and this concern grows directly out of his concept of grace. Only if the being who meets us in our lowly human condition is truly God's unique Son, the Logos, can we receive from him the οἰκειότης that he has with the Father and the incorruption and holiness that come from him as the source of life. This is the idea of God's gracious relationship to humanity that Cyril finds in Scripture, and he uses the slogan 'one incarnate nature of God the Logos', the title *Theotokos*, and the word ἴδιος to proclaim this idea.

4.5. CONCLUSIONS

Several scholars have seen a marked development from Cyril's early thought to his mature teaching during the Nestorian controversy,[48] whereas others have argued for the basic consistency of his thought throughout his life.[49] The examination of Cyril's understanding of grace and christology that I have undertaken lends strong support to the view that Cyril did not change markedly as a result of the Nestorian controversy. If one considers his terminology and his technical christology alone, then certainly a development is discernible; but when one considers the soteriological concerns that lie behind his christology, it becomes apparent that the guiding principles of his thought

[47] e.g. Galtier, 'Cyrille et Apollinaire', 601–2; Grillmeier, *Christ in Christian Tradition*, 481–2; McGuckin, *St. Cyril of Alexandria*, 207–10.

[48] e.g. Liébaert, *La Doctrine christologique de Cyrille*, 78, 145; Kelly, *Early Christian Doctrines*, 322–3; Grillmeier, *Christ in Christian Tradition*, 415–17, 474–6.

[49] e.g. Weigl, *Christologie*, 202; H. Chadwick, 'Eucharist and Christology', 150; and especially Angstenberger, *Der reiche und der arme Christus*, 189, who concludes a study of Cyril's use of 2 Cor. 8: 9 by writing, 'The notion that the early Cyril was sharply distinguished from the later Cyril is absolutely and completely false.'

remained constant throughout his career. Cyril holds unwaveringly to the idea that in Christ we have the personal presence of the Logos himself, since only this can ensure that we really receive God himself in grace when we receive salvation. This idea is the backbone for all his christological writing.

Furthermore, this study helps to corroborate the work of scholars who have noted Cyril's emphasis on the Eucharist and on Christ as the second Adam. Henry Chadwick, Gebremedhin, and Welch see Cyril's primary concern as the Eucharist, and his christology is closely related to his conviction that in the bread, we receive the Logos' own flesh which can make us alive.[50] Wilken argues that the consuming idea of Cyril's thought is that Christ is the new man, the second Adam from heaven, who alone is able to break the bonds of death and gain new life for humanity.[51] Both of these emphases require that Christ be a man who is more than a man, who is the Logos himself in human form. Only the Logos enfleshed can act as the second Adam to make us alive, and only if he is a single entity can his flesh be life-giving. Moreover, the concept of grace that has emerged from this study does not merely corroborate, but also enhances the work of these scholars. When Cyril writes that the second Adam makes us alive, when he insists that we receive the life-giving flesh of the Logos through the Eucharist, what he means by life becomes clearer from his concept of grace. To be alive is to partake of the one who is the source of life; to be holy is to receive the Holy Spirit, who is the *ἴδιον πνεῦμα* of the one who is holiness itself; to be incorruptible is to partake of the source of incorruption. In Cyril's thought, all these aspects of salvation are tied to the person of God the Son, since grace is not simply God's giving us gifts external to himself; it is God's granting us himself through his gift of his own Son to us. The second Adam does not give us life as if life were a created condition separate from himself; he gives us himself.

This consideration of Cyril's concept of grace also helps to clarify the question of what deification implies. Cyril's careful distinction between *ἴδιος* and *οἰκειότης* reveals which aspects of

[50] H. Chadwick, 'Eucharist and Christology', 153–5; Gebremedhin, *Life-Giving Blessing*, 111; Welch, *Christology and Eucharist*, 36.

[51] Wilken, *Judaism and the Early Christian Mind*, 224–5. Cf. Wilken, 'Cyril: The Mystery of Christ', 477.

himself God does and does not share with mankind when he gives himself to people. We do not become God's own sons (ἴδιοι υἱοί) in any ontological sense at all. Rather, there is only one ἴδιος υἱός, the Son who is eternally begotten from the Father and who thus possesses the substance of the Godhead. The ontological aspect of deification, according to Cyril, consists only of our sharing God's incorruption, holiness, and life through participation in the Holy Spirit and partaking of the Eucharist. This ontological element raises us beyond our *human* nature (and indeed, it restores us to the condition that God gave Adam by grace at creation), but it does not elevate us to the point that we possess the *divine* substance. Instead, Cyril sees the primary aspect of deification as humanity's sharing in the warm communion and intimacy that the persons of the Trinity have as a result of their ontological unity. By grace we receive the natural communion (οἰκειότης φυσική) of the Godhead because the Logos has brought his own humanity into the fellowship of the Trinity, in order to share this with us as well.

Finally, as I have mentioned throughout Chs. 3 and 4, this examination of Cyril's doctrine of grace throws into sharp relief the differences between his christology and that of Theodore and Nestorius. The Nestorian controversy was not primarily about *whether* there were two realities in Christ and *whether* he was a single person; the dispute concerned *who* that one personal subject was. Theodore and Nestorius saw the *prosopon* of Christ as a composite of deity and humanity. But more important, they saw the personal centre of Christ's being as a man who had become the unique recipient of God's gracious co-operation, a man who could thus help us to rise to the second age as well. In stark contrast, Cyril saw the one subject of Christ as the Logos, as God himself who had added a concrete humanity to himself and thus embarked upon human life in order to give us his natural communion with the Father. As a result, in Cyril's eyes, to see Christ as a composite *prosopon* was to deny the crucial truth that the Logos himself was personally present with us. It did not matter to him how well or poorly Nestorius expressed the composite/semantic unity of Christ. If that unity was a composite, then Christ was not the Logos himself. In that case, the effect was just as devastating as if Nestorius had actually intended to preach two sons. Any division in the person of Christ meant that he was no longer the natural Son, and thus that he could not give us his natural fellowship with the Father.

Once these differences stand exposed, the questions I raised in Ch. 1 come to prominence again: which of these understandings (if either) more closely reflected the faith of the entire early Church? Or was there any consensus at all? Can any view be said to represent the faith of the fifth-century Church? In order to shed some light on these difficult questions, I will now turn from Cyril's thought to that of John Cassian, the only Westerner who made a study of Nestorius' christology during the months leading up to Ephesus.

5

Grace as Deepening Communion with God in Cassian's Monastic Writings

If one looks at John Cassian's writings in the light of the issues I have considered thus far, there are several ways in which his thought seems similar to that of Theodore and Nestorius. He places great emphasis on the human task of pursuing moral perfection, and he frequently depicts grace as God's assistance or power to help us in that task. His christological language sounds Theodorean as well: he refers to Christ's humanity with the concrete *homo* rather than the abstract *humanitas*, and he occasionally uses the expression *homo assumptus*.[1] However, there are other ways in which Cassian's christology appears to be decidedly Cyrillian: he unflaggingly champions the title *Theotokos*, and he locates the unity of Christ's person in the Logos.

This tension is widely recognized among commentators, and Cassian is usually believed to have been an inconsistent thinker. Scholars argue that while he was a master of the spiritual life, he was not a theologian of any consequence.[2] It is generally agreed that Cassian's *De Incar. Dom.* had no influence on the course of the Nestorian controversy other than that of confirming Celestine's prior prejudice against Nestorius,[3] and historians are

[1] See Ch, 6, n. 38.

[2] e.g. Amann, 'L'Affaire Nestorius vue de Rome', 227; Grillmeier, *Christ in Christian Tradition*, 468; and especially Stewart, *Cassian the Monk*, 23, who writes, 'Cassian's own dogmatic statements veer between Nestorian and Cyrilline formulations; his grasp of the fine points of controversy was, to put it kindly, imprecise.'

[3] e.g. Brand, 'Le *De incarnatione Domini* de Cassien', 269–71; Kuhlmann, 'Ein dogmengeschictliche Neubewertung', 171. But see also Amann (*RevSR* 1950), 37–8, who argues that Cassian was responsible for shaping Celestine's opinion of Nestorius.

quick to point out that Cassian's only christological legacy was the dubious one of bequeathing to the entire Western Church his distorted impression of Nestorianism.[4] It is often argued that he made no positive contribution to the development of christology, an argument that carries considerable weight since Cassian is never quoted in later patristic discussions of Christ's person.[5]

In this chapter and the next, I will argue that this gloomy assessment of Cassian is harsher than the evidence warrants. He certainly did not possess the brilliance of Theodore or Cyril, and there are elements of his thought that only the most vigorous exegetical gymnastics could reconcile. Nevertheless, I believe there is a fundamental consistency underlying his thought, and a careful examination of the relation between his idea of grace and his christology will reveal this consistency. Accordingly, in this chapter I will elucidate Cassian's foundational concept of grace from his earlier monastic writings.[6] I will first consider the dominant scholarly opinion regarding Cassian's understanding of the monastic task, salvation, and grace. Then I will examine the evidence which I believe should lead one to reconsider this scholarly consensus. Finally, I will offer a view of Cassian's concept of grace that I think does better justice to the entirety of his monastic writings, an idea that centres around the deepening of the monk's communion with God. After I have dealt with

[4] e.g. Jugie, *Nestorius et la controverse nestorienne*, 199; Amann, 'Nestorius et sa doctrine', 101.

[5] See Brand, 'Le *De incarnatione Domini* de Cassien', 269–351, for a survey of the historical influence of *De Incar. Dom.* Brand concludes (p. 356) that such influence was only very modest and indirect.

[6] The chronology of Cassian's works is relatively straightforward. Correlation of statements in the prefaces to his monastic writings with information regarding the episcopal sees of Gaul leads one to conclude that Cassian wrote *De Inst. Coen.* prior to 426, published *Conlat.* 1–10 and *Conlat.* 11–17 in 426, and completed *Conlat.* 18–24 before January 429. See Gibson, 'The Works of John Cassian', 189–90, for an explanation of this evidence. O. Chadwick, 'Euladius of Arles', 200–5, has questioned this chronology and has attempted to place the second group of Conferences, containing the infamous *Conlat.* 13, after Augustine's *De Corrept. Grat.* reached Gaul in 427, but his conclusions have been rejected by Markus, *The End of Ancient Christianity*, 177–9, and Weaver, *Divine Grace and Human Agency*, 93–7. As significant as this disagreement about chronology is for a reconstruction of the semi-Pelagian controversy, it is of no consequence for this study. Cassian wrote *De Incar. Dom.* during the summer of 430, prior to the Roman synod of 11 August condemning Nestorius. See Brand , 'Le *De incarnatione Domini* de Cassien', 79–81.

Cassian's monastic writings, in Ch. 6 I will turn to *De Incar. Dom.* and show the relation between this idea of grace and his christology.

5.1. THE TYPICAL SCHOLARLY INTERPRETATION OF CASSIAN AND MONASTICISM

Most modern interpreters assert that Cassian, like monastics in general, saw Christian life in terms of gradual progress towards union with God through the pursuit of virtue in the regulated environment of the cenobium or the anchorite's cell. In this understanding, the ascent to God is a co-operative process, but one in which the initiative primarily rests with the human will. Grace is God's aid or co-operation that enables one to overcome vice and acquire virtue, and God gives his grace to those who strive for it and discipline themselves to receive it. Harper states this view most strongly when he writes:

> Cassian conceived the Christian life as a ladder at the end of which man reached salvation, the unceasing contemplation of God. The stuff of the Christian life is the battle of the spirit against the flesh in the pursuit of apathy or freedom from all passions which might distract from the act of contemplation. In the struggle of the spirit with the flesh the will holds the balance and by exercising itself it is strengthened. Thus the essence of the Christian life is the effort of the will against the flesh in behalf of the spirit so that grace may enter the soul. Grace is the reward of effort, and in the last analysis it is man's own capacity to free himself from original sin by effort and discipline.[7]

Here Harper alludes to the influence of Evagrius on Cassian (and indeed, on all monasticism). Origenism, as Evagrius sharpened and modified it, saw Christian life as a movement from the active sphere, in which one struggled to remove one's passions, to the contemplative realm, in which one could enjoy uninterrupted meditation on God. The transition point between these two realms is the achievement of passionlessness (ἀπάθεια),[8] freedom

[7] Harper, 'John Cassian and Sulpicius Severus', 371. For more recent assessments of Cassian that are similar, although less boldly stated, see Rea, 'Grace and Free Will in John Cassian', 114–16; O'Keeffe, 'The *Via Media* of Monastic Theology', 265; Weaver, *Divine Grace and Human Agency*, 2, 87–8.

[8] Cassian generally renders ἀπάθεια as *puritas cordis*, 'purity of heart': e.g. *Conlat.* 1.4 [42.81], which I will discuss in sect. 5.1.1.

from the delights of vice.[9] According to this understanding, Cassian generally follows Evagrius' form of Origenism: his focus is on human action, and grace is largely God's response to human striving after perfection.[10]

Furthermore, scholars assert that Cassian believed Christian life could be carried out *only* in the context of monastic discipline. Markus points out that Cassian thought the broader Church had fallen away from its initial purity,[11] and he concludes, 'Cassian's monastery is the gathered community of the faithful set in the midst of—or, rather, set apart from—an apostate Church, as had been the early Church in—and from—a pagan world.'[12] As a result, commentators generally see the idea that salvation comes from human initiative in seeking perfection with the help of grace as Cassian's dominant motif. If salvation is possible only through monastic perfection and contemplation of God, and if this task revolves around the monk's own initiative, then it follows that Cassian sees grace largely or even exclusively as divine assistance in such a task. Indeed, the vast majority of what Cassian writes in *De Inst. Coen.* and *Conlat.* corroborates this view, and I will now survey some of that evidence.

5.1.1. Salvation and the Monastic Task

Conlat. opens with a discussion between abbot Moses, Cassian, and his friend Germanus about the purpose of the monastic life.[13] Moses says: 'The ultimate goal of our profession, as we have said, is the kingdom of God or the kingdom of heaven; but

[9] The achievement of *ἀπάθεια* is the major focus of Evagrius' *Prac.* He dedicates chs. 6–33 to the vanquishing of the eight *λογισμοί*, chs. 34–56 to the struggle with passions and dreams, chs. 57–62 to the characteristics of one who is close to *ἀπάθεια*, and chs. 63–70 to the state of *ἀπάθεια* itself. Only once a monk has reached this point can he go on to pure contemplation, which is the subject of Evagrius' *Keph. Gnost.*

[10] Scholars who see Cassian's doctrine of the spiritual life as following that of Evagrius include Guillaumont, *Les 'Kephalia gnostica' d'Évagre*, 78–9; Chitty, *The Desert a City*, 52; Kline, 'Regula Benedicti', 102. These interpreters point out, however, that Cassian modifies Evagrius' terminology and removes the suspect elements from his system.

[11] See *Conlat.* 18.5 [64.14–16] for Cassian's discussion of this.

[12] Markus, *The End of Ancient Christianity*, 168. Cf. Munz, 'John Cassian', 2–3; de Vogüé, 'Monachisme et Église', 227; Christophe, *Cassien et Césaire*, 24, 40.

[13] Here I should mention the question of whether one may take the words of

the intermediate aim or *scopos* is purity of heart (*puritas cordis*), without which it is impossible for anyone to reach that goal. Therefore, fixing our gaze on this aim, as on a guide-mark, we shall take the most direct route' (*Conlat.* 1.4 [42.81]). Here we see the Evagrian distinction between the stages of Christian life: *puritas cordis* or ἀπάθεια is not the ultimate goal (*finis*) but rather the intermediate aim (*scopos*), the guide-mark that points one towards the kingdom of God. Notice that Cassian seems to tie salvation to the achievement of the monastic *scopos* by asserting that without it one cannot reach the ultimate end.

After sounding this note at the beginning of *Conlat.*, Cassian repeats the idea frequently. During a discussion of miracles, abbot Nesteros cites Jesus' words to the disciples after they exult that demons are subject to them (Luke 10: 17–20) and explains: 'They are warned that they should not dare to claim for themselves from it any of the blessing or glory which comes only from the might and power of God. Instead they may claim that inner purity of life and heart on account of which they deserve to have their names inscribed in heaven' (*Conlat.* 15.9 [54.219]). Although Jesus has said nothing about the basis on which the disciples' names are inscribed in heaven, Cassian interprets his words to mean that they deserve this because of their purity of life and heart. Similarly, during a discussion of promises, abbot Joseph says:

This invaluable judgement also teaches us above all that, although each

the fifteen abbots who speak in *Conlat.* to reflect Cassian's own views. Prosper of Aquitaine raised this issue at the beginning of his response to Cassian's *Conlat.* 13 and concluded that Cassian had made the abbots' teaching his own, to the point that one needed to deal not with the abbots, but only with the author (*Con. Collat.* 2.1 [218a]). O. Chadwick, *John Cassian*, 18–22, and Guy, 'Jean Cassien', 372, both argue that Cassian cannot be trusted historically. They conclude that while Cassian surely held conversations with numerous Egyptian monks, one must regard the substance of the Conferences as Cassian's own doctrine, not necessarily that of the 4th-cent. abbots in whose mouths he places his ideas. Corroborating these verdicts is the fact that there is only one place in *Conlat.* where Cassian attempts to distance himself from an abbot, and in this case he is hesitant not about the teaching, but only about the action of abbot Theonas, who left his wife in order to pursue his monastic calling (*Conlat.* 21.10 [64.85–6]). In all cases where teaching is concerned, Cassian is enthusiastic in his agreement with the abbots. Therefore, however close to or far from the teaching of the historical monks Cassian's portrayal is, we may be confident that *Conlat.* is intended to represent Cassian's own views.

person's end may be known to him before he was born, he disposes everything with order and reason and, so to say, human feelings, in such a way that he determines all things not by his power or in accordance with his ineffable knowledge but, based upon the actions of men at the time, either rejects or draws to himself each one, and either grants or withholds his grace daily. (*Conlat*. 17.25 [54.278])

Here we see that God's gift of grace is a response to our efforts, and Cassian's insistence that God does not act in accordance with his foreknowledge gives striking emphasis to the priority of human action. Another example of Cassian's link between human action and salvation comes as he tells the story of abbot Theonas in *Conlat*. 21. As soon as Theonas decided to enter monastic life, he tried unsuccessfully to persuade his wife to join him, and Cassian adds: 'Consequently, he had determined and decided for himself to renounce secular life and even to die to the world, so as to be able to live to God. And if he was unable to have the blessing of joining Christ's company with his wife, he preferred to be saved even at the expense of one member and as it were to enter the kingdom of heaven crippled, rather than to be condemned with a sound body' (*Conlat*. 21.9 [64.83]). Here we see that at least in Theonas' case, Cassian ties salvation not simply to human action, but specifically to the monastic task.

In these passages, the pattern is that one reaches salvation through the monastic path of achieving purity and contemplation of God, and God's role is largely to respond to the monk's efforts with grace.[14] Of course, this does not mean that God is merely responsive, since Cassian insists that God begins the process of salvation by calling a person to the monastic life.[15] But as a person walks the pathway to salvation, he must continually take the initiative to purify himself, and God responds by drawing the monk to himself more fully.

[14] Among the many other passages that give the same impression, cf. *De Inst. Coen*. 12.8 [462] and *Conlat*. 11.13 [54.118], both of which link salvation to our following the example of Christ. Cf. also *Conlat*. 21.32 [64.107], which connects grace to the pursuit of a higher morality than that of the law, and *Conlat*. 24.26 [64.200–1], which ties adopted sonship to one's renouncing the world in order to pursue the monastic vocation.

[15] e.g. *Conlat*. 3.10 [42.155], in which abbot Paphnutius uses God's calling of Abraham as a pattern for monastic life. Cf. *Conlat*. 3.19 [42.162–3].

5.1.2. Grace and the Monastic Task

As Cassian discusses grace in connection with the monastic pursuit of purity, he considers three major aspects: grace as divine assistance and power, as divine forgiveness, and as God's granting blessings that are far greater than the effort people have put forth to gain them. These facets of grace are closely intertwined, and all of them depend on the priority of human action. I will consider each in turn.

During an extended discussion of pride in *De Inst. Coen.* 12, Cassian insists that the monk depends completely on God, so there is no room for him to think that his own efforts alone have produced perfection. But he continues, 'When we say that human efforts cannot secure it [i.e. perfection] on their own, apart from God's help (*sine adiutorio Dei*), we thus insist that God's mercy and grace are bestowed only upon those who labour and exert themselves' (*De Inst. Coen.* 12.14 [468]). Here Cassian identifies grace with God's *adiutorium* that assists the monk's efforts, and God grants this help in response to those efforts. In *Conlat.* 2, abbot Moses explains why monks need to be compassionate towards the moral struggles of others by saying that no one can achieve perfection on his own: 'For no one could endure the snares of the enemy or the seething emotions of the flesh which burn like real fires, nor could anyone extinguish and smother them, unless the grace of God helped our frailty (*fragilitatem*) and protected and defended it' (*Conlat.* 2.13 [42.129]). Notice here Cassian's awareness of the frailty of human will: even when our intention is pure, we need God's grace to come to our aid and to protect our *fragilitas* in that intention. Grace and the human will are not in an adversarial relation, as if grace needed to overcome a recalcitrant will; they are in a co-operative relation. Grace strengthens a weak will, providing the power that the monk needs to do what he purposes.[16]

Similarly, while discussing the three renunciations with which a person begins monastic life, abbot Paphnutius says, 'No righteous person is able by himself to obtain righteousness unless the divine mercy offers the support of its hand to him every time he stumbles and trips, lest he be overthrown and perish when he has fallen because of the weakness of his free

[16] Cf. Rousseau, *Ascetics, Authority, and the Church*, 232–3.

will' (*Conlat.* 3.12 [42.157]). He concludes the discussion by declaring, 'We wish not to do away with man's free will by what we have said, but only to establish that God's assistance and grace (*adiutorium et gratiam*) are necessary to it every day and hour' (*Conlat.* 3.22 [42.165]). Again, Cassian connects grace to divine *adiutorium* and insists that we need this aid at all times. The task of salvation is not one which we have the strength to complete; we depend on God's assistance and power to carry it out.[17] This idea of grace as divine assistance in the monastic task is Cassian's most frequently repeated emphasis,[18] and a number of scholars have noted it.[19]

Another idea that receives repeated treatment in Cassian's monastic writings is that of grace as forgiveness, which he generally links to the monk's repentance. Cassian devotes an entire conference to penitence, and he emphasizes that its goal is the removal of all desire for the sin in question. Abbot Pinufius declares:

> The surest judge of repentance and the mark of forgiveness resides in our conscience, which reveals the absolution of our sinfulness before the day of revelation and judgement and discloses to us who are still living in the flesh the conclusion of reparation and the grace of forgiveness (*remissionis gratiam*). Let what has been said be expressed still more precisely: We should believe that the stain of former vices is forgiven us only when both the desires and the passions associated with present sensual pleasures have been expelled from our heart.
>
> (*Conlat.* 20.5 [64.62])

This passage shows the same pattern that we have seen elsewhere: God gives grace in response to human intention. In the case of *gratia remissionis*, the monk can be confident of God's

[17] The prominence of the petition from Ps. 70: 1 (69: 1 in Vulg.), 'O God, come to my aid; O Lord, make haste to assist me,' in Cassian's doctrine of prayer further underlines this idea of grace as divine assistance. See *Conlat.* 10.10 [54.85–90].

[18] Cf. *De Inst. Coen.* 6.5 [268] and *De Inst. Coen.* 12.13 [466–8], which emphasize that one's ability to overcome vice and acquire virtue depends on God's assisting grace. Cf. also *De Inst. Coen.* 5.16 [216] and *Conlat.* 7.8 [42.254], 7.23 [42.266], which assert that God's grace fights triumphantly on our behalf against vice and demonic powers.

[19] e.g. Amann, 'Semi-Pélagiens', 1805; Holze, *Erfahrung und Theologie im frühen Mönchtum*, 155; Pristas, 'The Theological Anthropology of John Cassian', 144–8.

forgiveness only upon a repentance so thorough that he has eliminated all desire for a certain sin. Later, abbot Theonas distinguishes different types of confession/repentance for different grades of sins. He says, 'For whoever falls upon *the body of death* [Rom. 7: 24] after having been baptized and having known God should realize that he will not be cleansed by the daily grace of Christ—that is, by the easy forgiveness that our Lord is accustomed to grant to our misdeeds when he is beseeched at particular moments—but by the extended suffering of penance and by the anguish of purgation' (*Conlat.* 23.15 [64.158]). Again, grace is connected with forgiveness, but one can gain remission through simple confession only in the case of mild sins. Greater sins (falling on the body of death) require more strenuous, lifelong penance. In either case, however, Cassian ties the grace of forgiveness to the monk's confession/repentance. God's grace is given in response to human intention.[20]

A third way in which Cassian describes grace is by asserting that God gives great rewards for small actions on our part. Abbot Chaeremon says that God does not want to seem unreasonable by bestowing blessing on the lazy, so he stirs up our desire to strive. Nevertheless, he explains why God's grace can still be called grace in such cases: 'God's grace continues to be gratuitous since in return for some small and trivial efforts it bestows with inestimable abundance such glory of immortality and such gifts of everlasting bliss' (*Conlat.* 13.13 [54.168–9]). Likewise, during a discussion of the means by which the monk may expiate his sins, abbot Pinufius writes:

> No one should allow the obstinacy of a hardened heart to turn him away from a salutary healing and from the source of so great a mercy, for even if we did all these things they would be ineffective for the expiation of our crimes unless the goodness and mercy of the Lord destroyed them. When he has seen the services of a devout effort rendered by us with a humble mind, he supplements these feeble and small efforts with his own immense generosity. (*Conlat.* 20.8 [64.67])

In both of these passages God requires action on the part of the monk first, but he gives blessing or pardon in a way that vastly

[20] Cf. *De Inst. Coen.* 12.11 [464], which asserts that God forgives in response to our confession of sin, and especially *Conlat.* 20.8 [64.64–7], which describes various means by which we can obtain forgiveness of sins.

transcends the merit of the action itself. In this way Cassian makes clear that God never simply rewards people according to what we deserve; he is always gracious, even though he responds to prior human action.[21]

The ideas of salvation, the monastic task, and grace as divine assistance that we have seen in these passages dominate Cassian's monastic writings, and there is good reason to believe, as do the scholars I have cited above, that this strand of thought is the primary one in Cassian's mind. If in fact Cassian sees God's primary role as assisting the monk's efforts to pursue perfection, then his idea of grace shows a great deal of similarity to Theodore's thought. In this view, both understand salvation largely as a human task (although there are important differences in the way they view the nature of that task) and see God's role in a co-operative, auxiliary sense. If this is correct, one would expect to see in Cassian's writings a strong emphasis on Christ's humanity and on his role as a teacher and example, a pioneer who blazes the trail that the monks follow. It is true that in his monastic writings, Cassian makes much of Christ's example,[22] and many scholars believe this is the full extent of his depiction of Christ. For example, Munz argues that Cassian sees Jesus exclusively as an example and teacher and has no place for his sacrificial death.[23] Brand claims that Christ is practically an afterthought in *De Inst. Coen.* and *Conlat.* and concludes, 'One would search in vain in the work of the Abbot of Saint Victor's prior to his *De incarnatione* for a christocentric spirituality, a mysticism connected with Christ incarnate or Christ crucified.'[24]

[21] Cf. *De Inst. Coen.* 12.11 [464], where Cassian writes that God's grace superabounds in granting abundant forgiveness upon the confession of only a single word. Amann, 'Semi-Pélagiens', 1804–5, notes that this is a major part of Cassian's idea of grace.

[22] e.g. *De Inst. Coen.* 12.8 [462]; *Conlat.* 9.34 [54.70], 11.13 [54.118], 16.6 [54.228].

[23] Munz, 'John Cassian', 14–16. Cf. Olphe-Galliard, 'Cassien (Jean)', 228.

[24] Brand, 'Le *De incarnatione Domini* de Cassien', 59. On the other hand, Codina, *El Aspecto Christologico*, 187, asserts against Brand that for Cassian, asceticism and mysticism are tied to the person of Christ. Similarly, Azkoul, 'Peccatum originale', 40, argues that Cassian's primary frame of reference was christological, but by 'christological' he means that Cassian preserved a proper synergism between divine and human action in the person of Christ and in human salvation. Azkoul is following Lossky, *The Mystical Theology of the*

However, the evidence on which this interpretation rests is not everything Cassian writes about grace and salvation in his monastic writings. There is a smaller, but still significant, body of evidence that points in a different direction and that should force a reconsideration of the picture I have developed thus far.

5.2. EVIDENCE THAT UNDERCUTS THE TYPICAL INTERPRETATION

We have seen that even if salvation is largely a human task, any reconstruction of Cassian's thought must assert that God begins the process by calling people to himself. However, there are passages in Cassian's monastic writings that seem to indicate that he sees the monk's action as a response not simply to what God has done in *calling* him to salvation, but to what God has done in *saving* him. These passages give the impression that throughout Christian life, the priority rests with God's action. As I consider this evidence from Cassian's monastic writings, I will look first at passages that suggest that salvation is something God has already accomplished in the monk, and then at passages that depict grace as that which produces virtue, rather than simply that which assists the monk's efforts to achieve virtue.

5.2.1. Human Action as a Response to God's Prior Salvific Action

In *De Inst. Coen.* 12, Cassian deals with the sin of pride, and here his thought is markedly different from what he has written previously. For most of the work, he has urged monks to vigilance and strenuous effort in extirpating their vices, but in this last book, he insists that the monk's salvation and achievement of virtue come not from his own efforts but from God's mercy. Cassian uses the repentant thief on the cross (Luke 23: 39–43) as an example of this by writing, 'If we recall that thief who was admitted into paradise by reason of a single confession, we will recognize that he did not acquire such bliss by the merits of his life, but obtained it by the gift of a merciful God' (*De Inst. Coen.* 12.11 [464]). He also asserts that David received forgiveness through God's merciful gift, and he adds:

Eastern Church, 199, although Lossky does not use the word 'christological' when referring to Cassian's synergistic understanding of salvation.

If we consider also the beginning of the human call and salvation, in which, as the apostle says, we are saved not of ourselves, nor of our works, but by the gift and grace of God, we will be able to see clearly how the height of perfection is *not of him who wills, nor of him who runs, but of God who has mercy* [Rom. 9: 16], who makes us victorious over our faults, without any merits of works and life on our part to outweigh them, or any effort of our will availing to scale the arduous heights of perfection, or to subdue the flesh that we have to use.

(*De Inst. Coen.* 12.11 [464])

Here Cassian mentions the thief in order to show that one cannot attribute his salvation to his own virtue: the thief did not live to make any significant progress in virtue, yet God mercifully received him into paradise on the basis of his confession alone. In the light of this, when Cassian refers to 'the beginning of the human call and salvation' (*principium uocationis et salutis humanae*), he does not mean that God calls us to achieve virtue so as to gain union with God. Instead, he means that God freely accepts us, and on the basis of this acceptance he calls us to the pursuit of perfection. Furthermore, God is the one who makes us victorious over our faults; the key element is not our own effort (although Cassian still insists that such effort is necessary), but God's enabling. As a result, this passage reveals a pattern rather different from that which Harper has suggested. Christian life is not primarily a ladder we must climb in order to reach salvation; it is our response to God's merciful action of bringing us to himself and enabling us to root out our sins and seek perfection.[25]

Another important passage in this connection comes in *Conlat.* 1, where abbot Moses discusses the purpose of monastic life. We saw in sect. 5.1.1 that Moses says no one can reach the kingdom of God without purity of heart, thus giving the impression that Christian life is a path of ascent leading to God. But later in the same conversation, Moses considers the monk's contemplation of God and asserts that we can arrive at such contemplation by reflecting on what he has done. During this discussion Moses says that true contemplation of God comes to us

[25] For similar ideas later in the book, see *De Inst. Coen.* 12.15 [470], in which Cassian asserts that the virtuous monks ascribe their virtue to God's mercy, not to their own exertions; and *De Inst. Coen.* 12.19 [478], in which he indicates that the monk's actions are the evidence of his faith, not the means to union with God.

when we look with a kind of overwhelming wonder at the call through which he has claimed us as his own (*adsciuit*), thanks to his mercy and not to our preceding merits (*nullis praecedentibus meritis*), and finally at the many occasions of salvation that he has bestowed on us who were to be adopted (*quot occasiones salutis tribuit adoptandis*)—because he commanded that we should be born in such a way that grace and the knowledge of his law might be given us from our very cradles, and because he himself, conquering the adversary in us, bestows on us eternal blessedness and everlasting rewards for the sole pleasure of his good will; and when, finally, he accepted the dispensation of his incarnation for our salvation and extended the marvels of his mysteries to all peoples. (*Conlat.* 1.15 [42.97])

Two things about this passage are striking. First, Cassian links our *uocatio* to the fact that God has claimed us as his own (*adsciuit nos*). The verb *adscisco*, when used with a personal object, refers to the act of receiving, uniting, or adopting someone to oneself.[26] Cassian uses the word seven times, always in the perfect tense and always in reference to a person's having been admitted to a certain status before God or other people.[27] God's calling consists of the fact that he has already claimed the Christian as his own; he has already made one an adopted child.[28]

The second noteworthy aspect of this passage is that Cassian asserts God has made us his own by grace, 'with no preceding merits' (*nullis praecedentibus meritis*).[29] God does not call people

[26] See LewSh 171–2.

[27] The perfect passive participle *adscitus* refers to a person's having been admitted to the office of king (*De Inst. Coen.* 12.21 [480]), apostle (*Conlat.* 3.5 [42.144]), or bishop (*Conlat.* 11.2 [54.101]). The same participle refers to a person's having been drawn to the monastic task (*Conlat.* 3.3 [42.141], 3.4 [42.142]), and to a person's having been admitted by God from slavery to adopted sonship (*Conlat.* 4.18 [54.55]). This last passage directly parallels the one I am discussing now.

[28] The statement *quot occasiones salutis tribuit adoptandis* is puzzling. It could mean either that Christians are not yet adopted but are given opportunities to gain adoption and salvation, or that unbelievers who *were* yet to become Christians and thus to be adopted were given opportunities to believe (the sense reflected in my translation of the passage). In the light of the fact that Cassian always uses *adscisco* in the perfect tense, the latter seems more likely, and I will demonstrate in sect. 5.3.3 that Cassian sees adoption in connection with the beginning of faith, rather than with its consummation.

[29] This assertion is also one of Augustine's favourites. Among the many passages in Augustine's later writings stressing that God saves us apart from any

to the pursuit of perfection so that he may later accept them; he claims them as his own and on this basis calls them to perfection. Cassian further emphasizes this point by asserting that God is the one who conquers the adversary in believers and gives them eternal bliss. He ties all this to the mystery of the incarnation for salvation, and in doing so, he significantly modifies the impression he has given at the beginning of *Conlat.* 1. There we saw a strong emphasis on the upward path the monk must follow. Here we see that contemplation (the highest rung on the ladder of monastic spirituality) involves looking back at what God has himself done for the monk, not just looking ahead to what the monk needs to do with God's help.

In *Conlat.* 21, abbot Theonas talks about the difference between the lower prescriptions of the law and the higher perfection of the gospel, and he urges monks to follow the latter. Near the end of the conference, he says:

> Whoever strives to hold to the perfection of the gospel teaching lives under grace and is not oppressed by the dominion of sin, for to be under grace means to fulfil what is commanded by grace. But whoever does not wish to be subject to the fullness of gospel perfection should realize that, although he may seem to himself to be baptized and a monk, he is not under grace but is still bound by the fetters of the law and weighed down by the burdens of sin. For he, who by the grace of adoption accepts all those who have received him (*qui omnes a quibus receptus fuerit gratia adoptionis adsumit*), aims not to destroy but to build upon the Mosaic requirements, not to abolish but to fulfil them.
>
> (*Conlat.* 21.34 [64.110])

This passage might appear to imply that one must hold to the perfection of the gospel in order to be under grace, but in actuality, the fact that a monk seeks this perfection is evidence that he is already under grace rather than law. The phrase 'he who by the grace of adoption accepts all those who have received him' shows the pattern that Cassian wishes to establish. Christ graciously adopts all those who receive him, and since he came not to destroy the law but to fulfil it, those whom he has adopted also seek to adhere to the perfect morality of the gospel. Again we see that the monastic task is a result of what God has already done

preceding merits, see e.g. *Ep.* 194.7, 32 [181–2, 201–2]; *Ep.* 215.4 [390–1]; *De Grat. Lib. Arb.* 10 [887–8]; *De Praed. Sanct.* 6 [963].

in adopting and accepting a person; it is not the means to such acceptance.[30]

5.2.2. Grace as That Which Produces Faith and Virtue

In keeping with his idea that the monastic task is a response to what God has already done in the monk's life, Cassian sometimes describes divine grace not merely as God's assistance in the pursuit of perfection, but as that which actually produces the monk's virtue. While discussing the battle between the flesh and the spirit, abbot Daniel indicates that when a monk encounters dejection, only God's grace can pull him out of the depths. He continues:

> Sometimes this grace does not refuse to visit the negligent and the lax with the holy inspiration of which you speak and with an abundance of spiritual understanding. Instead, it inspires the unworthy, arouses those who are sleeping, and enlightens those who are held in the blindness of ignorance. Mercifully it reproves and chastises us and pours itself into our hearts, so that thus stirred up by its compunction we might be prodded to rise up out of inactive slumber.
>
> (*Conlat*. 4.5 [42.170])

Although Cassian has written elsewhere that God gives grace to those who labour, his words here indicate that God does not give grace *only* to those who strive. Instead, he is free to work in anyone's life, whether that person is seeking him or not. This passage shows that grace is what prompts us to action; it produces the strivings by which we gain virtue.

At the beginning of the infamous 'semi-Pelagian' discussion of grace and free will in *Conlat*. 13, Germanus cites the illustration of a farmer who works hard to produce a crop, and he asks why the monk cannot similarly say that his virtue is the result of his own labour. Abbot Chaeremon replies that in the illustration, it is God, rather than the farmer, who produces the crop. He continues: 'From this it is clear that the beginning not only of good acts but even of good thoughts is in God. He both inspires in us the beginnings of a holy will and grants the ability and the opportunity to bring to fulfilment the things we rightly desire' (*Conlat*.

30 Other passages that show much the same pattern include *De Inst. Coen*. 3.3 [98]; *Conlat*. 10.7 [54.81], 11.7 [54.107], 13.18 [54.180], 17.9 [54.255], 23.17 [64.162–4].

13.3 [54.150–1]). Chaeremon then quotes Jas. 1: 17 and 2 Cor. 9: 10 in support of this idea, and he adds, 'But our task is to conform humbly to the grace of God which daily draws us on' (*Conlat.* 13.3 [54.151]). Here as well, we see that the pattern is one of human response to God's grace, not God's response to human action. God produces the desire for holiness, grants the ability to carry out this desire, and daily draws the monk on (*adtraho*) as he pursues perfection. The human responsibility is to follow (*subsequor*) the divine initiative.[31]

During abbot Theonas' discussion of the difference between the law and the gospel (cited above), he comments that the monk who is under grace is far above the law, since God's love, poured out on him through the Holy Spirit, removes all desire except that which drives him towards perfection. He continues, 'Those whom the Saviour's grace has inflamed with a holy love for incorruption consume all the thorns of carnal desires by the fire of the Lord's love, so that no dying ember of vice diminishes the coolness of their integrity' (*Conlat.* 21.33 [64.108]). Here we see that grace does not simply require perfection and help the monk to attain it; grace produces purity of desire and itself destroys the longing for vice. One should also notice that grace is connected not with power but with the fire of the Lord's love (*ignis dominicae caritatis*). Christ's love is given through the Holy Spirit, and this love consumes all other desires by focusing the monk's attention on Christ alone. Theonas concludes the chapter by citing Rom. 6: 14 and writing that the monk who lives by the light of the gospel is not under law, '*but under grace*, which not only cuts off the branches of iniquity but completely pulls up the very roots of the evil will' (*Conlat.* 21.33 [64.110]). Grace does not simply assist a person; it changes him. The initiative lies not with human action to seek union with God, but with divine action.[32]

[31] In Prosper's response to this conference (*Con. Collat.* 2.2–5 [218–21]), he heartily endorses what Cassian writes here, but he insists that Cassian departs from this principle in the rest of the conference by asserting that people can make the first move towards God. I will not deal directly with the semi-Pelagian controversy, but in sect. 5.4 I will discuss some of the potential implications of my research for the interpretation of that dispute.

[32] Cf. *De Inst. Coen.* 12.9–10 [462–4]; *Conlat.* 3.16 [42.160], 6.16 [42.240], 12.4 [54.124–5], 12.15 [54.144], 23.10 [64.153].

One can see an apparent tension within Cassian's monastic thought. His dominant idea seems to be that salvation is the end product of the human ascent towards perfect contemplation, and grace is God's assistance in this task and his action of crowning human effort with rewards far greater than the effort warrants. But a significant undercurrent in his writings is the idea that all monastic life is a response to an already-present salvation and that grace initiates the struggle towards perfection by giving the monk both the desire and the ability to pursue it. Of course, this tension has not escaped the attention of scholars, and some interpreters contend that Cassian resorts to the latter of these ideas only when discussing pride. His main idea, they assert, concerns the monk's striving against vice and towards God, but a large part of the struggle against vice involves conquering pride, and the best remedy for this is the belief that one's own efforts (however heroic they may be) are not the cause of one's victories over sin. Instead, God's grace has produced these victories, since grace has produced the desire and ability to strive against vice. In short, scholars argue that what Cassian writes about the need for effort and what he writes about pride are inconsistent with each other, or at least paradoxical.[33] This explanation of the tension is certainly possible, but on the other hand, it may be that the very presence of such tension is an indication that the image of a ladder ascending to God is not the best way to view Cassian's understanding of salvation. Instead, the passages in which he gives priority to God's action may represent his fundamental picture of salvation, rather than being simply a tool for staving off a monk's pride. In order to give a clearer picture of Cassian's idea of salvation and grace, I will examine more carefully what Cassian means by union with God. As I do this, I will suggest what I believe is a more plausible resolution to the tension that scholars have noted in Cassian's thought.

5.3. RECONCILING THE EVIDENCE: UNION WITH GOD IN CASSIAN

As we have seen, when scholars argue that the view of the monastic task as an ascent to God under human initiative is Cassian's foundational view of salvation, part of the reason is that

[33] e.g. O. Chadwick, *John Cassian*, 110–11.

they assume he sees monasticism as the sole viable form of Christian spirituality. Only with this assumption can one completely equate the monastic endeavour and the task of salvation, and thus regard what Cassian writes to monks as a comprehensive expression of his doctrines of salvation and grace. If this assumption is not correct, then the occasional nature of Cassian's writings becomes very significant for any assessment of his soteriology. The overwhelming dominance of references to monastic striving and to grace as divine aid in our struggles may not imply that this is Cassian's foundational idea of grace. Rather, this may imply simply that Cassian sees divine aid as the aspect of grace most relevant to that portion of Christian life with which monasticism is concerned. In that case, passages that seem to indicate a different pattern may actually provide a glimpse into Cassian's broader assumptions regarding the nature of and path to salvation. That these passages are a minority may not mean that they are less significant for his thought; instead, they could represent the assumed, but rarely stated, foundations of his thought. In this section, I will explore this possibility and attempt to explain and reconcile the evidence I have surveyed.

5.3.1. The Monastic Task: Deepening an Already-Present Union with God

Scholars have noted that in *Conlat.* Cassian rarely exhausts a given topic in one discussion, but instead returns to the same theme at various times so as to consider his subject from different angles. The overall effect is thus cumulative, and one must look at the whole in order to gain a balanced picture of his teaching.[34] More specifically, de Vogüé argues that Cassian structures his work around pairs and trilogies of conferences. The pairs consist of one conference that concerns progress towards the monastic goal, followed by one that deals with avoiding extremes on one side or another (e.g. *Conlat.* 1–2, 3–4, 5–6, 14–15, 16–17). The trilogies (*Conlat.* 1–3, 11–13, and 21–3) all deal with the relation between grace and the monastic task: the monk must strive for perfection by avoiding extremes, but he must rely on God's grace to do so.[35] As a result, *Conlat.* 23 is perhaps the climax of the entire work. It is the last section of the final trilogy on grace,

[34] Cf. Pristas, 'The Theological Anthropology of John Cassian', 132–3.
[35] de Vogüé, 'Pour comprendre Cassien', 250–2.

it comes very close to the conclusion of the whole work, it deals with the question of whether the perfection that constitutes the goal of monastic life is attainable, and it is the conference that deals most thoroughly with contemplation, the highest rung on the ladder of monastic striving.[36] Thus I would like to concentrate on this conference as I probe the foundations of Cassian's understanding of union with God, salvation, and grace.

Conlat. 23 begins with the question of whether Rom. 7: 14–25 refers to Paul or to non-Christians. Germanus has argued in 22.15–16 that since Paul had reached perfection and thus there was no inner conflict within him, he could not have been referring to himself in this passage. In response, Theonas declares in 23.1–4 that neither Paul nor anyone else except Christ has ever been sinless,[37] that the passage does refer to Paul, and that the good that Paul wants but cannot achieve is *theoria*, perfect contemplation of God. Then in 23.5 Theonas explains that part of the reason even Paul was sometimes distracted from contemplation of God was that his ministry itself distracted him, and he describes the conflict within the apostle as follows:

> He realized that he was endowed with many practical gifts, but on the other hand, when he considered in his heart the good of *theoria* and in a sense weighed on one scale the progress made from so many labours and on the other scale the delight of divine contemplation (*delectationem diuinae contemplationis*), and so to speak, with the vast rewards of his labours pleasing him sometimes and the desire for union and inseparable communion with Christ (*unitatis et inseparabilis Christi societatis*) moving him to depart from the flesh at other times, he ultimately cried out and said anxiously, *I do not know which to choose* [Phil. 1: 22]. (*Conlat.* 23.5 [64.145])

Here one should note that Cassian contrasts Paul's active life of ministry with the life of *theoria* or *contemplatio*, and he describes the latter as both 'union' (*unitas*) and communion (*societas*) with God. Clearly, Cassian sees *societas Christi* as a description of union with God. I will deal below with the question of what

[36] Stewart, *Cassian the Monk*, 32–5, offers a structure for *Conlat.* similar to the one de Vogüé proposes, and he concurs in arguing that Conferences 21–3 provide the final word on chastity and grace.

[37] Cf. other passages where Cassian directly states that no one except the Saviour has been sinless: *Conlat.* 11.9 [54.109–11], 22.7 [64.125–6], 22.9 [64.127], 23.17 [64.164].

Cassian means by *societas*, and for now my translation of the word as 'communion' should be regarded as merely provisional. At this point the important thing is that the reason Paul sought death was not so that he might gain this *unitas/societas* with God. Paul certainly realized that he was not perfect, and Cassian interprets this to mean that his *contemplatio* was not yet perfect. If union with God were something Paul had to gain by perfecting his contemplation, then he would not have longed for death, since it would have cut short his efforts to aspire to such union. Rather, one can conclude that Paul already possessed *societas* with God, but he was not always able to enjoy this *societas* uninterruptedly. He longed to depart from the body so as to have *inseparabilis societas Christi*, rather than a somewhat distracted *societas Christi*. For Paul, the goal was to enhance a union with God that he already possessed, not to gain *unitas/societas* with God.[38]

Also noteworthy in this passage is the fact that Theonas speaks very favourably of Paul's practical ministry gifts, and he avers that Paul could look forward to vast rewards (*stipendia immensa*) as a result of his missionary work. This missionary activity was not directly connected to the task of pursuing perfect *contemplatio*; indeed, it detracted from that task. Yet Cassian does not denigrate this work at all; he depicts Paul's choice as one between two good options, not between a good and a bad option. (Of course, Paul himself also depicts the choice this way; hence his indecision about which option he prefers.) As a result, one cannot claim that Cassian sees the monastic task as being the only important aspect of Christian life, nor is the monastery the only place where one can find salvation. His understanding of salvation and the Church is not as exclusively monastic as some interpreters believe.[39]

Immediately after this, Theonas explains that for the sake of his preaching ministry, Paul was willing not only to forgo

[38] Rousseau, 'Cassian, Contemplation, and the Coenobitic Life', 115–16, offers a concurring interpretation of this passage when he writes that Germanus sees contemplation as the result of the monastic endeavour, but Theonas (and thus Cassian) sees it as the ultimate goal, but yet a goal which is guaranteed by Christ's redemptive sacrifice.

[39] It is worth noting that according to Cassian, one of the many means by which one may make absolution for sins is by bringing people to conversion through preaching. See *Conlat*. 20.8 [64.65–6].

uninterrupted *contemplatio*, but even theoretically to be condemned himself so that others might be saved. He quotes Rom. 9: 3 and explains:

> I would wish to be delivered over not only to temporal but even to everlasting punishment, if it were possible for all people to enjoy communion with Christ (*Christi consortio*). For I am certain that the salvation of all people is more beneficial to Christ and to me than mine is. Therefore, in order to be able to acquire perfectly this highest good—that is, enjoying the vision of God and clinging constantly to Christ—the apostle desired to be rid of his body, which was weak and overwhelmed by the many burdens of its own frailty and which could not help but keep him from communion with Christ (*Christi consortio*). (*Conlat*. 23.5 [64.146])

In this passage, the fact that Cassian mentions Paul's willingness to undergo eternal punishment indicates that he is dealing with salvation in its broadest sense, and there is no ghost of a connection between salvation and the monastic task. Rather, Cassian sees God as offering salvation to all people through the preaching of Paul, and he describes this salvation with the expression 'enjoying communion with Christ' (*frui consortio Christi*). Here *consortium* appears to be another synonym for *unitas* and *societas*, and I will return below to the question of what Cassian means by it. In the latter half of the quotation, Theonas returns to Paul's desire for death, and he argues that the highest good, that which is even greater than seeing other people come to salvation, is to enjoy the vision of God and to cling to Christ constantly. As a justification for this, he argues that the frailties of the body cannot fail to separate one from *consortium Christi*. In the light of his earlier discussion, one should read this as implying that his mortal condition distracts him from uninterrupted *consortium Christi*, not as implying that he cannot gain this *consortium* at all until after he leaves his mortal body.

As I have noted, this discussion of Paul comes at a crucial juncture in the structure of *Conlat*., and it provides a rare but important glance at the Christian world outside the confines of the cenobium. As such, it demonstrates that for Cassian, salvation is not simply something one needs to achieve, but rather something the Christian possesses and should strive to enjoy more perfectly and with less interruption. Paul already possessed *societas/consortium* with God while he was in his mortal body, and this salvation is available to all through the preaching of the gospel. But whoever receives it recognizes that it is the highest good and thus longs to experience it more fully. As a result, the monastic pursuit of perfection in order to enjoy uninterrupted *contemplatio* comes from the desire to deepen the experience of *unitas* with God, to enhance the *societas/consortium* that the Christian has already been given. The rest of Theonas' discussion in 23.5 bears out this pattern. He says that the mind cannot enjoy the divine vision constantly, and he gives examples of worldly concerns that interrupt a monk's prayers, his meditation on Scripture, and his contemplation of God. In all of these cases, the question is not one of gaining something; it is a matter of seeing more clearly what one already has, or better, *whom* one already has.

This view of the relation between salvation and monasticism is corroborated by the fact that Cassian elsewhere argues that the monastic task is to anticipate the perfect contemplation of God that all Christians will enjoy eternally. Abbot Serenus uses the following argument in urging the monk to pursue virtue:

> No one will reach this full measure in the coming age except the one who has reflected on it and been initiated into it in the present and who has tasted it while still living in this world; the one who, having been designated a most precious member of Christ, possesses in this flesh the pledge (*arram*) of that union through which he is able to be joined to Christ's body; the one who desires only one thing, thirsts for one thing, and always directs not only all actions but even all thoughts to this one thing, in order that he may already possess in the present what has been pledged him and what is spoken of with regard to the blessed way of life (*conuersatione*) of the saints in the future—that is, that *God may be all in all* to him [1 Cor. 15: 28]. (*Conlat*. 7.6 [42.253])

Notice that in this passage, Serenus is referring not to the means by which a person can attain to the future age, but to the way one can attain to the full measure (*plenitudo mensurae*) of that world. That is, he is discussing how one can most fully deepen the union with God that will characterize the age to come. He says that the monk has already been designated a member of Christ and already possesses the pledge of union that joins him to the body of Christ. The monk's desire for perfection grows out of the fact that he has already been given this seal, and his goal is to anticipate in the present time the perfect way of life (*conuersatio*) that the saints will have in the future world. In that world, all the saints will be fully dedicated to the contemplation of God and will be united to him. The monk's special role is to dedicate himself completely in the present to the task that will belong to all Christians in eternity, and in this way, the monastery serves as an emblem of the coming age.

In a very similar passage, abbot Isaac discusses the life of continual prayer that the anchorite leads: 'This should be the anchorite's goal and whole intention, to deserve to possess the image of future blessedness in this body and as it were to begin to taste the pledge of that heavenly way of life (*arram caelestis illius conuersationis*) and glory in this vessel' (*Conlat.* 10.7 [54.81–2]). Here we see that what the anchorite seeks to deserve (or perhaps, 'to attain') is not the future blessing itself, since he already possesses the pledge of that blessedness. Rather, what he seeks to attain is the image of that blessedness, the *conuersatio* or 'heavenly way of life' that will characterize the future age. He seeks in his earthly body to live the blessed life of the future age. Again, the monastic task is not an attempt to gain salvation; it is an effort to live as fully as possible the life most appropriate to a Christian, the life of contemplation of God. One seeks not to achieve union with God but to deepen an already-present union so as to anticipate the age to come.

One can conclude that there are substantial grounds for revising the typical scholarly opinion of Cassian. The attention he gives to the pursuit of perfection should not lead one to think that he sees salvation only in terms of moral purity or that he believes union with God is something the monk achieves himself. The passages I have considered give a glimpse into his broader soteriology, and this glimpse enables one to place his constant attention to monastic striving in proper perspective. But if it is true that the monk seeks to deepen and foster a union with God that he already possesses, we must ask what Cassian believes that union to be. I will now turn to this question as I consider his use of *societas*, *consortium*, and other synonyms for *unitas*.

5.3.2. *Union as Communion with God*

Louth argues that in the Evagrian strand of monasticism, contemplation (which Evagrius himself calls θεολογική) is absolutely imageless and results from the monk's completely stripping his mind of thoughts so that the knower and the Known are one.[40] In the light of Evagrius' influence on Cassian, one might expect a similarly imageless understanding of union, but in fact, Cassian's idea is a good deal more personal, as an examination of the words he uses to describe this union will show.[41]

Cassian uses the noun *unitas* and the verb *unio c.*62 times in his writings, *c.*40 of which refer to the christological union. The 22 other occurrences refer to various kinds of relationships among people or between people and spirits or God. The words can connote general interaction between people, friendship or fellowship, and even physical inhabitation of a person by a spirit. Cassian uses the words three times to refer to the unity within the Trinity and four times to refer to the monk's union with Christ.[42] Of these latter four passages, two describe a person's union with Christ in largely mental terms: the monk thinks in the same way as Christ by concentrating on heavenly things, rather than earthly. Abbot John affirms that the monk's purpose is to crucify his desires, to turn from his own will, and to glorify the Lord. By stripping his mind of all earthly things, the monk will be able, as far as human frailty allows, to unite (*unire*) his mind to Christ (*Conlat.* 19.8 [64.46]). Similarly, abbot Theonas comments on the conflict within the monk by saying that in the inner man, the monk delights in the law of God (Rom. 7: 22) and longs to be continually united to God alone (*deo soli semper uniri*), but there is another law that wars against this desire and leads the monk to think of earthly things (*Conlat.* 23.11 [64.153]). It is clear that in Cassian's thought, part of what it means to be united with God is to set one's mind on the things above (Col. 3: 2), the things of God.

The other two passages both depict the monk's union with God in terms of communion or friendship. In sect. 5.3.1, I considered *Conlat.* 23.5 and asserted that there Cassian regards both *societas* and *consortium* as synonyms for *unitas*. The other passage

[40] Louth, *The Origins of the Christian Mystical Tradition*, 108–9. Cf. Tugwell, 'Evagrius and Macarius', 172–3.

[41] Codina, *El Aspecto Christologico*, 189, concurs with this assessment that Cassian's and Evagrius' perspectives on spiritual life are very different.

[42] For a complete list of the passages where Cassian uses the words *unitas* and *unio* in each of these ways, see Table 5.

comes much earlier in the work, as Cassian describes the zeal of abbot Paphnutius. Not only did the young Paphnutius overcome all his vices, but he also longed for the solitary life of the desert. Cassian writes that he did this 'so that, no longer hindered by any human companionship (*humano consortio*), he would more easily be united (*uniretur*) with the Lord to whom, although surrounded by a large number of brothers, he longed to be inseparably linked' (*Conlat*. 3.1 [42.140]). One should notice the parallel between union with the Lord and human companionship. Paphnutius found that his fellowship with people was hindering his friendship with God, and he longed to remove that human concourse so as to facilitate union with God. This parallel gives an important glimpse into Cassian's understanding of union: *unitas* is not a contentless absorption into God, utterly unlike anything one experiences in other situations. Rather, union with God is something akin to one's friendships with other people, but certainly of a much deeper intensity and greater value. Cassian also uses *unitas* to indicate the close friendship between monks in *De Inst. Coen*. 4.8 [130] and *Conlat*. 24.26 [64.200], and the fact that he can use the same word to refer both to human friendship and to union with God corroborates the parallel that we see in this passage about Paphnutius.

When one turns to Cassian's use of *societas* and *consortium*, the same pattern is evident. He can use both words to refer to an association of ideas, but much more often, he employs the words (and their corresponding verb and adjective forms) to refer to human interaction, whether it be general social concourse with people, marriage, or close friendship such as that which monks share with one another. In the case of *societas* and its related forms, 18 of the *c*.27 occurrences refer to interaction between people, and two occurrences refer to the Christian's interaction with God. In the case of *consortium* and its related forms, 46 of the *c*.56 occurrences refer to interaction between people, and 5 occurrences refer to the believer's relationship with God.[43] Clearly, both of these words, as well as *unitas* itself, refer primarily to human companionship, and Cassian sees a Christian's union with God to be something of the same sort. A glance at several passages will illustrate this.

[43] For a complete list of passages where Cassian uses these words in each of these ways, see Tables 6 and 7.

As abbot Moses discusses the contrast between the joys of heaven and earthly pleasures, he writes, 'Everyone who lives in this body knows that he must be committed to that special task or ministry to which he has given himself in this life as a participant (*participem*) and a labourer (*cultoremque*), and he ought not to doubt that in that everlasting age he will also be the friend (*consortem*) of him whose servant (*ministrum*) and companion (*sociumque*) he now wishes to be' (*Conlat.* 1.14 [42.93]). Here Moses describes Christians not only with servant imagery (*cultor* and *minister*), but also with imagery indicative of friendship with God (*consors*, *socius*, and perhaps also *particeps*, although this last word is ambiguous). Furthermore, one should note that Cassian uses friendship imagery to refer not merely to the future age but also to the present. The one who is now *socius Christi* will in the age to come be *consors Christi*. Communion with God is not the end result of serving him; it is something in which the Christian takes part now, and as a result the Christian then desires to serve God. Similarly, during a discussion of whether one is allowed to break a promise, abbot Joseph writes of Peter: 'Because he departed from the definitive statement that he had made with almost sacramental force when he said, *you shall never wash my feet* [John 13: 8], he was promised communion with Christ (*Christi consortium*) forever, whereas he would certainly have been deprived of the grace of this blessedness had he clung obstinately to his statement' (*Conlat.* 17.9 [54.255]). In this passage Joseph connects Peter's gaining communion with Christ (*Christi consortium*) with his willingness to allow Jesus to wash him, a fact that shows Cassian's belief that Christ gives salvation and fellowship with himself to those who are willing to receive him. This *consortium* is not something that must wait until one achieves monastic perfection.[44]

Further corroboration that Cassian sees union with God primarily as communion comes from the fact that he uses the

[44] I should mention that *Conlat.* 21.9 [64.83], which I have discussed in sect. 5.1.1, seems to indicate the contrary: only by renouncing everything and seeking perfection can the young Paphnutius gain *consortium Christi*. In the light of the argument I have developed in this section, this passage and other similar ones can perhaps be interpreted to mean that pursuit of perfection enables one to deepen the fellowship with Christ that God has already given, rather than implying that such fellowship does not begin until one reaches perfection.

very personal words *amicitia* and *familiaritas* and their related forms to describe the monk's relationship to God. In Cassian's writings, *amicitia* and *amicus* refer to personal friendship between people in 25 of their occurrences, compared with only 4 occurrences that refer to one's love for an object, and 7 times Cassian refers to friendship between God and people with these words. In the same way, he uses *familiaritas*, *familiaris*, and *familiariter* of an impersonal relation 9 times, compared with 9 occurrences that refer to friendship between people and 8 that refer to friendship between God and people.[45] Thus both groups of words refer primarily (but hardly exclusively) to personal relationships. Especially noteworthy are the three passages where Cassian uses the comparative adverb *familiarius* and the superlative *familiarissime*. In the first, abbot Moses describes a conversation in which Antony asks several elders what is most necessary in the pursuit of perfection, and they answer that one must retire to the desert, since 'someone living there [in solitude] would be able to address God more familiarly (*familiarius*) and cling to him more closely' (*Conlat*. 2.2 [42.112]). In the second passage, abbot Isaac uses the beginning of the Lord's Prayer to speak of pure prayer, formed by perfect contemplation, as that prayer 'by which the mind, having been dissolved and flung into love for him, speaks most familiarly (*familiarissime*) and with particular devotion with God, as with its own father' (*Conlat*. 9.18 [54.55]). Finally, abbot Nesteros says that by virtue of living in the desert, Antony and others like him were able to 'cling most familiarly (*familiarissime*) to God through the silence of solitude' (*Conlat*. 14.4 [54.185]). In these three passages, the use of the comparative or superlative shows that the monks are seeking to enhance a familiarity they already have with God, rather than trying to gain a familiarity that is not yet present. One cannot seek to know God *more* familiarly unless one already knows him. In particular, the second of the passages shows the warmth of love that characterizes the Christian's relationship to God; he is able to call God his own Father, and as he pursues prayer, he can speak with him in the most familiar way possible.

45 For a complete list of the passages where Cassian uses these words in each of these ways, see Tables 8 and 9.

The various words that Cassian uses to describe salvation and union with God show that *unitas* is not an impersonal absorption into the divine being or a state of mindless ecstasy devoid of any thought. In fact, Cassian gives no hint that his idea of unity even approaches such an extreme. Rather, unity consists primarily of friendship or communion with God, and the Christian receives this from Christ as a gift. The desire of the monk is to strip away all other concerns and distractions so that he may enjoy this fellowship to the greatest degree possible, so that he may undistractedly contemplate the Friend and Father who is most truly worth knowing. Therefore, although Cassian is far from a monistic mode of thought, he is also very far from Theodorean/Nestorian thought, which sees salvation largely in terms of an ascent to a higher human age, to a state of partnership with the *homo assumptus*, and which maintains such a sharp distinction between God and humanity that any significant human fellowship with God is impossible.

Furthermore, if this reconstruction is correct, Cassian's soteriology is consistent with, and even remarkably similar to, that of Cyril. Of course, the monk has none of the terminological precision that we saw in the Alexandrian bishop, who has made the word *οἰκειότης* into a virtual technical term to refer to communion between personal beings. Cyril never uses the word of an impersonal association, and in the vast majority of cases the word refers to the Christian's fellowship with God. On the other hand, Cassian's words for union or fellowship do not refer exclusively to personal relationships; they are all used in a variety of ways. Since Cassian is a monk and thus perhaps more prone to being understood in an absorptionist way than Cyril, it is probably better that Cassian has no term comparable to Cyril's *οἰκειότης*. By using several very ordinary words, words that can refer to one's love for an idea as well as one's love for God, Cassian avoids giving the impression that salvation is a state of impersonal absorption into God, a condition devoid of either thought or content. But although he has no single word with which to describe communion with God, Cassian does make clear that salvation consists largely of such friendship. This raises the question of whether Cassian, like Cyril, sees this communion that God gives us as being that which the persons of the Trinity share with one another. To use Cyril's terminology, does Cassian see salvation as God's giving us his own natural communion (οἰκειότης φυσική)?

Of course, this is an unfair question to ask of one who, as far as we know, never met Cyril or read any of his early writings, although he may have seen Cyril's letter to the Egyptian monks.[46] It is certainly not Cassian's concern to describe our communion with God with the sort of specificity Cyril exhibits, but in spite of this, there is one passage in *Conlat.* that appears to be very close to Cyril's idea. In *Conlat.* 10 abbot Isaac discusses Jesus' prayer that all Christians be one, just as he and the Father are one (John 17: 21–4). Isaac says:

> Then after the fulfilment of this prayer of the Lord (which we believe can in no way be rendered void), God's perfect love, by which *he first loved us* [1 John 4: 19], will also have passed into our heart's disposition. This will be the case when all our love, our every desire, our every effort, our every undertaking, our every thought, everything that we live, that we speak, that we breathe, will be God, and when that unity that the Father now has with the Son and that the Son has with the Father will be transfused into our understanding and our mind, so that, just as he loves us with a sincere, pure, and indissoluble love, we too may be joined to him with a perpetual and inseparable love and be so united with him that whatever we breathe, whatever we understand, whatever we speak, may be God. (*Conlat.* 10.7 [54.81])

This is rather arresting language, since Cassian asserts that in pure prayer, everything about the monk can somehow be God. But one should note that the two threads that wind through this passage are the love with which Christ has loved us and the unity between the Son and the Father. What unites us to God is 'perpetual and inseparable love', and this is the same 'sincere, pure, and indissoluble love' with which Christ has loved us. But this love is said to be the same as the unity that the Father and the Son now have with each other. It thus appears that Cassian is referring to the personal unity of love and communion between the Father and the Son. This love that unites the Father and the Son in personal intimacy is what God shares with us when he gives us communion with himself, and the discipline of pure

46 Brand, 'Le *De incarnatione Domini* de Cassien', 145–7, notes the similarities between Cassian's *De Incar. Dom.* and Cyril's letter to the monks and suggests that Cassian had a copy of that letter. Cf. Vannier, 'Cassien a-t-il fait œuvre de théologien?', 348.

prayer is an attempt to heighten and deepen one's grasp of and appreciation for this fellowship.

Admittedly, this is only a single passage, and Cassian may not mean as much here as Cyril does in his interpretation of the same biblical text. But one may at least say that Cassian's thought is consistent with Cyril's, even if he does not have as full an idea in mind. God gives us communion with himself, and we seek through all aspects of Christian life to deepen that communion, to sense more fully the perfect love with which Christ has loved us.

5.3.3. Grace as God's Gift of Communion through Adoption

We have already seen that Cassian often appears to regard grace as God's assistance in the monk's efforts to pursue perfection, but that he sometimes seems to see it as that which produces the monk's desire for and ability to achieve virtue. In the light of my appraisal of Cassian's soteriology, it is important to ask whether he also has a more comprehensive understanding of grace than that which I have surveyed thus far. The emphasis he places on union with God implies that grace somehow involves God's giving himself to the monk, and there are a few places in Cassian's monastic writings where he indicates this more directly.

During *Conlat.* 16 on friendship, abbot Joseph uses 1 John 4: 16 to argue that love does not simply *belong to* God; love *is* God. Commenting on Paul's statement that God's love has been poured out in our hearts by the Holy Spirit (Rom. 5: 5), he explains, 'It is as if he were saying that God has been poured out in our hearts by the Holy Spirit who indwells us' (*Conlat.* 16.13 [54.233]). Closely connected with this idea is Cassian's belief that Christ gives himself to Christians by giving us his virtues. While pointing out that different monks possess different virtues, he indicates that the presence of each virtue is an indication of partial participation in Christ, and he concludes, 'Christ is now distributed, member by member, among all the saints' (*De Inst. Coen.* 5.4 [196]). Elsewhere, Cassian makes a sharp distinction between God (who is by nature eternal, immutable, and good) and creatures (who are not so by nature), and he says that we receive these qualities from him 'through participation in the Creator himself and in his grace' (*Conlat.* 23.3 [64.142]). In these scattered passages we find indications that Cassian believes grace is God's gift of himself to people by giving us qualities that he possesses.

More important, however, is the link that Cassian forges between grace and adoption. God gives himself to the monk by making him an adopted son, an imitator of the true Son and therefore a sharer in the relationship the Son has with the Father. I have already considered two passages (*Conlat.* 1.15 [42.97] and 21.34 [64.110], both discussed in sect. 5.2.1) in which Cassian states that adoption initiates the monastic life, and there are two others that I will now examine. During abbot Isaac's discussion of pure prayer in *Conlat.* 9 (discussed in sect. 5.3.2), he exhorts the monks to seek this perfect contemplation of God and adds, 'When we confess with our own voice that the God and Lord of the universe is our Father, we profess that we have in fact been taken from our servile condition and admitted (*adscitos*) into adopted sonship.' He then explains that we long for the heavenly dwelling-place of our Father, rather than for this present life, and he continues, 'Since we have been led to the rank and status of sons (*in quem filiorum ordinem gradumque prouecti*), we shall [henceforth] be inflamed with the piety that belongs to good sons, so that we shall direct all our effort to the advance not of our own profit, but of our Father's glory' (*Conlat.* 9.18 [54.55]). Notice that in the first sentence, as in *Conlat.* 1.15 [42.97], Cassian uses the perfect tense of the verb *adscisco* to indicate that we have already been claimed by God as his adopted children. In the light of this, one cannot take the second sentence to mean that we reach adopted sonship only through pure prayer. Rather, Cassian is indicating that through pure prayer we recognize more fully the sonship we already have. One should therefore take *in quem filiorum ordinem gradumque prouecti* to refer to the past, not the future. The sense is not '*once* we have advanced to the rank and status of sons, we will *then* burn with piety,' but '*since* we have been led to the rank and status of sons, we will burn with piety' (as is reflected in my translation through my addition of the implied 'henceforth'). Notice also that the desire to exhibit the piety characteristic of good sons indicates the prior presence of an adoptive relationship. The monk's longing for virtue is a desire to be a good son, to please his adopted Father. It is not an attempt to attain to sonship.

In a similar passage, abbot Chaeremon discusses three

motivations to pursue perfection: fear of hell (which he calls slavery), desire for rewards (which he equates with being a hireling), and love of goodness itself (which he links to adopted sonship). He says of the prodigal son (Luke 15):

> His father hastened to accept this statement of humble repentance with a love greater than that with which it had been spoken. Not content to grant him less, he passed over the other two degrees without delay and restored him to his former dignity of sonship. We also ought henceforth to hasten on, so that by means of the indissoluble grace of love we may mount to that third stage, the stage of sons, who believe that all the father has is their own, and so we may be counted worthy to receive the image and the likeness of our heavenly Father, and be able to say after the likeness of the true Son, *all that the Father has is mine* [John 16: 15]. (*Conlat*. 11.7 [54.106])

This passage certainly gives the impression that the monk is to seek adopted sonship, but if this were actually what Cassian meant, he would be flagrantly at odds with his own exposition of the biblical text: Chaeremon has directly said that the father *gave* the prodigal son's former sonship back to him. In the light of this fact and of the overall context, when Cassian writes that we should mount up to the stage of sonship, he is referring to our motivation for seeking perfection. We should not seek perfection merely out of fear or desire for rewards, since we are not slaves or hirelings. God has made us sons, and so we should act in a manner worthy of sons by seeking perfection purely for the love of goodness itself. This is what motivates the true Son, and when this motivates us as well, we will be imitators of the true Son. Thus we see not only that the monk's desire for virtue grows out of what God has already done in adopting him, but also that the monk's obedience has a strongly relational element. He is trying to be perfect so as to imitate the true Son, the one whose adopted brother he is.

Olphe-Galliard argues that for Cassian, adoption comes only after one succeeds in being united to God through contemplation.[47] There are certainly passages in Cassian that seem to indicate this,[48] just as there are many passages that emphasize the monk's striving after perfection. However, in the preceding

[47] Olphe-Galliard, 'Cassien (Jean)', 228.
[48] e.g. *Conlat*. 24.26 [64.200–1].

discussion I have sought to demonstrate that adoption is what produces the monk's striving for virtue, rather than what follows from it. Once a person is adopted as a child of God, he should seek to be a worthy child, to act in the same way Christ, the true Son, acts. Although Cassian devotes most of his attention to what a monk does, one can see that the monk's own efforts are not the basis for his thought. Rather, the foundation is what God has already done in giving himself to the monk: sharing his immortality and virtue with him, and even more, making the monk his own child. In making us his children, God gives us the gift of fellowship with himself, a communion that may be the very love the Father and the Son share with each other.

This is the heart of Cassian's thought, even though the specific purpose for which he writes means that he rarely addresses this issue at length. He is not writing a systematic theology, nor is he preaching to the unconverted. He is writing to men who are among the most devoted of Christians, and he seeks to lead them to recognize more fully the greatness of the God who has redeemed them, the one who has given himself to them so that they might call him their own Father. Because of Cassian's purpose, his assumptions about what God has already done are often hidden beneath his exhortations to the monks, and it is not surprising that many commentators have lost sight of them. But these assumptions surface from time to time in his writings, and when they do appear, it is clear that the monk's task is to deepen an already-present communion with God, not to attain such fellowship or union.

In the conclusion of a work on the origins of Christian mysticism, Louth writes that whereas Platonic mysticism sees God as an impersonal ultimate to which one aspires, Christian mysticism seeks not an experience of an ultimate idea, but an experience of the personal God. God is deeply concerned with the soul's search for him, and God's grace is his gift to the soul of communion with himself, without which the soul could not even seek him.[49] If Louth intends 'communion' in the same personal, relational sense in which I have been using the word, then whatever may be said of other early Christian monks, this assessment is true of Cassian.

[49] Louth, *The Origins of the Christian Mystical Tradition*, 195.

5.4. IMPLICATIONS OF CASSIAN'S CONCEPT OF GRACE AND SALVATION

One can conclude that Cassian's idea of grace as God's co-operative assistance in response to the monk's effort is a derivative idea, rather than his primary concept of grace. It is significant that he discusses co-operation or divine aid only when considering the monk's efforts to strive after virtue; he never mentions these ideas when discussing Christ. Theodore uses these ideas to describe the God-man, to elucidate the union between deity and humanity in the person of the Saviour, and in doing so he indicates that divine aid in response to human action is his primary notion of grace.[50] In contrast, Cassian stands much closer to Cyril in that he sees the decisive aspect of grace as God's gift of himself to people by giving us adoption into a relationship with the Father. Cyril and Cassian both believe that human striving after virtue follows and grows out of this initial, and primary, gift of grace.

However, Cassian rarely elaborates the connection between the adopted sonship that Christians have and the true sonship of Christ. Whereas Cyril spends much time discussing the way God the Son gives his *οἰκειότης φυσική* to his own humanity and thence to all people, Cassian's monastic writings give little hint of how God gives himself to people. Again, the occasional nature of his writings can explain the lacuna: Cassian's purpose is not to describe the basis of salvation or even the basis for grace; it is to incite monks to seek virtue. Because Cassian leaves the issue of how God gives himself to people unexplored, one cannot venture to speculate about whether he would have said the same thing as Cyril had he written more. We may say only that in so far as he writes about grace as adoption and as the gift of communion, his thought is consistent with Cyril's.

At this point, it is worth mentioning that although I have not discussed the semi-Pelagian controversy, my reconstruction of Cassian's soteriological thought does have implications for that dispute. Most of the discussion related to the controversy concerns whether Cassian and the other so-called 'semi-Pelagians' believed that the source of good will (*ortus bonae*

[50] See especially *De Incar.* 7 [293–8].

uoluntatis) always came from God or could sometimes originate unaided in the human will. It seems to me that this entire question derives from the assumption that the desire for the good is the first step along the path of salvation, an assumption that is in turn based on the notion that Cassian sees salvation primarily as a human ascent towards virtue.[51] Whether one holds that God rewards human merit by granting salvation in return for virtue or believes that God rewards his own grace which produced the virtue,[52] one is still assuming that salvation comes at the end of a process of gaining perfection. But what I have argued implies that one should not consider Cassian's discussion of the human pursuit of perfection to be the foundational aspect of his soteriology. Whether or not a person can begin to will the good apart from the assistance of grace (and Cassian seems to believe one can), such desire is not the beginning of salvation. If I am correct, the will towards the good necessarily follows God's prior gift of himself to people through Christ. The good will, in Cassian's thought, is that of the Christian who seeks to purify himself so as to appreciate more fully the relationship he already has as a child of God; it is not that of one seeking to gain such union. Therefore, the semi-Pelagian debate may misunderstand Cassian by dealing only with the portion of his thought that concerns human striving, a portion that is not the foundational part. Admittedly, this does not solve all the problems *Conlat.* 13 poses, since several passages in that conference seem to indicate that Chaeremon is talking about the very beginning of salvation,[53] but a reconsideration of that debate in the light of what I have asserted may help to resolve some of the issues.

Even though Cassian's monastic writings do not treat the

[51] As an example of the pervasiveness of this assumption, see Weaver, *Divine Grace and Human Agency*, 7–8, where she asserts that Augustine's emphasis on grace was the result of realism about how little progress most Christians were making in gaining virtue, and 44–5, where she suggests that Prosper and Hilary may have been more confident of God's graciousness than of their own ability to advance in virtue. Throughout this generally excellent summary of the semi-Pelagian controversy, Weaver assumes that at least the monks, if not also everyone involved, believed salvation was the result of one's advance in perfection. Cf. the same assumption in Rea, 'Grace and Free Will in John Cassian', 126–46.

[52] See Augustine's insistence on the latter of these in *Ep.* 214.4 [384]; *Ep.* 215.1 [387–8]; *De Grat. Lib. Arb.* 15 [890–1], 20 [892–3], etc.

[53] e.g. *Conlat.* 13.15 [54.175], 13.18 [54.180].

workings of grace as much as one might like, his christology may help to show the degree to which his charitology is the same as Cyril's. Cassian makes a sharp distinction between the true, natural Son and those who are sons by grace and adoption, just as Cyril does. The Alexandrian makes this distinction because he insists that the subject of Christ must be the Logos, since only one who is Son by nature can give us the communion that he naturally has with the Father. If Cassian is to follow this line of thought (even without explicitly stating it), we should expect him to adhere to a christology just as strongly unitive as that of Cyril and with just as much emphasis on the Logos as the sole personal subject of Christ. As I turn to Cassian's christological thought in Ch. 6, we shall see that this is exactly what he does.

6

Grace and the Saviour's Personal Subject in Cassian's *De incarnatione Domini*

In contrast to *De Inst. Coen.* and *Conlat.*, Cassian's *De Incar. Dom.* contains virtually no reference to monasticism, to the human struggle against vice, or to the pursuit of perfection. For the first time, Cassian shifts away from a narrowly monastic audience and writes for the Church as a whole, and he focuses not on the human task of attaining virtue but on God's role in salvation and thus on the person of Christ. In this chapter, I will consider the consistency of Cassian's thought in *De Incar. Dom.* with the understanding of grace and salvation that I have claimed is present in his monastic writings, and I will examine the ways in which Cassian develops this understanding of grace more fully in the later work. Then I will turn to his technical christology in order to demonstrate that what Cassian writes about Christ's person is directly linked to his understanding of grace as the gift of fellowship with God. Finally, I will consider several troublesome elements of Cassian's christology in the light of the ideas I have examined.

6.1. CONFIRMATION OF CASSIAN'S SOTERIOLOGY IN *DE INCAR. DOM.*

At the inception of his work against Nestorius, Cassian discusses the Latin monk Leporius, who had been guilty of a christological error and had been corrected by Augustine and others. Cassian connects Leporius' christological mistake to Pelagianism by writing that both make Christ into a mere man who was sinless and thus imply that all people can be sinless with God's help. He continues:

They said that our Lord Jesus Christ had come into this world not to bring redemption to the human race but to give an example of good works. That is, [he came so that] by following his teaching, and by walking the same path of virtue, people might arrive at the same reward of virtue. Thus they destroyed, as far as they could, the entire gift of his holy advent and the entire grace of divine redemption, since they declared that people could by their own lives obtain that which God had wrought by dying for human salvation. (*De Incar. Dom.* 1.3 [240])

Cassian then links Nestorius directly to these ideas by asserting that he also believes we can reach the heavenly kingdom by following Christ's example, not by his redemption (*De Incar. Dom.* 1.3 [240]). Cassian reiterates this connection between Nestorius and Pelagius at several points in the work, most notably in 6.14, where he writes:

If Christ who was born of Mary is not the same one who who was born of God, you undoubtedly make two christs, according to the impious Pelagian error, which by asserting that a mere man was born of the virgin, said that he was the teacher of the human race rather than the redeemer, for he came to bring to people not redemption of life but [only] an example of how to live, so that by following him, people should do similar things and so come to a similar state.

(*De Incar. Dom.* 6.14 [341])[1]

Scholars have pointed out that there is no known historical link between Leporius and Pelagianism and that it is wrong for Cassian to make a connection between Nestorius and Pelagius,[2] but be that as it may, Cassian's words in these passages are important because of what they indicate about his own thought. What he condemns here is something very close to what the typical scholarly interpretation of his monastic writings claims *he* believes. Cassian insists that if one makes Christ into a mere example and teacher and views salvation as the result of human action in walking the same path of virtue (*uia uirtutis*) as Christ

[1] Cf. *De Incar. Dom.* 2.1 [246], 5.1–3 [301–4], 7.6–7 [361–3].

[2] e.g. Amann, 'L'Affaire Nestorius vue de Rome', 229–30; O. Chadwick, *John Cassian*, 138, 147; Grillmeier, *Christ in Christian Tradition*, 468. Cf. Turner, *Jesus the Christ*, 115, and Wickham, 'Pelagianism in the East', 211, both of whom argue that there was no definite historical connection between Pelagianism and Nestorianism, even if there was a connection between the ideas. But Gibson, 'The Works of John Cassian', 190, argues that Cassian was correct in linking Pelagianism and Nestorianism.

did, then one eliminates the value of the incarnation and Christ's death. Would Cassian write this so boldly if he himself actually saw salvation as the end result of the human task of striving after virtue? Brand believes so, and he argues that it is ironic that one who sees Christian life as a gradual process of union with God can accuse Nestorius of saying that Jesus gained deity by progress in virtue. Brand conjectures that the reason Cassian is so vehement here is that he is already feeling the heat of Prosper's accusation that *he* is a Pelagian, and thus he is on the defensive.[3] As ingenious as this explanation is, it hardly does justice to Cassian's soteriology. It is much simpler to assume that the reason Cassian makes this accusation is that he genuinely believes it is wrong to say one can attain union with God through progress in virtue. Salvation depends on the redemptive work of Christ, which requires that he be God, not a mere man (*solitarius homo*). However unfair Cassian's invective may be to Nestorius, Leporius, and even Pelagius, his comments concur with the view of his thought that I elaborated in the previous chapter. Cassian sees salvation predominantly as a gift that comes to us through Christ's redemption, not primarily as something to which we aspire through our own virtue.[4]

Cassian's emphasis on God's role in salvation is consistent with his condemnation of a view that turns Christ into a mere example. In 5.7, he quotes Col. 1: 12–20 in order to show that the one who is the image of the invisible God is the same one who lived and died on earth. Cassian writes, 'For he commands us to give thanks to the Father and adds a great reason for giving thanks, namely that he has made us worthy to be allotted a portion among the saints and *has delivered us from the power of darkness and transferred us to the kingdom of his beloved Son* [Col. 1: 13]' (*De Incar. Dom.* 5.7 [311]). Notice here that God is the one who makes us worthy to be allotted a portion among the saints. God's action, rather than ours, is decisive in the drama of

[3] Brand, 'Le *De incarnatione Domini* de Cassien', 155.

[4] Codina, *El Aspecto Christologico*, 187, concludes a study of Cassian's spirituality by writing that the denial of Christ's deity is the ultimate in demonic rebellion against God. The incarnation is the source of Christian humility, and a denial of the deity of Christ (and therefore of a real incarnation) constitutes the assertion of the creature above the creator through the claim that we are able to aspire to salvation on our own.

salvation.[5] Similarly, when Cassian discusses the human role in salvation, he emphasizes that faith is what makes us worthy of God's acceptance. Commenting on Paul's conversion, he writes, 'Because of his [Paul's] most earnest and devoted faith, he was at once worthy (*meruit*) of never lacking the presence of the one whom he had faithfully believed, and that he [Christ], to whom he had passed in heart, should himself pass into his [Paul's] heart' (*De Incar. Dom.* 3.6 [269]). Later, Cassian indicates that in Peter's case, what merited heaven and the keys to the kingdom of heaven was his faith that Christ was God's Son (*De Incar. Dom.* 3.14 [279]).[6] In these passages, merit or worthiness to be united to God is connected with God's action and with our faith in Christ's person, not with our pursuit of the monastic task or achievement of virtue. Especially noteworthy is Cassian's statement that Paul would never lack Christ. Salvation, as Cassian sees it, was the gift of Christ himself to Paul, a gift that God gave him when he began to believe, not merely after he progressed in virtue.

De Incar. Dom. contains little direct evidence that Cassian sees salvation in terms of communion with God, since he does not use *unitas*, *societas*, *consortium*, *amicitia*, or their related forms to refer to the relationship between the Christian and God. However, there is one important passage in which he describes believers as God's friends (*familiares deo*). Cassian explains that the Old Testament saints longed for the incarnation

> since indeed they knew that the hope of all men lay in it, and that the salvation of all was bound up in it, because no one could release the prisoners except one who was himself free from chains; no one could set sinners free except one who was himself without sin; for no one can in any case set anyone free unless he is himself free from that particular thing from which he frees another. And so when death had passed to all, all were lacking in life, so that by dying in Adam, they might live in Christ. For although there were many saints, many elect, and even [many] friends (*familiares*) of God, yet none could ever be saved of themselves, had they not been saved by the coming of the Lord and his redemption. (*De Incar. Dom.* 5.15 [324])

[5] Cf. *De Incar. Dom.* 4.12 [300], 5.15 [324], and 6.14 [341], in which Cassian argues that no one except God could accomplish redemption from sin.

[6] Cf. *De Incar. Dom.* 5.4 [305], in which Cassian asserts that all who believe become sons of God by adoption.

This passage provides an excellent summary of Cassian's soteriology. The hope of all people for salvation comes from the incarnation, since only one who is divine and therefore sinless can free us from sin. Only one who is not subject to that death which came through Adam can make us alive. Cassian concludes by implying that those who are saints, elect, and friends of God are such because of God's advent and the redemption he brought about. Cassian strongly links our salvation to Christ's presence and action, asserts that Christ's action is that of God (a point to which I will return below), and shows that salvation is, among other things, friendship with God.

One can see that the same concept of salvation pervades both Cassian's monastic writings and *De Incar. Dom.*, and the differences between them are due to the different situations Cassian is addressing. His monastic corpus focuses on the pursuit of virtue that enables a monk to deepen and appreciate more fully the gift of communion with God that he has been given, and his christological work concerns the foundation of that gift, the person of Christ. In both cases, Cassian sees salvation as a gift based on God's action and our faith in the Son of God, and he rejects the idea that we attain it only through a gradual process of union with God. In both cases, Cassian sees salvation as fellowship with God, although this element of his thought is more marked in the monastic writings than in *De Incar. Dom.*

6.2. CASSIAN'S DEVELOPMENT OF HIS CHRISTOLOGICAL CONCEPT OF GRACE

In *De Incar. Dom.*, Cassian does not merely corroborate the soteriology of his monastic writings but also develops it substantially. Specifically, he looks at what I call christological grace, the questions of what God gives us in salvation and of who Christ must be in order to give us this grace. These are the questions I will address in this section.

Cassian's most extended treatment of grace in *De Incar. Dom.* comes in 2.5 as he defends the use of the title *Theotokos*. He begins by quoting Acts 15: 10–11 and asserting that grace is given through Jesus Christ. Cassian asks whether this grace is given by a man or by God, and he answers from Titus 2: 11 that it is given by God. Therefore, Christ is God and Mary must be called *Theotokos* (*De Incar. Dom.* 2.5 [257]). Cassian then bolsters his case by discussing the fact that grace and truth came by Christ (John 1: 17). He writes:

> If Christ is a mere man (*solitarius homo*), how did these [i.e. grace and truth] come by Christ? Where did the divine power (*uirtus*) in him come from, if, as you say, he possesses only the human condition? Where did heavenly largesse (*largitas*) come from, if he possesses [only] earthly poverty? For no one can give what he does not already have. Since Christ gave divine grace, he already possessed what he gave.
>
> (*De Incar. Dom.* 2.5 [257])

Notice here that Cassian equates grace with divine power and heavenly largesse. He argues that Christ must have already possessed these in order to give them, and the implication is that Christ could not have possessed them if he were not God. He could not have gained them as a man and then passed them on to us. The assumption behind this argument is that God would not give his power and largesse to someone else in such a way that that person can mediate these to other people.[7]

Near the end of the work, Cassian makes the same point while speaking of divine power and righteousness. He accuses Nestorius of interpreting 1 Tim. 3: 16 to mean that Christ was filled with righteousness by the Holy Spirit as if he were devoid of that righteousness in his own right. In response, Cassian quotes 1 Cor. 1: 30 and 6: 11 and argues:

> How far he was from needing to be filled with righteousness, since he himself filled all things with righteousness and since his very name justifies all things. Thus you see how inept and insane are your blasphemies, since you are trying to take away from the Lord our God what he constantly pours forth upon all believers in such a way that in its continual supply it is still never diminished (*numquam in ipso tamen iugi largitate minuatur*). (*De Incar. Dom.* 7.18 [375])

One should notice Cassian's claim that Christ gives righteousness to all believers in such a way that it is never diminished. If he were himself devoid of righteousness and needed to be filled

[7] As I mentioned in Ch. 3 n. 16, Athanasius has used this argument in *De Syn.* 51 [784b]. One who receives grace has only enough for himself; he cannot then give grace to others.

from the Holy Spirit, then he could not give righteousness continually to others without being himself diminished. Christ must be the source of righteousness in order to give it to us; he could not have received it and then transmitted it to us.

Shortly after this, Cassian distinguishes between the apostles, who healed with a power received from Christ, and Christ himself, who healed in his own name and with his own power. He concludes: 'You must admit one of two alternatives, either that a man could possess and give divine power, or if no man can do this, that the one who could do it was God. For no one can grant divine power from his own liberality except the one who possessed it by nature' (*De Incar. Dom.* 7.20 [378]). Here the issue is not simply that of possessing divine power, since the apostles themselves did that. Rather, Cassian's concern is with possessing divine power in such a way that one can give it to others. He dismisses out of hand the possibility that a mere man could do this, and so the one who does possess this power so as to be able to give it to others must be God. He must have divine power by nature.

I have asserted that a key component of Theodore's thought, and thus very likely of Nestorius' as well, was the idea that Christ is the unique recipient of divine grace (as power and aid in becoming righteous), and thus the one who can mediate it to us.[8] In both *De Incar. Dom.* 2.5 and 7.18–20, Cassian rejects that possibility outright, as Cyril does as well. However, Cassian's rejection of the Theodorean idea is more problematic than Cyril's. We have seen that for the Alexandrian, grace is not some*thing* (in which case one who had received it from God could pass it on to others), but some*one*. Grace is God's gift of himself, and thus only God can give grace to humanity. But if Cassian sees grace as *things*, as power, largesse, and righteousness, why does he insist that one who can give them to us must therefore be God? It could be that Cassian is merely using a Christianized version of the common Neoplatonic idea that only the source of power can furnish an inexhaustible supply of that power to others.[9] If Christ were not God and thus the very source of power, he could not give this grace to us.

[8] See *Hom. Cat.* 3.9 [65], 15.12 [479–81]. (In this chapter, all references to Theodore's and Nestorius' writings are to passages discussed in Ch. 2.)

[9] The 3rd-cent. philosopher Plotinus compares the One to a spring that gives

However, when one considers *De Incar. Dom.* 2.6, it becomes apparent that earlier in 2.5 (where Cassian discusses grace as power and largesse) and later in 7.18–20 (where he considers power and righteousness), he means more than this. While entertaining the possibility that the man Jesus could have gained grace through his actions, he addresses Nestorius and writes:

> Perhaps you will say that this grace of our Lord Jesus Christ, of which the apostle writes, was not born with him, but was later infused into him by the descent of divinity upon him, since you say that that man Jesus Christ our Lord, whom you call a mere man, was not born with God, but afterwards was assumed (*assumptus*) by God; and that through this, grace was given to the man at the same time that divinity was given to him. But we say nothing else than that divine grace descended with the divinity (*diuina gratia cum diuinitate descenderit*), because the divine grace of God is in a way the bestowal of actual divinity (*ipsius diuinitatis*) and the gift of abundant graces (*munificentiae gratiarum*).
>
> (*De Incar. Dom.* 2.6 [258–9])

Here we see that for Cassian, grace is not simply the gift of abundant graces, but more importantly, the bestowal of divinity itself. He goes on to ask whether divinity descended onto the man Jesus at his conception or later, as he incorrectly thinks Nestorius believes. Cassian insists that the issue is not simply one of timing; he cites Luke 1: 35 and asserts: 'Do you see that Jesus Christ is first proclaimed to be Son of God, so that he might become the son of man according to the flesh? . . . Since he was born by means of the descent of the complete fullness of divinity (*totius diuinitatis plenitudine*) upon the virgin, he could not be the son of man unless he had first been the Son of God' (*De Incar. Dom.* 2.6 [259–60]). These two passages show that Cassian rejects the entire view of Christ's life that he believes Nestorius teaches. If one says that God gave divinity to an already-existent man Jesus, then this implies that the man somehow attained to divinity. Cassian insists that this is impossible. Grace is the gift of divinity, but it did not descend onto a man; it descended to earth when the Son, the one who possessed the fullness of divinity (*plenitudo diuinitatis*), was incarnated in the virgin's

itself to all the rivers flowing from it without being diminished in itself, to a root that is unmoved but gives life to the whole tree, and to a central fire that radiates heat to every receptive body around it while still maintaining the heat essentially inherent in itself. See *Enneads* 3.8.10, 5.1.3.

womb. In order to preserve this understanding, Cassian insists that Christ must have been the Son of God first in order to become the son of man later.

In a similar passage, Cassian writes that if God had simply dwelt in Christ, he would have been no different from the Old Testament saints. He explains:

> All the prophets and saints received from God some portion of the divine Spirit as they were able to bear it. But in Christ *all the fullness of divinity* dwelt and still *dwells bodily* [Col. 2: 9]. And therefore they are all far short of the fullness of the one from whose fullness they receive something. Their being filled is the gift of Christ, because they would all be empty if he were not the fullness of all.
>
> (*De Incar. Dom.* 5.14 [323])

Here it is clear that Christ has not merely received *of* the fullness of deity; he *is* the fullness of deity. Furthermore, we could not have received of his fullness if he had not been the fullness of all (*plenitudo omnium*).[10] This passage helps to clarify what Cassian writes about grace as power, righteousness, and largesse. He does not see these as being things that exist in themselves and can be detached from the one who possesses them. Instead, they are part of the *plenitudo*, part of who Christ is as God. To receive God's power by grace is to receive God himself, to receive of the fullness of God. Therefore, only one who is God himself can give grace to us. In addition, Cassian's discussion in 2.6 shows that the way God gives himself to us in grace is by his downward movement towards us. He does not simply assist us in aspiring to union with him, and not even in Christ's case is it true that a man has attained divinity. Therefore, the reason Cassian can argue that Christ must be God is that only God could have always possessed divine power, largesse, and righteousness, and thus only God could have given these to us by giving us himself in grace.[11] No one could have given us divinity that he had himself acquired, precisely because no one could have acquired divinity by his virtue.

The fact that these passages tie God's gift of himself to his power, largesse, and righteousness seems to imply a less

[10] Cf. *De Incar. Dom.* 5.4 [306].

[11] Cf. ibid. 2.4 [254], where Cassian also implies that grace is God's giving us himself when he equates the expressions, 'the grace of God has appeared from Mary' and 'God has appeared from Mary.'

relational notion of grace and salvation than I have contended is present in Cassian's writings. However, this is not all that Cassian means when he writes that grace is God's giving us himself. He also indicates that God gives us communion with himself, and he generally does this in passages where he makes a sharp distinction between Christ and us. Like virtually all patristic writers, Cassian discusses biblical texts such as Exod. 7: 1 and Ps. 82: 6 (81: 6 in Vulg.) in which people are called gods. He follows the traditional argument that the word *deus* is used differently when referring to Moses or other leaders of Israel than when referring to Christ. In the former case, it denotes God's favour (*indultum*) and shows the power of God rather than that of the recipient. Cassian continues:

> But when it [the statement that he is God] is said of our God and Lord Jesus Christ, *who is over all, God blessed forever* [Rom. 9: 5], the fact is at once shown by the words, and the meaning of the words is demonstrated by the name given; because in the case of the Son of God the name 'God' does not denote an adoption by favour (*adoptionis indultae*), but what is truly and really his nature.
>
> (*De Incar. Dom.* 3.2 [263])

In a similar passage, Cassian explains the difference between Christ and other holy people:

> They all had God within them, and all were made sons of God, and all were receivers of God, but in a very different and dissimilar way. For all who believe in God are sons of God by adoption (*per adoptionem*), but the Only-Begotten alone is Son by nature. He was begotten not of any material substance, but of his Father, for all things and the matter of all things exist through the only-begotten Son of God; and he was not [created] out of nothing, because he is [begotten] from the Father.
>
> (*De Incar. Dom.* 5.4 [305])

Notice here that the saints were all *made* sons of God and that this took place by adoption and because they believed. Cassian sharply contrasts this way of being sons of God with the way Christ is Son.[12] He is Son by nature, begotten of the Father, rather than created from nothing. Both these passages reveal an unequivocal distinction between Christ and us, both use the word 'adoption' to refer to our sonship, and both insist that

[12] The context makes clear that in this passage Cassian is not distinguishing *Christus* from *filius dei*. His point is that the man Christ is the Son of God; he is not simply one in whom the Son of God dwells as in the saints.

Christ's sonship is natural rather than adopted.[13] In making these points, Cassian shows that God's gift of himself includes more than power and righteousness; it also involves sonship. This sonship implies not merely the status of being children, but also a warm intimacy and the right to call God 'Father', so it is clear that for Cassian, grace involves God's gift of fellowship with himself as well. Moreover, we see another obvious parallel with Cyril's thought. Christ cannot be simply a man in whom the Logos dwells, because if he were such a man, he would be merely a son by adoption as we are, not the Son by nature.

In this section, we have seen that Cassian's portrayal of grace in *De Incar. Dom.* is consistent with, but goes significantly beyond, what he has written in his monastic writings. Grace is tied to God's gift of himself, so that even when Cassian discusses power, righteousness, or largesse, he sees these in connection with the Christian's participation in God. In fact, all these gifts are tied to a person's becoming an adopted child of God and his consequent entrance into the communion that the Father and the Son have with each other. Because grace is connected to God as a person, only this person can give himself to others. Someone who has received grace can only possess it/him; he cannot in turn give it to another. Here Cassian is very close to Cyril and stands in marked contrast to Theodore and Nestorius. Since Cassian's soteriology hinges on the belief that Christ is God and Son of God by nature, one would expect him to resist any hint of division within Christ and to locate Christ's unity in the person of the Logos. I will now examine the way he does this in his christology proper.

6.3. GRACE, SALVATION, AND CASSIAN'S TECHNICAL CHRISTOLOGY

If one looks at *De Incar. Dom.* as a whole, it is clear that Cassian's major goal is to demonstrate Christ's deity, and in Books 2–5 he adduces a host of Old and New Testament citations to do so. But as the work continues, Cassian moves from simply arguing

13 Other passages in which Cassian marks Christ off from us include *De Incar. Dom.* 5.14 [323] (which I have quoted earlier in this section) and 7.17 [373], in which he insists that Christ's power is his own and is not received from the outside from the Holy Spirit.

for Christ's deity to asserting the unity of Christ. He returns repeatedly to the idea that the one who was born of Mary was the same one who had been begotten eternally from the Father, and in doing so he locates the unity of Christ in the person of the Logos. As a result, by the time Cassian's attention shifts from biblical passages to evidence from the Antiochene baptismal formula (which Nestorius himself presumably recited at his baptism)[14] in Book 6 and from various Church fathers in Book 7, his emphasis falls on the person of God the Word. A number of illustrations of these points will enable one to gain a feel for Cassian's christology.

6.3.1. Christ is God

It is clear that Cassian believes Nestorius sees Christ as a man who attained deity through progress in virtue. In *De Incar. Dom.*, he uses the expression *solitarius homo c.*37 times to characterize Nestorius' christology, and his shock that anyone could call Christ a mere man is what propels him to amass such a volume of evidence in support of the Saviour's deity. Not surprisingly, scholars have been quick to point out that Cassian is incorrect to call Nestorius a psilanthropist or adoptionist. For example, Amann asserts that this charge could be disproved merely from the sermons by Nestorius that Cassian certainly had in his possession.[15] Technically speaking, Amann is correct,

[14] This symbol was probably written by Melitius about the year 363. See Hahn, *Bibliothek der Symbole*, 141–3.

[15] Amann, 'L'Affaire Nestorius vue de Rome', 238. Cf. Grillmeier, *Christ in Christian Tradition*, 468. It is worth noting here that there is some disagreement regarding which of Nestorius' writings Cassian had on hand as he wrote *De Incar. Dom.*, although all agree that he did not have the dossier that Cyril sent to Rome via Posidonius. Schwartz, *Konzilstudien*, 7–12, argues that Cassian must have had Nestorius' first letter to Celestine, since only from this could he have learned that Julian of Eclanum was in Constantinople and thus deduced a link between Nestorianism and Pelagianism. Schwartz argues further that Cassian possessed copies of *Ser.* 8, 9, and 16, in which Nestorius explains his reasons for rejecting the title *Theotokos*. Virtually all scholars agree that Cassian had these four documents, and several have suggested others as well. Cappuyns, 'Cassien (Jean)', 1332, argues that Cassian also had Nestorius' second letter to Celestine, and Kuhlmann, *Eine dogmengeschichtliche Neubewertung*, 27, agrees. Amann, 'L'Affaire Nestorius vue de Rome', 231–2 n.; Brand, 'Le *De incarnatione Domini* de Cassien', 93; and Kuhlmann, *Eine dogmengeschichtliche Neubewertung*, 33, suggest that Cassian also had *Ser.* 14.

since Theodore and Nestorius insisted that the assumed man was united to the Logos from the moment of his conception.[16] However, in Cassian's mind, the question is not simply *when* the man was united to the Logos, but more importantly, *why* he was so united. Cassian writes:

> We said in the first book that the heresy that is the pupil and imitator of Pelagianism strives and contends by all means to make people believe that the Lord Jesus Christ, the Son of God, when born of the virgin, was only a mere man; and that having afterwards taken the path of virtue, he merited by his pious and devoted life that the divine majesty should associate (*sociaret*) itself with him; and thus by excluding him completely from the honour of his sacred origin, it only left to him an election on the basis of his merits. (*De Incar. Dom.* 5.1 [301–2])

Cassian goes on to assert that in saying this, Nestorius is taking away from God what rightfully belongs to him and holding out to people false promises. As we have seen, Cassian does not believe that *any* person can mount up to the level of deity; salvation can be accomplished only through God's descent to humanity. Therefore, Nestorius does not escape this criticism simply by asserting that the christological union began in the virgin's womb. If the union was based on merits (and at least Theodore did write that it was based on the Logos' foreknowledge of what kind of person the assumed man would be[17]), then for Cassian, that was the same thing as arguing that the man Jesus earned union with God later in his life. If one is concerned only about the *timing* of the union, then Cassian has read Nestorius' thought incorrectly, but if one is concerned with the *reason* for the union, then he does have a valid criticism.

In this connection, it may be noteworthy that Cassian uses the verb *socio* to refer to Nestorius' understanding of the christological union. In sect. 5.3.2, I asserted that in Cassian's works this word usually refers to a personal relationship, and it may be that he is implying here that Nestorius sees Christ not as a single person, but as an association, a relationship between two personal beings, God the Logos and the assumed man. However, one should be cautious about inferring too much from Cassian's word choice here, because he is not careful with his own terminology. In *De Incar. Dom.* 4.5 [290], he uses the word

[16] See Theodore's *De Incar.* 7 [296–8], Nestorius' *Ep.* 9 [192].

[17] See *De Incar.* 7 [296–8].

consortium to refer to his own understanding of the christological union, and since *societas* and *consortium* are basically synonyms for Cassian, his use of *socio* here in describing Nestorius' christology may not be significant.

A passage from 7.8 helps to make Cassian's attitude clearer. Commenting on Nestorius' infamous statement, 'I divide the natures, but I unite the worship' (*Ser.* 9 [262]), Cassian writes:

> By a subtle and impious skill you say that he is to be worshipped together with God, so that you will not have to confess that he is God, and by the very statement in which you seem deceptively to join him with God, you actually sever him from God. For when you blasphemously say that he is certainly not to be adored as God, but, as it were, to be worshipped together with God, you thus grant him a close conjunction to God (*diuinae uicinitatis coniunctionem*), in order to reject the truth of his divinity. (*De Incar. Dom.* 7.8 [364])

Here Cassian is certainly not arguing against what Nestorius actually says, since the latter's point is that despite the diversity of natures, Christ is a unity of God and man. Rather, Cassian is arguing against the implication of Nestorius' thought. If the assumed man possesses simply 'a close conjunction to God' (*coniunctio uicinitatis diuinae*), then this man is not himself God. Cassian believes that this actually separates the man Christ from God and makes salvation, as he understands it, impossible.

Therefore, it is this understanding of the implications of Nestorius' thought that drives Cassian's insistence on the deity of Christ. It may not be that he has misheard Nestorius so badly as to think that he *says* Christ is a mere man who was adopted to deity, but rather Cassian believes Nestorius' thought amounts to this. If Christ is merely a man united to the Logos, and if this union depends, even to some degree, on the man's (foreseen) virtue, then the incarnation is no longer purely God's act of giving himself to us. In order to safeguard his understanding of salvation and grace from the perceived threat that the implication of Nestorius' thought poses, Cassian insists that the man whom the Gospels describe is God. Such assertions come on virtually every page of *De Incar. Dom.*, but especially noteworthy are Cassian's statements in Book 3. He describes the statements of Peter (Matt. 16: 16), Thomas (John 20: 28), and God the Father (Matt. 3: 17) about Christ and takes pains to show that the person to whom the statements are addressed is the man Christ, but the speakers proclaim that he is Son of God or Lord and God.[18] This is the force of Cassian's insistence on the deity of the Saviour: Christ is not simply a man united to God; he *is* God.[19]

6.3.2. *Christ is a Unity*

Cassian's belief that the man who appears in the Gospels is God leads him to a repeated emphasis on the unity of Christ. Spurred on by Nestorius' distaste for the title *Theotokos*, Cassian argues that the same one who was begotten of the Father was born of Mary:

> He was the same one (*idem*) on earth who was also in heaven, the same one in his humility who was also in the highest [glory], the same one in the meanness of manhood as in the majesty of God. And so the apostle was right when he called God's grace 'the grace of Christ', for Christ was everything that God is. At the moment of his conception as man there came the power of God, all divinity, all the fullness of divinity; for all the perfection of divinity originated with him. Nor was that man ever without God, since he indeed received from God what he was.
>
> (*De Incar. Dom.* 2.7 [260])

One should note how carefully Cassian safeguards the unity of Christ. He insists that both divine exaltation and human humiliation apply to the same one (*idem*); he asserts that Christ was everything God was; he argues that the power of God, all divinity, and the fullness of divinity were his from his conception. Furthermore, when he turns to Christ's humanity, Cassian argues that that man[20] received his very existence from God. This last statement seems to be a way of guarding against any possibility that Christ's humanity could be viewed as an independent man. It is clear that Cassian sees everything that took place in Christ's life as happening to the same subject, who is God and has always had the fullness of deity.

Furthermore, Cassian indicates that this person who is one and the same is not a composite person formed in Mary's womb,

[18] See *De Incar. Dom.* 3.12 [277], 3.15 [281–2], 3.16 [283].

[19] It is true that Cassian sometimes uses expressions such as *Christus unitus deo* and *homo unitus deo*, which seems to belie the point I am making here. I will deal with his use of these expressions in sect. 6.4.1.

[20] I will consider Cassian's frequent use of the concrete noun *homo*, rather than the abstract *humanitas*, in sect. 6.4.1.

but rather an eternal person who has added humanity to himself at the incarnation. He addresses Nestorius and writes, 'You ought to believe that the one who was fully God before his corporeal birth, was man and God after his corporeal birth; and that the same one (*eundem*) who was God the Word before his birth from the virgin, was God in a body after he had been brought forth by the virgin' (*De Incar. Dom.* 4.1 [286]). Here the priority of the Logos in Cassian's christology is very apparent. The one who was purely God became God and man; the one who was the bare Logos became God enfleshed. Later, Cassian explains why Nestorius' thought implies a denial of this truth:

> Here you have Jesus Christ the Son of God, but you say that the one who was born of Mary was not the same (*eundem*) Son of God. Therefore, there is one (*alter*) Christ of God and another (*alter*) of Mary. In your teaching, then, there are two christs. . . . But if you will confess in the Creed that Christ is the Son of God, you must also confess that Christ, the Son of God, is the same one (*eundem*) who was born of Mary. Or if you assert another (*alium*) christ of Mary, you certainly blaspheme in saying that there are two christs.
>
> (*De Incar. Dom.* 6.15 [342])

In this passage, as in the previous ones, Cassian uses masculine pronouns to indicate the personal unity of Christ.[21] Nestorius says that one was born of the Father and another (*alter*) of Mary, that the two are not the same person (the accusative form *eundum* shows unambiguously that the pronoun is masculine rather than neuter) but one and another (*alius et alius*). But Cassian insists that Nestorius must confess that Christ, the Son of God, is the same one (*eundem*) who was born of Mary. The charge that Nestorius makes two christs is a common one, and as with Cassian's other accusations, it is not technically accurate, since Nestorius uses the word 'Christ' to refer to the one *prosopon* of union composed of both the Logos and the assumed man.[22] But again, Cassian is concerned not so much with the technicalities of Nestorius' thought as with its implications; he insists that if one makes Christ out to be one and another, he is actually not a single entity but an association of two personal entities.

[21] I should point out that Cassian is not entirely consistent in his use of masculine pronouns. He calls Christ *nihil aliud deo* in *De Incar. Dom.* 2.4 [254] and asserts that he is *unum atque idem* (neuter) in *De Incar. Dom.* 4.5 [290].

[22] See *Ep.* 5 [175] and other passages discussed in sect. 2.6.3.

Throughout *De Incar. Dom.*, Cassian frequently repeats the idea that Christ is one and the same,[23] and as we have seen, he does so in order to stress the divine in the Redeemer's person. This is completely consistent with Cassian's understanding of grace and salvation. Since God gives us himself, God must be the one who acts in the life of Christ and the one to whom the key experiences pertaining to redemption are ascribed. This leads Cassian directly to the idea that the single subject of all Christ's actions (and thus the one who is one and the same) is God the Logos.

6.3.3. *Christ is the Logos*

The ascription of all the human events of the Gospels to the Logos is precisely what Nestorius' christology is designed to avoid,[24] and at this point Cassian and his adversary part ways most dramatically. While discussing the Antiochene symbol, Cassian refers to Nestorius' common insistence that we would be shocked to hear of God dying and being buried, and that the Son who was eternally begotten of the Father could not possibly be born a second time and still be God. Cassian then concludes: 'If all these things cannot possibly be, how is it that the Creed of the Chuches says that they did happen? How is it that you yourself said that they did?' (*De Incar. Dom.* 6.9 [336]). What Nestorius is shocked to consider, Cassian claims to be the assertion of the Creed: God the Logos was born, died, and was buried. He seems to be unaware that Theodore and Nestorius interpret the Creed to mean that the titles 'Lord' and 'Jesus Christ' apply to both natures and that these natures are then successively described.[25] Rather than responding to this interpretation, Cassian simply declares that the Creed means that the same one who is of the Father was also born, suffered, and died. In the following chapter, Cassian again interprets the Creed to mean that all the actions apply to the same personal subject, and he concludes:

[23] e.g. *De Incar. Dom.* 1.5 [242–3], 3.1 [262], 4.6 [293], 5.4 [305–6], 5.6 [310], 5.7 [310], 5.7 [312–13], 6.13 [340–1], and particularly 7.24–30 [382–90], in which Cassian argues that all the Church fathers whom he cites believed that the same one who was eternally begotten of the Father was also born of Mary in time.

[24] See *Ser.* 9 [262] and other passages discussed in sect. 2.6.1.

[25] See Theodore's *Hom. Cat.* 3.6 [61], Nestorius' *Ep.* 5 [174–5].

'Do you see then how you are utterly destroying and wiping out the whole faith of the Catholic Creed, the whole faith of the Catholic mystery? . . . Do you think then that the faith of our salvation and the mystery of the Church's hope are a shock to your ears and hearing?' (*De Incar. Dom.* 6.10 [338]). It is important to note here that Cassian does not see Nestorius as simply misinterpreting the Creed. Rather, by trying to protect God from suffering, Nestorius is destroying the entire faith and is shocked at the very mystery that alone can bring him salvation. For Cassian, the redemptive acts of Christ's life must be divine actions (as opposed to human actions aided by God) for salvation to be possible. He cannot shrink from stating that God was born and died, and it is largely in order to preserve this confession that he locates Christ's unity in the person of the Logos.

We see the same pattern in the final book. Cassian responds to Nestorius' assertion that no one can give birth to one older than herself by writing:

> If it can seem unreasonable to you that Mary could give birth to God who was anterior to her, how will it seem reasonable that God was crucified by men? And yet the same God who was crucified himself predicted, *Shall a man afflict God, for you afflict me?* [Mal. 3: 8] If then we may not think that the Lord was born of a virgin because he who was born was anterior to her who bore him, how could we believe that God had blood? And yet it was said to the Ephesian elders, *Feed the Church of God, which he purchased with his own blood* [Acts 20: 28]. Finally, how could we think that the Author of life was himself deprived of life? And yet Peter says, *You have killed the Author of life* [Acts 3: 15].
>
> (*De Incar. Dom.* 7.4 [358])

In this passage, Cassian again embraces the very ideas Nestorius has shunned: that God could be born, be crucified, shed blood, and die. Later, he interprets Heb. 7: 3 (one of Nestorius' favourite texts) similarly:

> The apostle wants to make clear to everyone the double birth of God, and in order to show how the Lord was born in deity and in flesh, he says, *without father, without mother*. For one is proper to the birth of divinity, the other to that of the flesh. For just as he was begotten in his divine nature without mother, so also is he begotten in a body without father.
>
> (*De Incar. Dom.* 7.14 [370])

Nestorius has used this text to argue for a strong distinction

between deity and humanity in Christ,[26] but Cassian uses it in precisely the opposite way, to argue for a personal unity. So strong is the unity in Christ that one can say God the Word was born twice, first in deity and then in flesh/in a body.

This claim that God the Logos was born twice expresses most clearly the idea that pervades Cassian's entire work.[27] He can assert that the man who walks in Galilee is God, is eternal, and is a unity because this same person who was born as a man from Mary is the eternal Son of God.[28] In maintaining this, Cassian is driven to paradox; he must say that God was born and died. But the paradox constitutes the heart of Cassian's faith because it ensures that it was God who brought about redemption; it is God who gives himself to us in salvation. Cassian's willingness to say what Nestorius will not say is tied to his understanding of grace and salvation: only the true Son of God can give us divine communion through the life, death, and resurrection of Christ. If Christ is not this true Son of God by nature, if he is not the Logos, then he cannot save us.

6.3.4. *Cassian's Meagre Treatment of Christ's Humanity*

In the light of Cassian's strong identification of Christ with the Logos, one might wonder whether there is any room for Christ's humanity in his portrayal. Grillmeier asserts that 'Cassian draws a very empty picture of the humanity of Jesus,'[29] and Kuhlmann comments that he seems to have little basis for a theology of Christ's humanity.[30] As observations, these statements are certainly accurate. Cassian does state that Christ had a genuine

26 See *Ser.* 5 [234–5].

27 Among the many other passages that stress the unity of Christ in the person of the Logos, see *De Incar. Dom.* 2.3 [253], 2.4 [255], 3.8 [271–2], 3.9 [272], 3.10 [275–6], 4.5 [291], 5.7 [312–13], 6.8 [334]. Cassian also conveys this idea through his discussions of the *communicatio idiomatum* (e.g. *De Incar. Dom.* 3.7 [269], 4.5 [290], 4.7 [293–4], 6.22 [349]) and his assertions that the Logos added humanity to himself while remaining what he was (e.g. *De Incar. Dom.* 2.2 [248], 5.15 [324], 6.19 [345]).

28 Many scholars have noted that Cassian locates the unity of Christ in the person of the Word: e.g. Brand, 'Le *De incarnatione Domini* de Cassien', 205; Grillmeier, *Christ in Christian Tradition*, 469–70; Vannier, 'Jean Cassien a-t-il fait œuvre de théologien?', 353.

29 Grillmeier, *Christ in Christian Tradition*, 471.

30 Kuhlmann, *Eine dogmengeschichtliche Neubewertung*, 173.

humanity,[31] but he does not even hint at how he understands the role of that humanity in salvation.

However, if one takes Grillmeier's and Kuhlmann's statements as indictments, then they are not warranted. Cassian's task in *De Incar. Dom.* is not to offer a comprehensive portrayal of salvation or even a comprehensive picture of Christ's person; it is to refute the Nestorian heresy.[32] He believes that Nestorius' teaching either constitutes or at least implies a denial of Christ's deity. That is to say, Nestorius' concept of the union of an independent man with the Logos because of the man's foreseen merits is a denial that the incarnation was a descent of God the Logos himself to earth. Thus Cassian enlists his considerable energy and invective to show that Christ is God the Logos, not simply a man united to God. Considering that this is the same person who could write mammoth works on the monastic task with very few references to his foundational doctrine of salvation, it is not surprising that he could write a long work on Christ's deity without much attempt to explain the place of the Saviour's humanity. While such an omission is not appropriate and may not be excusable, it is nevertheless understandable.

Given the overall similarity of Cassian's thought to that of Cyril, one might have hoped for some indication that through the life of Christ, God the Logos gave himself to humankind by giving himself to his own humanity. But no such discussions are to be found, and one can only guess what Cassian might have written on this subject. In spite of this ambiguity about the role of Christ's humanity, and thus about the way the Logos gives himself to people in grace, it is still apparent that Cassian's christology and his doctrine of grace go hand-in-hand. Both his thought on grace and his thought on Christ's person reflect a faith much closer to Cyril's than to that of Nestorius.

[31] e.g. *De Incar. Dom.* 5.10 [318], where he writes, 'This is the whole, true Catholic faith: to believe that just as the Lord Jesus Christ is God, so also is he man, and that just as he is man, so also he is God.' Cf. *De Incar. Dom.* 3.5 [265–6].

[32] See *De Incar. Dom.* Praef. [236].

6.4. TROUBLESOME ELEMENTS IN CASSIAN'S CHRISTOLOGY

Probably the most common criticism of Cassian's *De Incar. Dom.* is that he uses christological terminology very inaccurately,[33] and this sloppiness is one of the main reasons scholars argue that he makes no positive contribution to the development of the Church's doctrine of Christ's person.[34] Some of Cassian's language leans towards that of Nestorius, whereas other expressions appear to be very close to later Eutychianism. In this section I will look at these terminological difficulties in the light of the charitological and soteriological ideas I have considered.

6.4.1. Cassian's Use of 'Nestorian' Language to Describe Christ

There are three major ways in which Cassian's christological language approaches that of Nestorius. First, he uses *homo* to refer to Christ's humanity in a way that appears to suggest that this humanity is an independent man. Second, he uses *Christus* in a way that gives the impression that the humanity, rather than the Logos, is the personal subject of Christ. Third, he sometimes uses indwelling language to describe the christological union. So marked is this 'Nestorian' language that Amann comments, 'To be sure, if the bishop of Alexandria had held in his hands Cassian's *De incarnatione*, he would not have hesitated to rank it among the products of the "Nestorian" spirit.'[35] Conversely, Galtier argues that even though Cassian's language sounds Nestorian, his thought is much closer to that of Cyril,[36] and Owen Chadwick claims that there is no reason for calling him a Nestorian, in spite of his language.[37] What I have already asserted of Cassian's doctrine makes it very hard to side with Amann on this issue, and an examination of the 'Nestorian' language in Cassian's work will show that even this should be

[33] See Gibson, 'The Works of John Cassian', 190; Grillmeier, *Christ in Christian Tradition*, 468–9; Stewart, *Cassian the Monk*, 23.

[34] See Ch. 5 nn. 2–4.

[35] Amann, 'Nestorius et sa doctrine', 100.

[36] Galtier, *L'Unité du Christ*, 29.

[37] O. Chadwick, *John Cassian* (1950 edition), 157. He does not make this point in the 1968 edition.

explained in a non-Nestorian way in the light of his soteriology and understanding of grace.

Cassian uses *homo* to refer to Christ's humanity *c*.200 times in *De Incar. Dom.*,[38] but this is hardly his only expression. He also uses *corpus* of the humanity *c*.73 times and *caro* *c*.181 times. It is no more legitimate to argue that Cassian's use of *homo* necessarily makes him a Nestorian than it would be to call him an Apollinarian on the basis of the other two words. On the contrary, Cassian is simply using traditional Western language to describe Christ's humanity, probably without giving significant thought to any potential misunderstandings that could arise from it. Augustine was also fond of using *homo* to refer to Christ's humanity, although he was more careful than Cassian to make clear that this word referred to a human nature, not an independent man.[39] In a passage from *Lib. Emend.* which Cassian quotes, Leporius uses both *caro* and *homo* during a discussion of the *communicatio idiomatum*, a discussion that shows that one cannot interpret *homo* in a separatistic way.[40] In fact, the use of *homo* to refer to Christ's humanity was traditional in the West as far back as the time of Tertullian.[41]

Furthermore, there are a number of passages in which Cassian shows that by using *homo* he does not mean that Christ's humanity is an independent man. While asserting that the one subject of Christ is the Logos, he writes:

How was he the same one before the origin of the world, who was but recently born? Because he was the same one, who was recently born as

[38] One should take this figure as a rougher approximation than the others I list in this book, since it is sometimes difficult to judge whether Cassian is using *homo* to refer to the Saviour's human element or to the possibility that he is *merely* a man. In counting the occurrences of the word, I attempted to include only those in which he refers to his own understanding of Christ's humanity. I should also note that Cassian uses the expression *homo assumptus* to refer to what Christ does as a man in *De Inst. Coen.* 12.17 [472]; *Conlat.* 7.22 [42.265], 9.34 [54.70]. However, in *De Incar. Dom.*, he uses this expression only when referring to Nestorius' christology (*De Incar. Dom.* 1.2 [239], 2.6 [258]) or when quoting from Leporius' *Lib.Emend.* (*De Incar. Dom.* 1.5 [243]). He does not use it when describing his own christology.

[39] e.g. *Ep.* 219.3 [430–1]; *De Corrept. Grat.* 30 [934]; *De Praed. Sanct.* 30 [981–2]; *De Don. Pers.* 67 [1034].

[40] *Lib. Emend.* 5 [116], quoted in *De Incar. Dom.* 1.5 [242–3].

[41] e.g. *De Car.* 14 [48]; *Adu. Prax.* 30 [128].

man (*in homine*), who was God before the beginning of all things. And so the name 'Christ' includes everything that the name 'God' does; because the union between Christ and God is such that no one, when he uses the name 'Christ', can help speaking of God under the name 'Christ', nor, when he speaks of God, can he help speaking of Christ under the name 'God'. And since through the majesty of his holy nativity, the mystery of each substance is united in him, whatever there was—that is, both man and God—all is regarded as God.

(*De Incar. Dom.* 5.7 [310])

Here we see that Cassian uses not only *homo*, but also *Christus*, to refer to the Saviour's humanity. But when he writes that the same one who was God before all things was born *in hominem*, his thought cannot be that the Logos was born by indwelling an independent man, since that would not have constituted a birth of the Logos. Instead, Cassian's idea is that the Logos was born as a man (reflected in my translation), and the phrase *in hominem* is reminiscent of Cyril's use of 'as man' (ὡς ἄνθρωπος) to refer to what the Logos did in human form. The final sentence of this passage also makes clear that there is no separation. *Homo* and *deus* are the two substances of Christ, but they can be said to be all God because the Logos is the sole subject of Christ.

In a similar passage, Cassian boldly asserts that one can speak of the man Christ as eternal and of God as suffering, and he explains how this is possible:

This is what we established from the previous Scriptures: that God, being united to humanity (*homini*), that is, to his own body, does not allow any separation to be made in people's thoughts between man and God. Nor will he permit anyone to believe that there is one son of man, and another Son of God. But in all the holy Scriptures he connects and incorporates the Lord's man (*dominicum hominem*) into God, so that no one can sever man from God in time, nor God from man at his passion.

(*De Incar. Dom.* 6.22 [348])

Here Cassian uses the word *homo* to refer to Christ's humanity 6 times, but the entire thrust of his argument is that there is no separation between deity and humanity. One cannot say that man and God are one son of man and another Son of God, nor may one sever them from each other in Christ's passion. Notice also that Cassian describes the incarnation as God's being united 'to humanity, that is, to his own body' (*homini, id est suo corpori*). This expression makes clear that the humanity is the Logos' own; not an independent man who could be considered a separate subject of attribution.[42] As a result, it is clear that even when Cassian uses the word *homo*, he is referring to the Logos' humanity, not to a separate assumed man.

Cassian also seems to approach Nestorianism in that his use of 'Christ' in opposition to 'God' makes it appear that the Saviour is a man to whom the Logos is united, rather than being the Logos inhominated.[43] If Cassian were using the word *Christus* to refer to the entire being of the Saviour, then such statements as 'Christ united to God' (*Christus unitus dei*) could hardly fail to imply that Christ is a man who has become associated with the Logos in some sort of moral union. In actuality, however, Cassian generally uses *Christus* to refer not to the combination of both natures (as Nestorius does), but only to his humanity, or more specifically, to the one who appears before people as a man.[44] For example, while discussing Rom. 9: 5, Cassian states that the essence of spiritual life consists

> simply in this, as he [Paul] himself says, that they might know God, the Christ born according to the flesh, of their own flesh. . . . Clearly he lays down that from them according to the flesh was born that Christ *who is over all, God blessed for ever*. You certainly do not deny that Christ was born from them according to the flesh. But the same one who was born from them is God. (*De Incar. Dom.* 3.1 [261–2])

When he writes that even Nestorius cannot deny that Christ was born from the Jews, he is referring to the man whom people saw, heard, and touched. Cassian goes on to insist that this Christ, this man who was born from the Jews, is not just a man; he is God. As we saw in sect. 6.3.1, Cassian uses the same argument when discussing the statements of Peter, Thomas, and God the Father about Christ. They address their words to Christ, that is, to the man, but they declare that he is God and Son of God.[45]

In *De Incar. Dom.* 4, Cassian argues on the basis of Ps. 107: 20 (106: 20 in Vulg.) and John 17: 3 that God sent his Word, but the one who was sent was Jesus Christ. He concludes, 'Separate this,

42 Cf. *De Incar. Dom.* 2.7 [260].

43 e.g. *De Incar. Dom.* 5.7 [310], quoted just above, 3.7 [269], 4.4 [290].

44 Amann, 'L'Affaire Nestorius vue de Rome', 239, makes this point in passing, but he does not develop it.

45 See *De Incar. Dom.* 3.12 [277], 3.15 [281–2], 3.16 [283].

if you can, although you see that the unity between Christ and the Word is so great that the Word was not simply united with Christ, but in virtue of the unity itself, Christ may even be said to be the Word' (*De Incar. Dom.* 4.5 [291]). Here again we see the suspicious reference to 'the unity between Christ and the Word' (*unitas Christi et uerbi*), but Cassian interprets this to mean not that Christ the man is united to the Logos, but that Christ the man *is* the Logos. Cassian's purpose in using the word *Christus* is not at all to imply that an independent man was conjoined to the Logos and that the man is the personal centre of the Saviour's being. Rather, his purpose is to argue that the one who appears to be simply a man is actually much more than this; he is God the Logos in human form. In spite of the similarity between Cassian's language and that of Nestorius, their ideas are vastly different.

The third way Cassian seems to be close to Nestorius is that he describes the incarnation in terms of an indwelling of the Logos in the assumed man. He sometimes uses expressions such as 'Christ in God', 'God in Christ', and 'God in him'.[46] Furthermore, Cassian interprets Isa. 45: 14 to refer to Christ: 'When the prophet says, *God is in you*, he rightly points not merely to the one who was visible (*qui praesens esset*), but to the one who was in the visible one (*qui esset in praesente*), distinguishing the indweller from the one in whom he dwelt by pointing out the two natures, not by denying the unity' (*De Incar. Dom.* 4.11 [299]). This is probably the closest Cassian ever comes to Nestorius' thought. He uses masculine forms to refer to both the indweller and the indwelt one, and although he uses the word 'natures' to denote Christ's deity and humanity, it is difficult to avoid the impression that the Logos and the man are independent subjects. However, immediately after this sentence, Cassian returns in 4.12 to his more customary mode of argument by writing that the man Christ is the Saviour, but it does not lie in the power of a man to save people from their sins, so Christ must be God. In the light of this, it appears that Cassian's prior indwelling language was intended not to distinguish the indwelling Logos from the man who is indwelt, but to identify them as the same person.

[46] e.g. ibid. 2.3 [252], 3.1 [262], 3.7 [269], 5.9 [316].

In fact, elsewhere in the work Cassian specifically shows that his indwelling language should be read in terms of the Logos' possession of his own humanity. While discussing Gal. 1: 1, Cassian emphasizes that Jesus Christ is not merely a man by writing, 'That renowned and admirable teacher [Paul], knowing that our Lord Jesus Christ must be proclaimed as true man as well as true God, always proclaims the majesty of divinity in him in such a way that he will not lose hold of the confession of the incarnation.' Cassian quotes the biblical passage and adds that it 'teaches that it was a real body of the incarnate God that was raised from the dead' (*De Incar. Dom.* 3.5 [265–6]). In the light of what we have seen above, one should take 'divinity in him' (*diuinitas in eo*) to mean not that an independent man has God dwelling in him, but that divinity (considered as a quality) dwells in the one who appears to be simply a man because he is actually not a mere man: he is God. Cassian argues that the Saviour's humanity is that of the incarnate God, the Logos.[47] It is not the case that a man possesses divinity, but that God possesses humanity, and so the man who appears in the Gospels has divinity within himself precisely because that man *is* God the Logos.

Similarly, Cassian explains why Christ and the Word can be said to be the same:

> You see that the Word was sent to heal men, for though healing was given through Christ, yet the Word of God was in Christ, and healed all things through Christ; and so since Christ and the Word of God were united through the mystery of the incarnation, Christ and the Word of God were made one Son of God from both substances (*ex re utraque*).
> (*De Incar. Dom.* 4.4 [290])

Here again *Christus* refers not to an independent man or to the entire being of the Saviour, but to the humanity. Christ and the Word are two different substances (*res*), but they are one Son. Therefore, one should take the expression 'the Word of God was in Christ' (*uerbum dei in Christo fuit*) to mean that the Logos dwelt in the humanity or even that the Logos lived on earth in human form. It is not necessary to take Cassian's indwelling language to mean that the Word dwelt in an independent

[47] Here one should take *corpus* as one of the traditional Western ways to refer to Christ's full humanity, not as an indication that his humanity is merely a body.

man, and in fact, such an interpretation would contradict his repeated insistence that the Redeemer is one and the same, that the personal subject of Christ is the Logos.

One may conclude that none of Cassian's allegedly Nestorian language actually reflects a divisive christology. Because of his belief that only God can give us fellowship with himself, he seeks to demonstrate that God the Logos is the sole personal subject in Christ. Admittedly, the terminology he uses in pursuing this aim is sometimes careless and misleading, but only if one considers the terminology alone can one believe that Cassian's thought is Nestorian. If one bears in mind the soteriological concerns that guide his thought, one will not fail to see that the monk's christology is decidedly unitive.

6.4.2. *Cassian's Use of Absorptionist Language to Describe Christ*

In addition to using language that sounds Nestorian, Cassian occasionally vacillates to the other extreme by seeming to imply that Christ's humanity has been completely absorbed into his deity. In an infamous passage in 3.3, he uses Rom. 9: 5 and 2 Cor. 5: 16 to argue that believers know Christ only as God:

> We formerly knew him as man as well as God, yet now we know him only as God. For since the frailty of flesh (*infirmitate carnis*) has come to an end, we no longer know anything in him except the power of divinity (*uirtutem diuinitatis*), for the power of divine majesty is fully in him, where the weakness of human infirmity (*infirmitas imbecillitatis humanae*) has ceased. (*De Incar. Dom.* 3.3 [264])

Shortly after this, he continues:

> The nature of flesh has been transformed into spiritual substance, and that which formerly belonged to man has all become God's. And therefore *we no longer know Christ according to the flesh*, because when bodily infirmity (*infirmitate corporea*) has been absorbed by divine majesty, nothing remains in that holy body from which weakness of the flesh can be recognized in it. And thus whatever had formerly belonged to a double substance has become attached to a single power.
> (*De Incar. Dom.* 3.3 [264–5])

This is admittedly very dangerous language, but two things are noteworthy. First, Cassian does not say that Christ's humanity *itself* has been absorbed into his deity; he writes that 'the weakness of human infirmity' has come to an end, that 'bodily infirmity' has been absorbed by divine majesty. He does not mean that Christ's humanity has been abolished, but that it has been changed at the resurrection from a weak, fleshly substance to a permanent, strong, spiritual substance.[48] In other words, Cassian is referring to the Logos' rendering his own humanity incorruptible at the resurrection.[49] A second thing one should note is that the context of this passage is Cassian's assertion that Nestorius has no excuse not to recognize Christ as God. He argues that before the resurrection one might have had such an excuse, but after the resurrection has demonstrated Christ's divine power, no one could fail to see that he is God himself, not merely a man. The resurrection was not a change whereby one who was God and man became purely God; it was an event that made clear that the one who seemed to be an ordinary man was actually God as well.[50]

Shortly after this, Cassian begins his lengthy examination of Gal. 1: 1 which I discussed in sect. 6.4.1. He argues that Christ is God and is the one who, along with the Father, sent Paul as an apostle. He asserts, 'There is no longer room for the name "man" in the one whom divinity claims entirely' (*De Incar. Dom.* 3.4 [265]). In the light of the overall context, Cassian may be using the word *homo* here as a synonym for *solitarius homo*. Since Paul declares that Christ is God, Nestorius cannot claim that he is a mere man. In any event, however poorly Cassian expresses himself in 3.3–4, it is clear that he does not mean to deny the continued existence of Christ's humanity, since he goes on in 3.5 to argue that Paul knows Christ must be preached as true God and true man (*De Incar. Dom.* 3.5 [265–6]).

[48] Cf. Paul's discussion in 1 Cor. 15: 35–55 of a similar transformation of Christians at our resurrection.

[49] Cf. Brand, 'Le *De incarnatione Domini* de Cassien', 167.

[50] It is worth noting that in *Conlat.* 10.6 [54.79–80], Cassian also comments on 2 Cor. 5: 16. There he argues that only one who has advanced in purity and contemplation can see Jesus' deity clearly, whereas others who are held by Jewish frailty (and thus see him only as a man) cannot aspire to this clarity of vision. If it is legitimate to see a connection between Cassian's thought in these two passages, the issue is not one of a fundamental change in Christ, but of a change in our perception of him. His resurrection and our pursuit of virtue both enable us to see him more fully the way he actually is, but just as Christ himself does not change when we improve in contemplation, so also he did not change fundamentally at his resurrection.

Cassian's absorptionist language, like his allegedly Nestorian language, reveals a great deal of terminological imprecision. Of course, Cassian is not the only pre-Chalcedonian writer whose terminology is inconsistent by later standards. Nestorius' use of *prosopon* to describe both the unity and the diversity of Christ and Cyril's occasional ascription in the same paragraph of both one nature and two natures to Christ also come quickly to mind. If Cassian's terminology is even sloppier than that of his contemporaries, it may be because he does not view technical christological terminology as the means by which to express his faith in Christ. Cassian's thought is driven not by an attempt to express the relation between Christ's deity and humanity, but by a desire to safeguard the truth that the man who walked in Galilee was the eternal Son of God. As Cassian understands grace, only God could give it to us; only God could save us. He is far more concerned with emphasizing this than he is with clarifying the relation between deity and humanity in the Saviour's person or even with delineating the role of the Logos' humanity in our salvation.

6.5. CONCLUSIONS

If one looks not simply at Cassian's christological terminology but also at the overall concerns that guide his thought, then I believe one may rate Cassian's theological acumen considerably more favourably than most scholars have. There is a consistency underlying his writings that modern interpreters have often missed by failing to read his interpretation of the monastic task in the light of his broader understanding of grace and salvation. This incomplete grasp of Cassian's soteriology has in turn led some scholars to misunderstand the intent behind what he writes about Christ. In these two chapters I have sought to correct these unbalanced judgements by arguing that for Cassian, the dominant aspect of salvation is not the human attempt to attain to God but God's condescension to give himself to us by granting us communion with himself. Only by entering human experience himself could God bring about the redemption that grants this fellowship to humanity, and Cassian's almost monotonous emphasis that Christ is the Logos grows out of this idea.

I have asserted that while Cassian has treated Nestorius'

technical christology poorly, one cannot be so quick to accuse the monk of having completely misread the spirit of the Constantinopolitan bishop's thought. Cassian is wrong in arguing that Nestorius says Christ is a mere man who was united to God sometime later in his life than at his conception. But can one say he is wrong in arguing that Nestorius sees the union as being, at least in part, the result of the assumed man's virtue? One may say that Cassian has caricatured Nestorius, that he has been too quick to condemn him by association with the vilified Pelagians. But I do not believe one can justly say that Cassian has completely misread him. However, even if one will not admit that there is much truth in Cassian's reading of Nestorius, it should be clear that Cassian's own understanding of grace and christology is vastly different from that of Theodore and Nestorius. Salvation is not a matter of advancing to a higher *katastasis*; it is for Cassian a matter of God's giving himself to humanity. Grace is not primarily assistance in the human task of pursuing virtue, although this is certainly part of Cassian's idea. Rather, grace is fundamentally God's sharing of fellowship with us. Christ is not the uniquely graced man, the supreme example of co-operation between God and man. He is instead the Logos himself, the same both before and after the incarnation, the one who has taken a full humanity into his own person in order to accomplish the redemption of all humanity. Cassian's confused and inconsistent terminology does not obscure the main outlines of his thought, and no terminology could mask such different conceptions of the faith as Nestorius' and Cassian's.

Equally important are the noteworthy similarities between Cassian's thought and that of Cyril, similarities that I have noted throughout Chs. 5 and 6. The two men share the same priority on God's action in salvation, the same emphasis on grace as communion with God, the same manner of sharply distinguishing the natural Son from those who are sons by adoption. There is the same stress on the Logos as the personal subject of Christ, the same insistence that the one begotten of the Father was also born of Mary, the same bold assertion that God the Logos suffered, died, and was buried. All of these ideas find clearer and more brilliant expression in Cyril's writings, but all of them are central in Cassian's work as well. Therefore, one can see Cassian as a representative of a Cyrillian type of thought in the West. He certainly did not advance this thought, and it is probably correct to argue, as many scholars do, that he had no positive influence on the development of the Church's christology. But it is not only the shapers of doctrine who are important, and I believe Cassian's thought is significant precisely because it represents the presence of doctrines about Christ, grace, and salvation very much like Cyril's, in a place where one would not have expected to find such ideas.

If this is the monk's primary doctrinal importance, one must enquire about the connection between Cyril and Cassian. There was doubtless no direct, personal link between them: at the time Cassian left Egypt (*c*.400), Cyril was still some dozen years away from becoming the bishop of Alexandria. Nor is there likely to have been a significant literary connection between the two, since the only Cyrillian document that Cassian was at all likely to have seen was the letter to the Egyptian monks.[51] Is it possible that Origen, as interpreted by Evagrius, was not the dominant Egyptian influence on the monk of Marseilles, but that Cassian also learned from the other great strand of Alexandrian thought, that which stemmed from Athanasius and later found its highest expression in Cyril? Or is it possible that Cassian's 'Cyrillian' thought did not actually possess (or need) a direct connection to Cyril or Athanasius? Is it possible that such thought was not simply Egyptian or even Eastern, but that it represented the consensus of the whole early Church? I will attempt to address this question as I conclude this study and discuss its broader implications.

[51] See Ch. 5 n. 46.

7
Grace and the Logos' Double Birth in the Early Church

I began this study with the question of the relation between the various christologies of the early fifth-century Church, and I argued that one's evaluation of these depends to a great degree on one's assessment of what the central issue of the controversy was. If one were to consider the primary question to be whether a given christology maintains that there is in Christ one person but two realities or natures, then one could argue that the theological differences between the major parties involved in the Nestorian controversy were not significant. If one were to consider christology largely in formulaic terms and to ask whether a given writer began with duality or unity in Christ, then one could perhaps regard Cassian's thought as closer to that of Nestorius than to Cyril's. However, if one considers christology to be the expression of grace, as I have done in this study, one will recognize that there was a fundamental contrast between two concepts of what God gives to humanity in grace through Christ, of how redemption is achieved, and therefore of who Christ must be (and is) in order to accomplish this salvation. As I conclude this study, I will summarize briefly what I have claimed concerning these two patterns of grace and christology, and I will then suggest what I believe these findings imply concerning the christology of the early Church as a whole.

7.1. GRACE AND THE SINGLE SUBJECT OF CHRIST

I have attempted to show that for Theodore, Christ is a graced man, the one who is both the supreme example and the unique recipient of the Logos' co-operative assistance. As such he is the mediator of grace to us, the one who has received divine aid from the indwelling Logos in such a way that he can pass this on to us. Furthermore, although Nestorius writes very little about the soteriological concerns that lie behind his christology, he nevertheless appears to follow Theodore's understanding. Both of them distinguish sharply between the Logos and the assumed man, both seem to regard the actual personal subject of Christ as the assumed man who receives the Logos' co-operation, and both appear to see the composite comprised of Logos and assumed man largely as a semantic or grammatical subject. This way of looking at Christ's person is possible because Theodore and Nestorius see grace as God's giving some*thing* (aid, power, co-operation) to us by first giving this to Christ the man.

In contrast, Cyril sees grace as God's gift of himself to humanity through Christ. God shares with us his immortality and incorruption, and more importantly, he shares his natural communion (*οἰκειότης φυσική*), the very fellowship he has between the persons of the Trinity. Cyril insists that only God's own Son (*ἴδιος υἱός*) can give this *οἰκειότης* to us, and therefore his portrayal of Christ's person centres around the idea that his single subject is God the Son, the Logos himself. From this starting point, Cyril elaborates the idea that at the incarnation, the Logos added a concrete humanity to who he already was, thus embarking on a human mode of existence without ceasing to be God or changing in his deity. The incarnation brought the Logos' own (newly created) humanity into the intimate fellowship which he, as the Son of God, had with the Father. Since his humanity represents ours, Christ's life, death, and resurrection bring us into that same relationship: we become children of God by grace and share in the *οἰκειότης* that God's only true, natural Son has eternally enjoyed with the Father. Because of Cyril's understanding of grace as God's giving himself to humanity, he cannot allow a conception of Christ as the recipient of grace. Only if Christ is the Logos himself, and thus the very source of grace, can he give grace to us.

I have argued that Cassian views the monastic task as a response to what God has already done in adopting the monk into his family and giving him communion with himself. The monk seeks to deepen that fellowship with God that he has already been given, not to attain to such communion through his ascetic efforts. Furthermore, Cassian hints that the fellowship

God gives us is the love between the Father and Son, the very communion he has within himself. Like Cyril, Cassian argues that Christ is not a mere man or a composite, but rather he is the Logos himself, who has taken humanity into his own person at the incarnation. Only the true Son of God, the Logos, could make us sons by adoption.

The findings of this study show that the Nestorian controversy was not at heart a debate about whether Christ had a complete humanity or whether he was a single person. It was a debate about whether God himself had entered personally into the experiences of human life. Theodore's and Nestorius' concept of grace did not require such a direct, personal presence of God in the world. For them it was enough that the Logos gave his co-operation to the pioneering work of the assumed man as that man blazed the trail to the second *katastasis*, and the graced man could then give that aid to those who followed. Because of this, Theodore's and Nestorius' concern for God's impassibility could rise above other considerations, and their insistence that the Logos did not suffer or die led them to a christology in which the personal subject was the assumed man. While Cyril and Cassian basically shared this understanding of the Logos' immutability, their idea of grace as God's giving himself to humanity demanded that they see the incarnation as a direct personal presence of God in the world, and thus that they see the single subject of Christ as the Logos himself, the one who took humanity into his own person.

Since this was the central issue of the controversy, then the key question that exposed this issue was whether the one born of Mary was the same one who had been begotten of the Father before the ages. Theodore and Nestorius so divided the Logos and the assumed man that there was no genuine sense in which the Logos could be said to take part personally in the man's birth, suffering, and death. The Logos was born of the Father and the man of Mary, and one could say that Christ was born twice only because the word 'Christ' referred to both Logos and assumed man. Cyril and Cassian insisted that it was the same person, the Logos, who was born twice; it was the Logos who suffered and died, and thus they maintained that Mary must be called *Theotokos*. The Logos went through these human experiences as a man, in the humanity that he assumed, rather than in his divine nature per se. But nevertheless it was the Logos who underwent these experiences. I have contended that part of the reason Cyril and Cassian made this bold claim was that their concept of grace demanded it. In the light of the prevailing view of God's impassibility, they would not have been likely to say that God was born if they had not been firmly convinced that the Scriptures taught it, the Church believed it, and it was necessary for salvation as they conceived it.

Because of this, it is appropriate to view the question of the Logos' double birth as a sort of theological shorthand for an entire complex of beliefs regarding grace, salvation, and christology. When a patristic writer affirms that the one born of Mary was the Logos who had previously been born from the Father, this assertion almost certainly means that he believes only God himself could bring about human redemption. Furthermore, the reason for this belief may well be that the writer in question holds to an understanding of grace consistent with (and perhaps even the same as) that of Cyril. Conversely, when a writer denies the double birth of the Logos or refuses to affirm it explicitly, it is likely that his view of salvation is closer to Theodore's. This question, rather than that of how strongly one distinguishes the human and divine realities in Christ, is the key interpretative tool for understanding the relation between the major players in the Nestorian and Eutychian controversies. With this question in mind, I will now look briefly at two key Orientals (so-called 'Antiochenes'), three key Western writers, and finally at the Chalcedonian Definition. In doing so I hope to show the plausibility of my claim that the Cyrillian way of looking at grace and christology was in fact the consensus of the whole Church in the years prior to Chalcedon.

7.2. THE ORIENTALS

At the beginning of this work, I pointed out that many scholars see the christological controversy as a clash between two rival (and equally represented) schools of thought, the Alexandrian and the Antiochene. Two of the key figures used to support such a reconstruction of the controversy are John Chrysostom and John of Antioch. Chrysostom spent most of his life at Antioch, studied with Theodore under the tutelage of Diodore, was said to practice the sort of literal exegesis characteristic of the Antiochene school,[1] and was overwhelmingly concerned with ethical instruction in all his homilies, just as Theodore was. One would expect his christology to be similar to that of his teacher and his fellow student, and if one were to find such a similarity, one would be able to argue for the presence of a genuine Antiochene school of thought. Furthermore, even though very few of John of Antioch's writings survive, his violent opposition to Cyril at Ephesus would obviously lead one to assume that his christology was closer to that of Theodore and Nestorius than to Cyril's. But when one examines Chrysostom's teaching on grace and christology, and when one looks at the handful of extant writings from John of Antioch's pen, one finds that just the opposite is the case. Both men held to a christology which was much more Cyrillian than Theodorean. In this section I will survey the evidence that leads to this conclusion.

7.2.1. John Chrysostom

The vast corpus of Chrysostom's sermons contains page after page of moral exhortations to his audiences, and he frequently argues that Christ is our example as we seek to purify ourselves morally. In the light of the close personal connection between Chrysostom and his fellow student Theodore, one might assume that the moralism of both men grows out of a christology in which Christ is our leader in the march to the second *katastasis*. Correspondingly, one might assume that Chrysostom would share Theodore's view of grace as God's aid, power, and co-operation in the task of aspiring to the higher age. However, neither in his view of grace nor in his christology proper does Chrysostom bear a resemblance to his classmate.

Rather than seeing salvation as an elevation from a state of mortality and imperfection to a higher one of incorruption and perfection, Chrysostom sees it largely as a restoration to the condition in which God created humanity, a condition lost through the fall. To use the terminology I have adopted, his view of the structure of salvation is decidedly a three-act scheme (similar to that of Athanasius and Cyril), not a two-act scheme such as Theodore's. Chrysostom makes this clear as he describes the body with which God originally created humanity:

[1] See Kelly, *Golden Mouth*, 95.

If you would learn what kind of body God formed us with at first, let us go to paradise and look at the man who was created at the beginning. For that body was not thus corruptible and mortal. . . . But when man did not bear his felicity soberly, but threw contempt upon his Benefactor, and considered the deceiving devil more trustworthy than God who had cared for and honoured him, and when he expected to become himself a god, and conceived thoughts above his proper dignity, then, then indeed it was that God, to humble him by decisive acts, made him mortal and even corruptible. (*Hom. Stat.* 11.2 [121])

In this passage mortality and corruption are clearly the results of the fall; they are not a part of humanity's original condition. Rather than being created mortal with the calling to aspire to incorruption (as in Theodore's thought), mankind was given immortality at creation and lost it through sin. In keeping with this emphasis on the fall as the loss of incorruption, Chrysostom views redemption and baptism as bringing about a refashioning of humanity, a restoration to the splendour of our original creation.[2]

Consistent with this view of redemption in terms of creation, fall, and restoration, Chrysostom places a great deal of emphasis on the changes that take place in a Christian's life at the beginning of faith. As he addresses catechumens who are about to be baptized, he asserts: 'At this time, through the words and the hand of the priest, the Holy Spirit descends upon you. Instead of the person who descended into the water, a different person comes forth, one who has wiped away all the filth of his sins, who has removed the old garment of sin and has put on the royal robe' (*Cat. 8 Bapt.* 2.25 [147]). Similarly, Chrysostom tells neophytes who have just been baptized:

Before yesterday you were captives, but now you are free and citizens of the Church. Formerly you were in the shame of your sins, but now in freedom and justice. You are not only free, but also holy; not only holy, but also righteous; not only righteous, but also sons; not only sons, but also heirs; not only heirs, but also brothers of Christ; not only brothers of Christ, but also joint heirs. (*Cat. 8 Bapt.* 3.5 [153])

These two passages show a strikingly different way of looking at baptism from what we saw in Theodore's *Hom. Cat.* For

[2] See *Cat. 3 Bapt.* 1.22 [136]. Cf. *Cat. 8 Bapt.* 2.3 [134–5], in which Chrysostom draws a sharp contrast between the original and fallen states of mankind.

Theodore, baptism is primarily the germ of a future reality, the sign of the perfection that will come about in the second *katastasis*. For Chrysostom, the results of redemption and baptism are present: Christians are *already* holy, righteous, sons, and heirs.[3]

Chrysostom's three-act portrayal of salvation and his stress on the changes that have already taken place in the life of a Christian dramatically influence his depiction of grace and the Christian life. While preaching on Rom. 6: 23, Chrysostom comments,

> After he [Paul] has spoken of *the wages of sin* and turned to the blessings, he has not kept to the same order. For he does not say, 'the wages of good deeds', but, *the gift of God*, so as to show that they were not freed of themselves, nor did they receive something owed them, neither yet a return or a recompense of labours, but by grace all these things came about. (*Hom. Rom.* 12.2 [496])

In this passage, grace does not assist our own efforts; it works apart from and prior to our efforts. Grace is not power that helps us to aspire to the second age, as for Theodore. Rather, it is that which makes us God's children at baptism. As a result, the moral improvement to which Chrysostom constantly exhorts his flock is not a means of aspiring to incorruption and salvation; it is a response to what God has already done in making us his children.[4] In this way, Chrysostom's overall picture of salvation and grace is far from Theodore's vision and much closer to Cyril's concept, and especially to Cassian's view of the monastic task as a response to God's salvific action.

[3] For a similar emphasis on the changes that take place at the beginning of faith, see *Cat. 3 Bapt.* 1.11 [134]; *Cat. 8 Bapt.* 4.11 [188]; *Hom. Rom.* 15.2 [542]. Trakatellis, 'Being Transformed', 225, points out that for Chrysostom, the transformation of the Christian is a present reality, not a future eschatological condition.

[4] For a similar emphasis on our action as a response to what God has already done in saving us, see *Cat. 8 Bapt.* 3.19 [162]; *Hom. Johan.* 10.3 [77]. Peasants, 'Making Christian the Christians', 392, notes that Chrysostom sees Christian life primarily as a response to what God has already done in the life of a believer. And Lawrenz, 'The Christology of John Chrysostom', 149, states: 'It should not be assumed that Chrysostom's ethical concern is necessarily accompanied by the same christological concern as Diodore, Theodore, and the like. The undeniable moralistic strain in his homilies is the consequence of his temperament and his role as pastor and preacher more than of his fundamental theology.'

We saw in Ch. 2 that Theodore views the second age in terms of perfect *human* life, not in terms of human participation in *divine* life. On this point as well, Chrysostom differs markedly from his fellow student. He interprets John 1: 17 to mean that Christians receive grace in a greater way than Old Testament saints did, and he explains: 'Not only was forgiveness of sins granted to us . . . but also righteousness, holiness, adoption, and grace of the Spirit—much more splendid and far richer gifts. Through this grace we have become dear (ποθεινοὶ) to God, no longer merely as servants, but as sons and friends (ὡς υἱοὶ καὶ ὡς φίλοι)' (*Hom. Johan.* 14.2 [94]). Here grace is connected with a variety of gifts, but foremost of these are adoption and friendship with God. For Chrysostom (as for Cyril, Cassian, and others), grace is God's giving people communion with himself by making them his adopted children.[5]

This emphasis on our adoption as sons of God leads Chrysostom (like Athanasius and Cyril) to distinguish between sonship by grace or adoption and true, natural sonship. He accuses an unnamed heretic (presumably an Arian) of making Christ the Son of God merely by grace and therefore of making him no different from us. He continues: 'You say that he has shared in adoption by grace as you have; for by maintaining that he is not Son of God by nature (φύσει), you declare that he is a son in no other way than by grace' (*Hom. Johan.* 3.2 [39]).[6] Chrysostom's reason for insisting that Christ must be the Son of God by nature is that only the true Son can make us sons of God by grace. While discussing Rom. 8: 29, he boldly declares:

> What the Only-Begotten was by nature (φύσει), they also have become by grace (κατὰ χάριν). And still he was not satisfied with calling them *conformed*, but even adds another point, *that he might be the firstborn*. And even here he does not pause, but again after this he makes another point, *among many brethren*. So he wishes to use all means of showing the kinship (συγγένειαν) clearly. Now you are to understand all these things as spoken of the economy. For according to his divinity he is Only-Begotten. (*Hom. Rom.* 15.1 [541])

This crucial passage lays out the main features of Chrysostom's

[5] For a similar emphasis on salvation as adoption, see *Cat. 8 Bapt.* 2.26 [148], 3.5 [153], 4.11 [188]. For a stress on salvation as friendship or communion with God, see *Hom. Rom.* 15.1–2 [541–2].

[6] Cf. (*Hom. Johan.* 15.2 [100]), where Chrysostom makes the same point.

soteriology and also provides the basis for his christology. Salvation consists primarily of our sharing by adoption in the natural relationship between the Son and the Father. In order for us to share by grace in that natural sonship, the true Son must have entered into brotherhood with us, and this was the purpose for the economy of the incarnation. The natural Son became our brother by grace, so that we could be adopted by grace into his sonship with the Father.[7]

From this brief overview of Chrysostom's understanding of grace and salvation, it should already be clear that his approach to christology must be essentially similar to that of Athanasius and Cyril, not that of Theodore. Theodore is able to see the assumed man as the personal subject of Christ because he sees salvation as our march from the first to the second age and grace as God's assistance and power as we follow the trail that Christ the man has blazed for us. Chrysostom sees salvation as God's action of rescuing us from our fallen condition and restoring us to the glory of our original creation, and he views grace as God's giving us himself by making us his adopted children. Such a view of salvation demands that the personal subject of Christ be God the Son, the Logos, since only the natural Son can make us sons by grace.

The fact that Chrysostom views the Logos as the subject in Christ becomes very apparent from his treatment of two key New Testament passages on the incarnation, John 1: 14 and Phil. 2: 6–7. He claims that the reason we could become children of God was that '*the Word became flesh* and the Master *took on the form of the slave*. He became the Son of Man although he was the true Son of God, in order that he might make the sons of men children of God. . . . He did not at all lower his own nature (*ἰδίαν φύσιν*) by this descent, but elevated us, who had always been in dishonour and darkness, to ineffable glory' (*Hom. Johan.* 11.1 [79]). Notice that in this passage, the Logos is the actor in the incarnation. He is the one who is the true Son of God. He is the one who descended to earth without doing violence to his own

7 Chrysostom also emphasizes that only the true Son of God could make us sons by adoption in *Hom. Johan.* 11.1 [79]. Cf. *Hom. Johan.* 39.3 [223], where he asserts that Christ has life and power in himself, as the Father does. Similarly, in *Hom. Phil.* 7.1 [229], Chrysostom argues that Christ possesses equality with God by nature.

nature. And he descended in order to make us God's children and bring us to glory. In a similar passage, Chrysostom declares:

> Speaking here of his divinity, Paul no longer says, *he became, he took*, but he says, *he emptied Himself, taking the form of a servant, being made in the likeness of men*. Speaking here of his humanity he says, *he took, he became*. He became (ἐγένετο) the latter [i.e. human], he took (ἔλαβεν) the latter; he was (ὑπῆρχε) the former [i.e. God]. Let us not then confuse or divide. There is one God, there is one Christ, the Son of God. When I say 'one,' I mean a union (ἕνωσιν), not a confusion (σύγχυσιν); the one nature (φύσεως) did not degenerate into the other, but was united (ἡμωμένης) with it. (*Hom. Phil.* 7.3 [232])

Several things are noteworthy here. First, Chrysostom equates God, Christ, and the Son of God ('there is one God, there is one Christ, the Son of God') in a way that makes clear that he sees the Logos as the subject of Christ's person. Second, he applies both being and becoming/taking to the person of the Logos. Third, he distinguishes being (who the Logos is in his deity) from becoming (what the Logos does in his humanity). The statements, 'he became' and 'he took' do not apply to Christ's deity: Christ did not become God or take deity upon himself, since he always was (ὑπῆρχε) God. Rather, the Son of God became (ἐγένετο) man and took (ἔλαβεν) the form of a servant upon himself.[8] Like Athanasius before him and Cyril after him, Chrysostom insists that the one born of Mary was in fact God the Son, the second person of the Trinity. The Logos who was eternally begotten from the Father was the one who personally descended to earth and was born, suffered, and died for our salvation.

In keeping with his emphasis on the Logos as the personal subject of Christ, Chrysostom distinguishes between what the Logos does as man and what he does as God. While discussing the raising of Lazarus in John 11, Chrysostom has Jesus say:

[8] Cf. other passages in which Chrysostom clearly shows that he views the Logos as the personal subject of Christ, the one who underwent incarnation and birth on our behalf: *Hom. Johan.* 6 [61], 10.2 [75], 39.3 [223], 64.2 [356], 15.3 [544], 6.2 [221]. Similarly, Chrysostom does not hesitate to assert that it was the Son of God who died on the cross in *Hom. Rom.* 15.2 [543]; *Hom. Phil.* 7.3 [232]. Scholars who recognize that Chrysostom sees the Logos as the person of Christ include Hay, 'Chrysostom and the Integrity of the Human Nature', 313–14; Grillmeier, *Christ in Christian Tradition*, 421; Lawrenz, 'The Christology of John Chrysostom', 151.

I have never left the assumed humanity (ἀναληφθεῖσαν ἀνθρωπότητα) unharmonized with the divine operation, acting now as a man, now as God, both indicating the nature (φύσιν), and bringing faith to the economy. . . . As God, I curbed nature, maintaining a fast for forty days, but afterwards, as man, I was hungry and tired. As God, I calmed the raging sea. As man I was tempted by the devil, but as God, I cast out demons. As man, I am about to suffer on behalf of people.

(*Hom. Laz.* 1 [642–643])

By using the phrases 'as God' (ὡς θεός) and 'as man' (ὡς ἄνθρωπος), Chrysostom is able to ascribe all the actions and experiences of Christ's human life to the Logos, while still insisting that the Logos did not change in his own nature. Of course, this is the same terminology that Athanasius and Cyril use to make the same point. Furthermore, Chrysostom uses language very similar to that of the Alexandrians when he writes that the Logos added humanity to himself while remaining what he was. While discussing John 1: 14, he asserts, 'When you hear that *the Word became flesh*, do not be troubled or downcast. His essence (οὐσία) was not transformed (μετέπεσεν) into flesh—for this is completely impious even to think of—but with it [i.e. his essence] remaining what it was, he thus took the form of a slave' (*Hom. Johan.* 11.1 [79]).[9]

From what we have seen, there can be little dispute that Chrysostom's christology is unitive and locates the personal subject of Christ with the Logos, and thus that he is much closer to Cyril than to Theodore.[10] We have also seen that Chrysostom's view of grace and salvation is similar to that of Cyril and that this charitology is part of what drives his christology. For Chrysostom, as for Cyril and others, the personal subject in Christ must be the Logos, because only then can God give himself to us by making us his adopted sons. Only if the one born of Mary is the same one who was eternally begotten from the Father is salvation (in Chrysostom's understanding) possible. Chrysostom describes grace, salvation, and Christ's person using language strikingly similar to that of Athanasius

[9] Cf. *Hom. Johan.* 31.1 [177]; *Hom. Phil.* 6.3 [223], 7.3 [232].

[10] Scholars are in agreement that Chrysostom's christology differs markedly from that of Theodore and is very similar to that of Athanasius and Cyril. See Hay, 'Antiochene Exegesis and Christology', 17, 19, 22; Lawrenz, 'The Christology of John Chrysostom', 149, 152.

and Cyril, in spite of the fact that there was no significant link between Chrysostom and the Alexandrians. That his thought could so closely mirror that of men with whom he had no connection and be so stunningly different from that of his teacher Diodore and his classmate Theodore lends support to my contention that Athanasian/Cyrillian thought mirrored the consensus of the Church at the turn of the fifth century. Since Chrysostom is reputed to be one of the prime representatives of the so-called Antiochene school, one must wonder whether one can even speak of such a school in any meaningful sense. As Grillmeier concludes, 'This Antiochene, so persecuted by the Alexandrians, is far more Alexandrian than Antiochene in his christology—a new indication of the care with which we must use a word like "school".'[11]

7.2.2. *John of Antioch Before and After the Council of Ephesus*

In the light of John's anger towards Cyril at Ephesus and his leadership of the rival council that deposed Cyril and Memnon, it would seem reasonable to assume that John's christology was much closer to that of Nestorius than to that of Cyril. However, a key document that indicates otherwise is John's letter to Nestorius just after the Roman synod of August 430. John urges his friend to accept the title *Theotokos*, because to deny what this appellation signifies would lead one away from the truth about the incarnation. He explains more specifically:

> If one suppresses this title or what it signifies, then it necessarily follows that neither is God the one who has taken on himself the unsearchable economy for our sake, nor is God the Logos the one who manifested such a great love for us in *emptying himself and taking the form of a servant* [Phil. 2: 7]. But these are things that the divine Scriptures affirm in connection with God's love for us, when they declare that the pre-existent, eternal, and only-begotten Son of God descended in an impassible manner to be born from the virgin. (*Ep. Nes.* [1.1.1.95])

Here John makes it absolutely clear that he believes Scripture teaches that the Logos himself was the one born of Mary, and the reason this is so crucial is that only then can God be the one who has accomplished our salvation, the one who has emptied himself and become incarnate on our behalf. John apparently believes

11 Grillmeier, *Christ in Christian Tradition*, 421.

that Nestorius will agree with him on this, that Nestorius' objection to the title *Theotokos* is based merely on the danger that its use will condone excessive devotion to Mary. But in urging Nestorius to accept the title, John assumes the very thing Nestorius refuses to admit.[12] Nestorius' doctrine does not demand that God the Logos be the actor in the drama of redemption, and the prominence he gives to the concept of divine immutability excludes the idea that the eternal Logos could be born of the virgin. This passage is of crucial significance, since it provides evidence that prior to Ephesus, John of Antioch held to a christology in which the Logos was the single subject of Christ, that soteriological concerns lay behind this christology, and that John mistakenly believed that Nestorius held to the same doctrine as he did.[13] One should not accuse John of political capitulation when he later agreed to depose Nestorius and to accept reunion with Cyril.

In addition, a comparison of two versions of the confession which would later be adopted as the Reunion Formula provides further evidence that John was concerned to uphold the Logos' double birth. The following passages are Theodoret's version of the confession from his letter to the Oriental monks in 431 and John's version from a letter to Cyril during the search for peace in 432. I italicize the important changes in John's version:

And we confess our Lord Jesus Christ, perfect God and perfect man, of a rational soul and a body, begotten before the ages of the Father according to his deity, in these last days for our sakes and the sake of our salvation [born] of Mary the virgin; the same one (τὸν αὐτὸν) consubstantial with the Father according to his deity and consubstantial with us according to his humanity. (Theodoret, *Ep.* 151 [1420a])

Therefore, we confess our Lord Jesus Christ, *the only-begotten Son of God*, perfect God and perfect man of a rational soul and a body, begotten before the ages of the Father according to his deity, *the same one* (τὸν αὐτὸν) in these last days for our sakes and the sake of our

[12] Even though Nestorius has grudgingly accepted the title *Theotokos*, he has not done so and will not do so for the reasons John offers here. Nestorius does not believe that redemption is something God has accomplished; he sees it as something the assumed man achieved with God's aid.

[13] Galtier, *L'Unité du Christ*, 54, makes this point in a more general way when he argues that the vigour with which John exhorted Nestorius to accept the *Theotokos* shows that he saw the central truth to be the fact that the Logos himself was born of Mary.

salvation [born] of Mary the virgin according to his humanity; consubstantial with the Father according to his deity and consubstantial with us according to his humanity. (John of Antioch, *Ep. Cyr.* [1.1.4.8–9])

The second of these is essentially identical to the confession found in John's letter to Sixtus shortly after the latter's accession to the Roman see in 432 (*Ep. Six.* [1.1.7.159]) and to that which is present in Cyril's letter to John accepting the Reunion Formula (*Ep.* 39 [1.1.4.17]). Both the important differences between these two versions relate to the question of whether the Logos is the single subject of Christ. In Theodoret's version, one could read the phrase 'our Lord Jesus Christ' as referring either to the Logos himself or to a composite *prosopon* created by the conjunction of Logos and assumed man. Similarly, the placement of 'the same one' in the clause that indicates that Christ is consubstantial with both the Father and humanity could imply that it is merely the grammatical subject, the composite denoted by the word 'Christ', who is both God and man. In contrast, John's version adds 'the only-begotten Son of God' in the first line, thus showing that the Lord Jesus Christ *is* the Only-Begotten (that is, that the Logos and the Lord Jesus Christ are the same subject). In so doing, this version makes clear that all the following assertions apply to the only-begotten Son of God, the Logos, whereas Theodoret's version does not necessarily require that reading. Similarly, the placing of 'the same one' in the section dealing with the birth of Christ from Mary makes clear that the one born from her is the same one who was born from the Father. Again, Theodoret's version could be read to imply that, but it does not make that identification explicit.

Interpreting the significance of these differences is complicated by the fact that there is an earlier version of the confession in the Eastern Anaphora (1.1.7.70) which includes the phrase 'the only-begotten Son of God', as John's version does, but places 'the same one' in the position where Theodoret's version has it. If Theodoret was working from the version in the Eastern Anaphora and deliberately dropped the phrase 'the only-begotten Son of God', there is good reason for thinking that he rejected the identification of Christ with the Logos, but if he was unaware of the phrase or omitted it by accident, his version remains inconclusive. If John was the one who re-added 'the only-begotten Son of God' and moved 'the same one' to a less ambiguous position, then it is very likely that his purpose was to make clear that the Logos was born twice. Romanides argues that John himself made the changes and insists that the faith of John and Cyril was not that of Theodoret; John upheld the double birth of the Logos, and Theodoret believed that only Christ was born twice (that is, that the word 'Christ' includes both the Logos born from the Father and the man born from Mary).[14] In contrast, Wickham suggests that Cyril was the one who added 'the same one' to the phrase describing the birth of Christ from Mary.[15] In either case, what is clear is that John did not simply agree to, but also actively promoted in his own letters, a confession which proclaimed that the personal subject of Christ was the Logos and that the Logos himself was the one who was born twice. The question of Theodoret's thought is an extremely debated one,[16] but there can be no ambiguity about John's. He, like Cyril, affirmed the Logos' double birth.

John's statements in these letters show that his support of Nestorius at Ephesus was not based on any actual sympathy for the latter's charitology and christology. In fact, when he insists that a rejection of the expression *Theotokos* constitutes a denial that God himself accomplished our salvation, John shows that even in Antioch itself, Theodorean/Nestorian thought was not the norm. Even there, the Church (as represented by Chrysostom earlier and John of Antioch at this time) believed that the personal subject in Christ was the Logos, a belief that may well have been connected with the idea that salvation consisted of God's giving us himself in grace. In the light of this, one should probably regard John's support of Nestorius at Ephesus as the result of his anger over the anathemas and over the fact that

[14] Romanides, 'Cyril's "One Physis" and Chalcedon', 93.

[15] Wickham, *Cyril: Select Letters*, 222 n.

[16] Some interpreters, such as McNamara, 'Theodoret and the Unity of Person', 326; Romanides, 'Cyril's "One Physis" and Chalcedon', 91–2; and Gray, 'Theodoret on the "One Hypostasis"', 303–4, see Theodoret as refusing throughout his life to identify the one subject of Christ with the Logos. Others, such as Grillmeier, *Christ in Christian Tradition*, 494–5, see in Theodoret a pronounced christological development and argue that by the time of Chalcedon he did identify the subject of Christ with the Logos. Still others, such as Jackson, 'The Ecclesiastical History', 5, and Mandac, 'L'Union christologique', 95–6, argue that even as early as Ephesus he was much closer to Cyril than to Nestorius.

Cyril had begun the council without waiting for him, coupled with the likelihood that John did not (yet) realize that Nestorius' belief was not his own. Although Sellers argues that if a different spirit had prevailed at Ephesus, both sides would probably have recognized the value of the other's position,[17] I suggest that the opposite would have been the case. If Cyril had not written his anathemas or had phrased them more cautiously and the bishops had been able to examine Nestorius' thought more dispassionately, I believe they would have found that he had very few sympathizers. Belief in the divine Son of God who himself achieved our salvation by taking humanity into his own person was the faith of virtually everyone in the Eastern Church, and it was only political and personal rivalry that prevented this from becoming apparent to all at Ephesus. Political rivalry did not *produce* the controversy, as some argue. Instead, it *obscured* the depth of the theological disagreement between Nestorius and almost everyone else.[18]

Scholars sometimes ask which was the real Cyril: the author of the anathemas or the signer of the Reunion Formula. Perhaps a more appropriate question would be that of which was the real John of Antioch: the opponent of Cyril at Ephesus or the man who had earlier pleaded with Nestorius to accept the title *Theotokos* and who later endorsed (and perhaps even shaped the final form of) the Reunion Formula. I contend that the latter was the real John and that his faith in the Logos' double birth was that of the Eastern Church as a whole. Further evidence of this comes from Cyril, as he sought to defend himself before his more exuberant supporters who believed that the expression 'two natures' in the Reunion Formula was tantamount to Nestorianism. Cyril sharply distinguishes John and the other Oriental bishops from Nestorius by writing: 'They [the Orientals] said distinctly that there is one Christ and Son and Lord, God the Word who was ineffably begotten of God the

17 Sellers, *Two Ancient Christologies*, 233.

18 Campenhausen, *The Fathers of the Greek Church*, 168, argues that at Ephesus Cyril engineered a condemnation of the very faith that most Greek theologians espoused, and he was thus forced to backtrack in accepting the Reunion Formula. However, John's letters show that this was not at all the case. Instead, Galtier, *L'Unité du Christ*, 62–6, is correct when he asserts that the groups that opposed each other at Ephesus did not disagree at all on the central point of the Logos' double birth.

Father before all ages, the same one (τὸν αὐτὸν) who was begotten in these last times of a woman according to the flesh, so that he is both God and man at once'(*Ep*. 50 [1.1.3.100]). Here we see that what Cyril seeks, and what he finds in John and others, is an unambiguous declaration that God the Logos himself personally entered human experience through the incarnation. This secures the understanding of grace and salvation that he affirms, and when he finds this confession, he is willing to be flexible about the rest of the terminology used to describe Christ's person.[19] In spite of the terminological differences between Cyril and the Orientals, their belief concerning the incarnation is the same, in contrast to that of Theodore and Nestorius.[20] One cannot justifiably speak of a well-represented Antiochene school, when in fact Chrysostom and John of Antioch, two of the major 'Antiochenes', both hold to a faith that is more Cyrillian than Theodorean.

7.3. THE LATIN CHURCH FROM LEPORIUS TO LEO

If one regards the confession that the Logos himself was born of Mary, rather than the degree of distinction between the two realities in Christ, to be the central point at issue in the christological controversy, then it becomes clear that the West also held to a christology much closer to Cyril's than to that of Nestorius. Not only Cassian, but also Leporius (as guided by Augustine and others) and Leo state unequivocally that the single personal subject of Christ is the Logos, and while Celestine writes nothing specific on this question, he does hint in several places that this is his belief as well.

[19] Cf. *Ep*. 40 to Acacius of Melitene (1.1.4.26–7), in which Cyril makes essentially the same point. Later in the letter to Acacius (1.1.4.30), Cyril cites John's earlier statement from a letter to the Oriental bishops (*Ep. Or*. [1.1.7.56]), where John affirmed that Cyril had interpreted the incarnation by drawing together the strands of tradition in the same way that tradition had come down to the Orientals.

[20] Cf. Florovsky, *The Byzantine Fathers of the Fifth Century*, 288, who argues that even though the Reunion Formula did not use Cyril's terminology, it did reflect his faith.

7.3.1. *Leporius and Augustine*

As the monk Leporius recants his earlier christological error in *Lib. Emend.*, he confesses that he previously balked at saying that God was born as a man because he did not want to ascribe human birth to the impassible divinity (*Lib. Emend.* 2 [113]). Turning to what he now believes after being corrected, Leporius writes, 'We confess Jesus Christ our Lord and God, the unique Son of God, who was born from the Father before the ages, and we believe that in the last time God was made man and was born from the Holy Spirit and the ever-virgin Mary' (*Lib. Emend.* 3 [114]). Later he asserts that since the Son truly became a man, 'we are not afraid to say that God was born from a human being, that God suffered as a man, that God died, etc. But we are proud to say that God was born and that the same God suffered as a man (*secundum hominem*)' (*Lib. Emend.* 6 [117]).[21] In these statements we see a close resemblance between the thought of Augustine/ Leporius and that of Cyril. In response to Leporius' understandable but misguided reluctance to ascribe suffering to God, Augustine insists that it truly was God the Word who was born, suffered, and died. The reason Leporius is willing to accept this correction may be that he now realizes that God must have entered personally into these human experiences in order for salvation to be possible. Leporius' statement that God suffered *secundum hominem* echoes Cyril's *ὡς ἄνθρωπος*: God the Son suffered not in his deity but as a man.

7.3.2. *Pope Celestine*

Celestine's letters shortly after the Roman synod of 430 are surprisingly vague; he gives little indication of what he believes Nestorius' error to be. However, there are several passages in which he indicates that Nestorius has denied 'the birth of Christ our God'. For example, he urges Cyril to rescue Nestorius from his fall by asserting: 'Christ, our God, about whose birth questions are being asked, taught us to work on behalf of one sheep, desiring to recall it even on his own shoulders, lest it be exposed as prey for the wolf' (*Ep.* 11.5 [1.2.6]). Later in the same letter, Celestine writes that for Nestorius to be reinstated, he must condemn his errors in writing and 'strongly affirm that he

[21] Cassian quotes both these passages in *De Incar. Dom.* 1.5 [242–4].

holds the same belief concerning the birth of Christ our God that the Church of Rome, and the church of your holiness [i.e. Cyril], and universal devotion uphold' (*Ep.* 11.7 [1.2.6]). While these two passages are not very specific, they seem to imply that Celestine sees Christ's birth as the birth of God himself. In his letter to the clergy and people of Constantinople, Celestine offers a bit more detail:

> Nestorius the bishop preaches atrocities concerning the virgin birth and the divinity of Christ, our God and Saviour, as if he has forgotten the reverence due to him [Christ] and the common salvation of all. . . . For he separates the human and divine natures in our Christ, sometimes asserting that he is a mere man (*solum hominem*), and yet at other times ascribing to him an association (*societatem*) with God, as he sees fit to do. (*Ep.* 14.2 [1.2.15])

Celestine thinks Nestorius views Christ as a man who has earned some sort of association or relationship (*societas*) with God, rather than as God himself who has become a man. Not surprisingly, this is very close to Cassian's view of Nestorius, and Celestine's statement shows that he sees soteriological problems behind Nestorius' refusal to say that God was born as a man. He believes Nestorius sees redemption as a human ascent to conjunction with God, not as the descent of God to the human sphere. While Celestine's vagueness prevents one from drawing any definite conclusions, it seems likely that his soteriological and christological ideas are consistent with those of Cassian and Cyril: God himself must have entered human history in order to give us communion with himself.

7.3.3. Pope Leo the Great

Leo's *Tome* has been the source of great controversy from the time of its composition until now.[22] At the Council of Chalcedon itself, there was heated discussion about whether

[22] We saw in sects. 1.1.2 and 1.1.3 that Harnack, *History of Dogma*, iv. 204–5, and Studer, '*Una Persona in Christo*', 454, view Leo and Cyril as being inconsistent with each other, and that Galtier, *L'Unité du Christ*, 75, 85, views their thought as consistent. Also noteworthy is the comment of Florovsky, *The Byzantine Fathers of the Fifth Century*, 293, that Leo barely even addressed the issues at hand and that his *Tome* was so ambiguous that one could see either Nestorius' or Cyril's views in it.

three statements from paragraphs 3 and 4 were Nestorian.[23] However, one should note that near the beginning and end of the *Tome*, Leo affirms that the one born of Mary was God the Logos, and his statements about the duality of Christ's natures should be understood against the backdrop of this affirmation. As Leo discusses the Nicene Creed's assertions about the Son, he writes:

> The same one who was the Only-Begotten of the eternal Father was also born eternal (*sempiternus*) of the Holy Spirit and the Virgin Mary. This temporal birth did not at all diminish, and added nothing to, that divine and eternal birth, but was intended completely for the restoration of man who had been deceived, in order that he [Christ] might both vanquish death and *overthrow* by his strength *the devil, who possessed the power of death* [Heb. 2: 14]. (*Ep*. 28.2 [2.2.1.25])

We should notice here that the one born of Mary is the Only-Begotten of the eternal Father. One could take *sempiternus* either as modifying 'Only-Begotten', in which case the sense is that the eternal Only-Begotten was born, or as a predicate adjective with 'born', in which case the idea is that the Only-Begotten was born eternal. In either case, Leo is asserting unequivocally that the Logos himself was born of Mary and that his deity remained undiminished in that birth. Furthermore, Leo indicates that the purpose of the Logos' birth was the restoration of humanity, the destruction of death and the power of the devil. Here again, soteriological concerns lie behind the confession that the Logos was born twice.

Towards the end of the *Tome*, Leo discusses the *communicatio idiomatum*, by which one can say that the Son of man descended from heaven and the Son of God took flesh from Mary. He explains: 'The Son of God is said to have been crucified and buried, although he actually suffered these things not in his divinity by which the Only-Begotten is co-eternal and consubstantial with the Father, but in the weakness of his human nature. And so also in the Creed we all confess that the Only-

[23] The statements are that Christ 'could die with the one [nature] and not die with the other' (*Ep*. 28.3 [2.2.1.27]); that 'each form does what is proper to it with the co-operation of the other' (*Ep*. 28.4 [2.2.1.28]); and that 'the source of the degradation that is shared by both is one, and the source of the glory that is shared by both is another' (*Ep*. 28.4 [2.2.1.29]). For the discussion of these statements at Chalcedon's third session, see *Ges. Chal*. 3.24–6 [2.1.2.81–2].

Begotten Son of God was crucified and buried' (*Ep.* 28.5 [2.2.1.29). Here we see the same way of dealing with Christ's death that we saw in Leporius and Cyril. God the Son, the Logos, was himself born, crucified, and buried, but all of these happened to him in his human nature, not in his deity per se. Even though Leo elsewhere ascribes more autonomy to Christ's human nature than Cyril's followers would like, he makes clear that all the human events in Christ's life are predicated of the same subject, God the Logos. For Leo, as for Celestine, Cassian, and Leporius/Augustine, the central christological affirmation is that the second person of the Trinity is himself the personal subject in Christ.

7.4. THE CHALCEDONIAN DEFINITION

If it is true that there was a consensus understanding of salvation requiring the Logos to be the personal subject of Christ, and if the major figures in the fifth-century Church affirmed the double birth of the Logos, then one should read the Chalcedonian Definition in the light of that background. While it is certainly correct to say that Chalcedon places more emphasis on the distinction between divine and human in Christ than Cyril did, one must see this emphasis within a framework provided by the belief that the Logos was the subject in Christ, simply because there was no one present at Chalcedon (except perhaps Theodoret) who could have intended anything else besides this. One can attribute Chalcedon's failure to state explicitly that the Logos is the subject of Christ to the fact that it is addressing the problem of Eutychianism, not that of Nestorianism.[24] The question of Christ's personal subject had already been resolved at Ephesus, and there was no need to address that issue again.

Although Chalcedon does not directly deal with this question, the assumption that Christ's single person is the Logos turns up implicitly in several statements in the Definition. The assertion 'Begotten before the ages of the Father according to his deity, the same one (τὸν αὐτὸν) in these last days for our sakes and the sake of our salvation [was born] of Mary the virgin, the bearer of God, according to his humanity' (*Ges. Chal.* 5.34 [2.1.2.129]) reflects

[24] Cf. Galtier, 'Cyrille et Léon à Chalcédoine', 386–7; Ortiz de Urbina, 'Das Symbol von Chalkedon', 408.

the same concern as the Reunion Formula to show that the one born of Mary was the same one who had been eternally begotten of the Father. The expression 'the same one' is in the place where it is found in John's and Cyril's versions of the Formula, not in the more ambiguous position it occupies in Theodoret's version. Furthermore, the entire Definition is framed by three statements declaring that Christ is 'one and the same' (εἷς καὶ ὁ αὐτός). Between the first and second such statements, the Definition asserts that Christ is both divine and human, and between the second and third, it details the union between the two natures without destroying their integrity. Thus the three statements serve to divide the Definition into two major sections and to begin and end each section with the assertion that there is but a single Christ. These 'one-and-the-same' statements become progressively more detailed as the Definition continues. The first reads 'to confess one and the same Son, our Lord Jesus Christ', the second 'one and same Christ, Son, and Lord, the Only-Begotten', and the third 'one and the same Son, the only-begotten God, the Logos, the Lord Jesus Christ' (*Ges. Chal.* 5.34 [2.1.2.129–30]). From the progression of these statements we see clearly that the expression 'one-and-the-same Christ' is not simply a semantic idiom referring to a co-operative union of the Logos and the man, but rather a description of the person of the Logos. It is the 'only-begotten God, the Logos' who is one and the same. These statements come from a council dominated by the thought of Cyril and Leo, both of whom had unambiguously affirmed that the Logos was the personal subject of Christ, and thus the statements cannot be read in any other way. This was the consensus of the Church in the mid-400s, and even though Chalcedon's primary purpose was to address another issue, it echoed this belief in the Logos' double birth.

7.5. CONCLUSIONS AND IMPLICATIONS

Writing in 1939, Galtier compares Leporius' *Lib. Emend.*, Cassian's *De Incar. Dom.*, and the Reunion Formula, and he asserts:

In spite of the diversity of words and formulae, in spite of their perhaps embarrassing and inelegant expressions, these men were committed to the affirmation of the intrinsic identity which exists between the Son of God and the son of Mary. So it becomes clear what the error attributed to Nestorius was: it was not God who, strictly speaking, was born as a man. So also the dogma of Ephesus is put forth: it was the very Son of God who, in being born as a man, became the son of the virgin.[25]

Later Galtier argues that Leporius, Cassian, Cyril, John of Antioch, Celestine, and everyone else affirmed that the Son himself descended into the virgin's womb and was born according to the flesh for our salvation. He states that this was the faith of the Church and that one cannot regard the christological controversy as being merely a matter of personality conflicts or political clashes.[26] My research on Cyril and Cassian and the brief sketch I have made in sects. 7.2–4 support Galtier's conclusions. If one steps away from purely terminological concerns and accepts the issue of the Logos' double birth as the decisive question in fifth-century christology, then one cannot justifiably argue that the West, the Reunion Formula, or even the Orientals themselves were closer to Nestorius than to Cyril. There were not two equally established 'schools' at Antioch and Alexandria, and thus there was no question of which school more closely resembled Western christology. Rather, in the early fifth century there was an unequivocal christological consensus, opposed by only two or three major figures: Theodore, Nestorius, and perhaps Theodoret.

My research also suggests that this consensus about Christ's person in the early Church was undergirded by a deep consensus understanding of what I call christological grace. For Athanasius, Chrysostom, Cyril, and Cassian, the declaration that the Logos was the subject of Christ was the primary way of safeguarding the understanding of grace that they believed to be biblical and to represent the Church's faith. Only if the Logos was born twice could the incarnation bring about God's direct, personal presence in the world. Only if Christ was God the Son himself could the incarnation be an act of divine self-giving. Only if the Logos was the one born of Mary could he give us participation in himself by giving us a share in his own communion with the Father. This was the concept of grace and salvation that lay behind the rallying cry that the Logos was Mary's Son,

[25] Galtier, *L'Unité du Christ*, 29. [26] Ibid. 69–70.

and this understanding reveals a very deep, specific consensus about grace and christology among these writers.

Accordingly, it is worth asking how widespread this consensus understanding of grace was. We have seen that other writers of the time insisted on the double birth of the Logos. Did they do so because they, like Cyril, believed that only God could give us his own communion with the Father, or did they affirm the Logos' double birth simply because they believed that only God could overcome human mortality and corruption? If the latter, then this understanding would concur with part of what Cyril and Cassian asserted, but one could hardly call it a specifically 'Cyrillian' concept of grace. In this case one might conclude that while there was a great deal of consensus in the early Church about who Christ had to be in order to save us, there was more variety of thought about what or whom he actually gave us in salvation. On the other hand, if other writers of the time affirmed the double birth of the Logos because they too saw grace as God's sharing with us the communion he has within himself, then one could reasonably argue that the doctrine of grace we find in Cyril is not simply his own, but is the belief of the early Church as a whole.

In connection with this question about how widespread and deep the consensus was, it is especially striking that there was no known personal or literary connection between Cyril and Cassian. Furthermore, Chrysostom's thought, and even his language and vocabulary, closely resemble Cyril's, with once again no significant connection between the two men. That there were such closely related understandings of grace and salvation in apparently 'independent' writers—indeed, writers from three different regions, thought to belong to different schools—suggests that the Cyrillian doctrine of grace was not simply Cyrillian or even Alexandrian, but that it reflected a deep and widespread consensus, just as his christology did. It is thus plausible to think that further research may find a similarly specific charitology in other writers from the same period. I suggest, and perhaps further research will establish, that faith in the divine Logos-made-man, who has given us his own natural communion (*οἰκειότης φυσική*) with the Father, represented the consensus faith of the whole Church in the early fifth century.

Whether or not my suggestion about the depth of the consensus on grace and salvation is borne out by research on other patristic writers, the early Church's unequivocal consensus regarding christology has important implications for the contemporary Church. Only those contemporary christologies that begin with the personal downward movement of the Logos to the sphere of humanity and that focus on divine self-giving as the heart of redemption can claim the sort of historical authority I mentioned in the Preface. Of course, to begin with the Logos' downward movement is to approach christology from above, and this approach consorts ill with the sensibilities of many nineteenth- and twentieth-century interpreters. Many today are more comfortable approaching christology from below, beginning with the obvious humanity of the Jesus whom the Gospels present to us and working towards an understanding of some sense in which this man can be said to be (or to become) divine as well. To these people, Theodorean/Nestorian thought about christology and grace is much more congenial. However, we need to recognize that adopting a view similar to that of Theodore is not to adopt the early Church's dominant view, or even a well-represented patristic view. The view of Christ as a graced man who leads humanity to a higher level was vigorously and uniformly opposed by the Church when it appeared in the fifth century. When similar views reappear today, we must acknowledge that they carry no historical authority, but only the censure of the historical Church. We who value and wish to follow the patristic faith must recognize that to do so requires the proclamation of God the Son's birth as a man, in order to give himself to humanity. Only such a view carries with it the authority of the early Church.

Epilogue

To a certain degree, the problems that confront us as we seek to understand and elucidate the mystery of the salvation we have in Christ remain much the same from one age to another. Christians have always believed that there is a sharp distinction between the transcendent triune God and the creatures he has made, yet we have also sensed that in some way, redemption spans this gulf. In Christ we are (or, some would say, 'will be') children of God, partakers of the divine nature, fellow heirs with Christ of the Father's kingdom. But to what degree and in what way is the gap between creature and Creator bridged? Where do the similarity and the distinction between the Redeemer and the redeemed lie? How does God (or how do we) span the gulf? It is one thing to be convinced from Scripture and the Spirit's witness that we *are* God's children in Christ; it is quite another to be able to *explain* what we know to be the case. This explanatory task is, in large measure, the unfinished vocation of Christian theology.

Of course, the path to a more complete understanding of the mystery of salvation is full of pitfalls, and Christian history exposes many occasions when we have distorted the truth of redemption or settled for inadequate explanations of what God has given us in Christ. We have often sought to explain the bridging of the Creator–creature gap in ways that are too impersonal to resonate with what we know of God and of ourselves. To turn Christian salvation into an absorption of the soul into the divine being forces one at least to depersonalize the saved one and perhaps also to depersonalize God as well. To see salvation exclusively as incorruption and immortality is to view the purpose of human life in terms that are too physical, as if only the body is fallen and needs redemption. To speak of salvation merely as a matter of legal status before God or as forgiveness of sins alone is to skirt the truth that neither God nor human beings are *primarily* juridical in nature. If we are to be fully faithful to the message of Christ, we must see the link between redeemed humanity and God in other ways as well as these.

Similarly, Christians have often failed to tie the achievement of redemption directly enough to the person of Christ. An overemphasis on the human aspect of salvation, on the march of people to a better age with the help of God, threatens to reduce Christian life to moralism and to relegate God to little more than an auxiliary role. Conversely, it has often happened that Christians have tied salvation so thoroughly to a secret decree of God that the incarnation and work of Christ seem to be little more than necessary formalities. With respect to both the content and the means of salvation, we have often failed to emphasize adequately the deeply personal and relational nature of God himself and of his interaction with his creatures.

As the contemporary Church seeks to avoid these pitfalls and to describe faithfully who Christians are in Christ, I believe we would do well to give heed to the vision that lay behind Cyril's thought, a vision that Cassian and others also shared and that may well have been the consensus of the whole early Church. It is a vision that may have succeeded better than any other perspective at maintaining the distinction between God and humanity while still showing clearly how Christians share in divine life. To be God is to be an eternal, loving communion of three equal divine persons. To be a child of God is to remain a finite, mortal creature by nature but to share by grace in that very fellowship and life that characterize God himself. In order to bring this salvation about, God the Son has himself stepped into human experience personally and has become our Brother in order make us adopted children, so that we too might share with him in the very joy, the very love that he has enjoyed from all eternity with his Father.

TABLES

In Tables 1–3, all figures are intended to give a sense of the relative frequency with which the various words appear in different writings by Athanasius and Cyril. The numbers should be regarded as approximations.

TABLE 1. *Overview of οἰκειότης, ἴδιος, and related forms in Athanasius' writings*

Work	οἰκειότης	οἰκεῖος	οἰκειόω	ἰδιότης	ἴδιος	ἰδιοποιέω
Con. Gen.	0	1	0	1	31	0
De Incar. Ver.	0	0	0	0	38	3
De Dec. Nic.	0	4	0	3	37	0
De Sent. Dio.	0	1	0	0	22	0
Apol. Arian.	0	11	0	0	23	0
Hist. Arian.	0	3	0	0	29	0
Apol. Const.	0	2	0	0	8	0
Con. Arian.	3	4	0	16	283	2
Ex. Pss.	2	25	5	0	43	3
Vita Anton.	1	1	0	0	15	0
De Syn.	0	7	0	2	23	0
Apol. De Fuga	0	2	0	0	12	0
Tom. Anti.	0	0	0	0	1	0
Ep.	0	2	0	4	104	1
Frag. Var.	0	0	0	0	13	1
TOTALS:	6	63	5	26	682	10

TABLE 2. *Overview of* οἰκειότης, ἴδιος, *and related forms in Cyril's early writings*

Work	οἰκειότης	οἰκεῖος	οἰκειόω	ἰδιότης	ἴδιος	ἰδιοποιέω
De Ador.	23	54	3	1	183	0
Glaph.	19	32	5	0	158	0
Ex. Pss.	13	31	3	1	86	2
Com. Proph. Min.	29	53	4	0	323	0
Com. Is.	61	41	2	1	244	0
Thes.	0	82	3	14	202	6
Trin. Dial.	11	23	1	7	340	0
De Incar. Vnigen.	0	2	2	1	47	0
Com. Matt.	5	8	0	0	30	0
Com. Luc.	8	36	2	1	102	1
Com. Johan.	48	308	9	20	888	1
Frag. Act.	0	1	0	0	8	0
Com. Paul. Ep.	7	6	9	1	117	0
Frag. Dog.	0	0	0	0	8	0
Frag. Ex.	0	0	0	0	11	0
Florilegium	1	10	9	4	132	1
Ep. Pasch. 1–16	3	55	1	0	45	0
TOTALS:	228	742	53	51	2924	11

TABLE 3. *Overview of οἰκειότης, ἴδιος, and related forms in Cyril's later writings*

Work	οἰκειότης	οἰκεῖος	οἰκειόω	ἰδιότης	ἴδιος	ἰδιοποιέω
Ep.	1	6	9	1	155	0
Hom.	0	2	5	0	23	0
Theot. Nol. Confit.	0	0	0	0	7	0
Con. Nes.	0	5	3	0	200	0
De Fide Theod.	0	3	3	1	48	0
De Fide Dom.	1	4	3	0	84	0
De Fide Aug.	1	3	5	0	73	0
Apol. Cap. Or.	0	8	1	1	64	2
Apol. Anath. Thdrt.	1	4	5	4	36	0
Expl. 12 Cap.	0	2	0	0	17	0
Apol. Theod.	0	5	0	0	6	0
Schol.	1	0	5	0	44	0
De Dog. Sol.	0	0	0	0	8	0
Resp. Tib.	0	1	0	0	19	0
Quod Vnus Christ.	0	3	8	1	75	0
Con. Dio. Theo.	0	0	0	1	8	0
Con. Julian.	0	7	0	1	26	0
Ep. Pasch. 7–30	3	10	1	1	36	0
TOTALS:	8	63	48	11	929	2

TABLE 4. *Οἰκειότης in Cyril's early writings (c.228 occurrences)*

Referring to the relationship between the persons of the Trinity (12 total):
Trin. Dial. 1 [SC 231.152], 3 [237.12], 4 [237.192], 6 [246.28] 2x, 6 [246.44]
Com. Johan. 2.1 [Pusey 1.159], 6.1 [2.231], 6.1 [2.232], 9.1 [2.438], 9.1 [2.442], 9.1 [2.451]

Referring to a relationship between God/Christ and people (206 total):
De Ador. 1 [*PG* 68.208a], 2 [212c], 2 [228a], 2 [237b], 6 [460d], 6 [477b], 7 [504b], 7 [525b], 7 [532a], 9 [628d], 10 [677c], 11 [725b], 12 [801c], 12 [804b], 12 [804d], 14 [913c], 14 [940a], 14 [941b], 15 [949a], 16 [1013b], 16 [1032b]

Glaph. Gen. 1 [*PG* 69.29b], 2 [80a], 2 [81a], 4 [184a], 6 [313c], 6 [332c], 6 [332d], 7 [337b]

Glaph. Ex. 1 [389b], 1 [408d]

Glaph. Deut. [*PG* 69.649d], [653c], [656a], [656b], [656c], [657b], [675d] 2x

Ex. Pss. 17 [*PG* 69.825c], 32 [873c], 32 [881a], 34 [896d], 34 [897d], 36 [936a], 36 [944a], 37 [964b], 41 [1000a], 41 [1000b], 44 [1040d], 78 [1197a], 117 [1269c]

Com. Os. 1 [Pusey 1.28], 1 [1.36] 2x, 1 [1.42], 2 [1.46], 2 [1.70], 2 [1.73], 2 [1.75], 2 [1.76], 5 [1.196], 5 [1.202], 5 [1.204], 6 [1.225], 6 [1.250]

Com. Amos. 1 [Pusey 1.394], 1 [1.395], 2 [1.418]

Com. Mich. 3 [Pusey 1.700]

Com. Nah. 1 [Pusey 2.21]

Com. Soph. 1 [Pusey 2.188], 1 [2.191], 1 [2.192], 2 [2.239], 2 [2.240]

Com. Zach. 1 [Pusey 2.323], 2 [2.347], 4 [2.441]

Com. Mal. 1 [Pusey 2.577]

Com. Is. 1.1 [*PG* 70.13a–b], 1.2 [100c], 1.3 [112b], 1.3 [144a], 1.5 [237d], 1.5 [244a], 3.1 [580c], 3.1 [584b], 3.1 [596d], 3.1 [601a], 3.1 [605b], 3.2 [660d], 3.2 [661d], 3.3 [701d–704a], 3.3 [713c], 3.3 [724c], 3.3 [728c], 3.3 [732c], 3.5 [820b], 3.5 [824b], 3.5 [832d], 4.1 [877c], 4.1 [884d], 4.1 [885d], 4.1 [888c], 4.1 [889a], 4.1 [889b], 4.3 [980d], 4.3 [985c], 4.3 [988a], 4.3 [1021b], 4.4 [1041c], 4.4 [1064c], 4.4 [1084c] 2x, 4.4 [1085a] 2x, 4.4 [1085b], 4.5 [1104b], 4.5 [1109c], 4.5 [1116b] 2x, 5.1 [1145d], 5.2 [1192b], 5.2 [1193c], 5.2 [1201a] 2x, 5.2 [1204c], 5.2 [1205c] 2x, 5.2 [1228c], 5.3 [1244b], 5.4 [1309a], 5.4 [1337d], 5.5 [1393b], 5.5 [1396a], 5.6 [1401a], 5.6 [1401b], 5.6 [1433a], 5.6 [1440d]

Trin. Dial. 1 [SC 231.154], 1 [231.182], 4 [237.22], 6 [246.16]

Com. Matt. [*TU* 61, frag. 201], [frag. 221], [frag. 246]

Com. Luc. [*PG* 72.560c], [609a], [777c] 3x, [780d], [784a], [820c]

Com. Johan. 1.9 [Pusey 1.132], 1.9 [1.135], 2.1 [1.189], 2.1 [1.237], 2.5 [1.284], 3.5 [1.446], 3.5 [1.449], 4.7 [1.630], 4.7 [1.631], 4.7 [1.632], 4.7 [1.641], 5.5 [2.85], 5.5 [2.86], 6.prooem.[2.110], 6.prooem.[2.111] 2x, 6.1 [2.167], 6.1 [2.212], 6.1 [2.231] 2x, 6.1 [2.232], 6.2 [2.233] 4x, 6.2 [234] 2x, 7.frag. [2.264], 9.prooem. [2.389], 10.2 [2.555], 10.2 [2.563] 6x, 11.8 [2.690], 11.12 [3.12], 11.12 [3.13], 12.prooem. [3.82]

Com. Rom. [Pusey 3.182], [3.223], [3.225], [3.237], [3.241], [3.242]

Com. 2 Cor. [3.250]

Ep. Pasch. 9 [SC 392.158], 10 [392.192], 13 [PG 77.700a]

Florilegium Cyrillianum, 1x

Referring to a relationship among people (10 total):

De Ador. 16 [*PG* 68.1045c], 17 [1077b]

Glaph. Gen. 4 [*PG* 69.184a]
Com. Os. 5 [Pusey 1.184]
Com. Is. 3.4 [*PG* 70.781d]
Trin. Dial. 1 [SC 231.156]
Com. Matt. [*TU* 61, frag. 225], [frag. 256]
Com. Johan. 6.prooem. [Pusey 2.131] 2x

TABLE 5. Unitas *and* unio *in Cassian's writings (c.62 occurrences)*

Referring to general interaction between people and spirits (2 total):
Conlat. 7.9 [SC 42.255] 2x

Referring to fellowship among people (2 total):
De Inst. Coen. 4.8 [SC 109.130]
Conlat. 24.26 [SC 64.200]

Referring to agreement, unity of faith or purpose (7 total):
De Inst. Coen. 5.4 [SC 109.196]
Conlat. 16.3 [SC 54.226] 2x, 16.6 [54.228], 18.10 [64.22]
De Incar. Dom. 7.28 [*CSEL* 17.386], 7.31 [390]

Referring to physical inhabitation of a person by a spirit or by God (4 total):
Conlat. 7.10 [SC 42.255], 7.11 [42.255], 7.12 [42.256], 7.13 [42.257]

Referring to the Christian's union with Christ (4 total):
Conlat. 3.1 [SC 42.140], 19.8 [64.46], 23.5 [64.145], 23.11 [64.153]

Referring to the christological union (40 total):
De Incar. Dom. 1.2 [*CSEL* 17.238], 1.2 [239], 2.3 [250], 2.4 [255], 3.1 [262], 4.4 [290], 4.5 [290–1] 7x, 4.13 [301], 5.5 [307], 5.6 [310] 2x, 5.7 [310] 2x, 5.7 [313] 2x, 5.8 [314] 4x, 5.9 [316] 2x, 5.10 [318] 2x, 5.11 [319], 5.12 [321] 2x, 6.20 [347], 6.22 [348] 3x, 6.22 [349] 2x, 7.17 [373], 7.17 [374]

Referring to the unity within the Trinity (3 total):
Conlat. 9.34 [SC 54.70], 10.7 [54.81]
De Incar. Dom. 7.17 [*CSEL* 17.374]

TABLE 6. Societas *and* socius *in Cassian's writings (c.27 occurrences)*

Referring to an association of ideas or a category/group of things (5 total):
De Inst. Coen. 2.5 [SC 109.66]
Conlat. 5.10 [SC 42.198], 12.1 [54.121], 22.3 [64.119]
De Incar. Dom. 6.5 [*CSEL* 17.330]

Referring to general interaction among people (7 total):
Conlat. 3.19 [SC 42.162–3] 2x, 5.23 [42.214], 8.21 [54.28], 14.14

[54.202], 16.2 [54.224]
De Incar. Dom. 6.5 [*CSEL* 17.330]

Referring to marriage and sexual union (4 total):
Conlat. 3.19 [SC 42.162–3], 21.9 [64.83], 24.26 [64.200]
De Incar. Dom. 5.11 [*CSEL* 17.319]

Referring to close friendship among people (7 total):
De Inst. Coen. 2.12 [SC 109.80], 7.17 [318]
Conlat. 16.1 [SC 54.223], 16.2 [54.223], 16.3 [54.225], 16.14 [54.233], 16.28 [54.247]

Referring to the Christian's fellowship with Christ (2 total):
Conlat. 1.14 [SC 42.93], 23.5 [64.145]

Referring to the christological union (2 total):
De Incar. Dom. 5.1 [*CSEL* 17.302], 7.27 [385]

TABLE 7. Consortium *and* consors *in Cassian's writings (c.56 occurrences)*

Referring to an association of ideas or a category/group of things (2 total):
Conlat. 16.2 [SC 54.224], 22.3 [64.118]

Referring to those who share something (5 total):
De Inst. Coen. 4.5 [SC 109.128], 5.26 [234], 12.33 [500]
Conlat. 9.17 [SC 54.57], 24.11 [64.182]

Referring to agreement among people (2 total):
Conlat. 7.19 [SC 42.261]
De Incar. Dom. 7.30 [*CSEL* 17.389]

Referring to general interaction among people (25 total):
De Inst. Coen. Praef. [SC 109.26], 2.16 [86], 8.18 [358], 9.7 [374], 11.6 [432]
Conlat. Praef. [SC 42.75], Praef. [42.76], 3.1 [42.140], 5.4 [42.192], 5.9 [42.197], 7.9 [42.255], 8.10 [54.18], 10.6 [54.80], 17.10 [54.256], 18.5 [64.15], 18.5 [64.16] 2x, 19.4 [64.41], 19.9 [64.47], 19.10 [64.47], 19.10 [64.48] 2x, 19.11 [64.48], 19.15 [64.54], 23.5 [64.146]

Referring to marriage and sexual union (2 total):
Conlat. 16.10 [SC 54.230–1], 24.26 [64.200]

Referring to close friendship among people (12 total):
De Inst. Coen. 2.5 [*CSEL* 17.66], 10.2 [386] 2x, 12.30 [496]
Conlat. 3.1 [SC 42.140], 16.11 [54.232], 16.17 [54.237], 18.16 [64.31], 18.16 [64.32], 23.2 [64.140], 24.26 [64.200], 24.26 [64.203]

Referring to the Christian's fellowship with Christ (5 total):
Conlat. 1.14 [SC 42.93], 17.9 [54.255], 21.9 [64.83], 23.5 [64.146] 2x

Referring to the christological union (3 total):
De Incar. Dom. 1.3 [*CSEL* 17.239], 2.3 [250], 4.5 [290]

TABLE 8. Familiaritas, familiariter, *and* familiaris *in Cassian's writings (c.26 occurrences)*

Referring to a close association or connection of things or ideas (3 total):
De Inst. Coen. 8.1 [SC 109.336]
Conlat. 5.10 [SC 42.199], 23.16 [64.161]

Referring to familiar affairs, worldly concerns, or possessions (5 total):
Conlat. 4.21 [SC 42.186], 8.12 [54.20], 21.26 [64.101], 21.26 [64.102], 24.23 [64.194]

Referring to a person's familiarity with a virtue (1 total):
De Inst. Coen. 5.4 [SC 109.194]

Referring to general interaction among people (5 total):
De Inst. Coen. 4.16 [SC 109.142], 11.18 [444]
Conlat. 7.26 [SC 42.269], 17.1 [54.250], 20.11 [64.70]

Referring to friendship among people or between people and spirits (4 total):
Conlat. 8.12 [SC 54.20], 8.13 [54.20], 8.19 [54.26], 20.4 [64.61]

Referring to close friendship between people or angels and God (8 total):
Conlat. 2.2 [SC 42.112], 6.10 [42.230], 8.15 [54.23], 9.18 [54.55], 9.35 [54.71], 14.4 [54.185], 23.5 [64.147]
De Incar. Dom. 5.15 [*CSEL* 17.324]

TABLE 9. Amicus *and* amicitia *in Cassian's writings (c.37 occurrences)*

Referring to love for a vice, virtue, or thing (4 total):
Conlat. 1.13 [SC 42.91], 1.20 [42.103], 10.10 [54.88], 21.28 [64.103]

Referring to friendship between people and demons (1 total):
Conlat. 8.10 [SC 54.19]

Referring to friendship among people (25 total):
De Inst. Coen. 4.16 [SC 109.142], 5.32 [240], 12.27 [490]
Conlat. 6.3 [SC 42.222], 8.24 [54.35], 9.34 [54.67], 11.13 [54.115] 2x, 16.2 [54.223] 3x, 16.3 [54.225] 2x, 16.6 [54.227], 16.6 [54.228] 2x, 16.8 [54.230], 16.18 [54.238] 2x, 16.18 [54.239] 2x, 16.28 [54.247] 3x, 22.12 [131]

Referring to friendship between people and God (7 total):
Conlat. 6.3 [SC 42.223], 7.21 [42.264], 11.12 [54.114] 3x, 11.13 [54.117], 21.18.[64.93]

BIBLIOGRAPHY

In both sections of this bibliography, only literature that is cited in the book is included. Entries under each author are arranged chronologically.

TEXTS AND TRANSLATIONS OF PATRISTIC WRITINGS

The bibliographical reference for each work includes:

1. The abbreviated Latin title by which I cite the work in the text.
2. The full Latin title of the work, following *CPG* or *CPL*.
3. The location of the work in *PG* or *PL*, if it may be found there.
4. The critical edition of the work which I have used, if any.
5. The translations of the work which I have consulted, if any.

The edition of each work which is printed in bold face type is the best edition and is the one to which references in the text and notes refer. (The reader is reminded that all quotations of patristic sources are given in English translations, but these translations are my own responsibility. They do not directly follow the English translations listed below.)

Athanasius

(*Con. Gen.*) *Oratio contra gentes*, *PG* 25.4–96. ***Athanasius: Contra Gentes and De Incarnatione***, ed. and trans. Robert W. Thomson (Oxford: Clarendon Press, 1971), **2–133** (text and E.T.). SC 18 (Text and Fr.T.).

(*De Incar. Ver.*) *Oratio de incarnatione Verbi*, *PG* 25.96–197. ***Athanasius: Contra Gentes and De Incarnatione***, **134–277** (text and E.T.). SC 199 (Text and Fr.T.).

(*Vit. Anton.*) *Vita Antonii*, *PG* 26.837–976. **SC 400** (text and Fr.T.). *NPNF* (2) iv. 195–221 (E.T.).

(*Ex. Pss.*) *Expositiones in Psalmos*, ***PG* 27.60–545**.

(*Con. Arian.*) *Orationes contra Arianos 3*, ***PG* 26.12–468**. *NPNF* (2) iv. 306–431 (E.T.).

(*De Syn.*) *De synodis Armini in Italia et Seleuciae in Isauria*, ***PG* 26.681–794**. *NPNF* (2) iv. 451–80 (E.T.).

Augustine
(*De Grat. Lib. Arb.*) *De gratia et libero arbitrio*, ***PL* 44.881–912**. *NPNF* (1) 5.443–65 (E.T.).
(*De Corrept. Grat.*) *De correptione et gratia*, ***PL* 44.915–46**. *NPNF* (1) v. 471–91 (E.T.).
(*De Praed. Sanct.*) *De praedestinatione sanctorum*, ***PL* 44.959–92**. *NPNF* (1) v. 497–519 (E.T.).
(*De Don. Pers.*) *De dono perseuerantiae*, ***PL* 45.993–1034**. *NPNF* (1) v. 525–52 (E.T.).
(*Ep.*) *Epistolae* 194, 214, 215, 219, *PL* 33.874–91, 968–74, 991–2. ***CSEL* 57.176–214, 380–96, 428–31** (text). FaCh 30.301–32; 32.57–68, 99–102 (E.T.).

John Cassian
(*De Inst. Coen.*) *De institutis coenobiorum*, *PL* 49.53–476. **SC 109** (text and Fr.T.). *NPNF* (2) xi. 199–290 (E.T.).
(*Conlat.*) *Conlationes*, *PL* 49.477–1328. **SC 42, 54, 64** (text and Fr.T.). *NPNF* (2) xi. 293–545 (E.T.). ACW 57 (E.T.).
(*De Incar. Dom.*) *De incarnatione Domini contra Nestorium*, *PL* 50.9–272. ***CSEL* 17.235–391** (text). *NPNF* (2) xi. 549–621 (E.T.).

Celestine
(*Ep.*) *Epistolae*, 11–14, *PL* 50.459–500. ***ACO* 1.2.5–12, 15–22** (text). *Ephèse et Chalcédoine: Actes des Conciles*, trans. A. J. Festugière, Textes, Dossiers, Documents, 6 (Paris: Beauchesne, 1982), 112–36 (Fr.T.).

John Chrysostom
(*Hom. Stat.*) *Homiliae 21 de statuis ad populum Antiochenum habitae*, ***PG* 49.15–222**. *NPNF* (1) ix. 331–489 (E.T.).
(*Cat. 3 Bapt.*) *Catecheses 3 ad baptizandos*, **SC 366** (text and Fr.T.). ACW 31 (E.T.).
(*Cat. 8 Bapt.*) *Catecheses 8 ad baptizandos*, **SC 50bis** (text and Fr.T.), ACW 31 (E.T.).
(*Hom. Johan.*) *Homiliae in Johannem*, ***PG* 59.23–482**. *NPNF* (1) xiv. 1–334 (E.T.). FaCh 33 (E.T.).
(*Hom. Rom.*) *Homiliae in epistolam ad Romanos*, ***PG* 60.391–682**. *NPNF* (1) xi. 335–564 (E.T.).
(*Hom. Phil.*) *Homiliae in epistolam ad Philippenses*, ***PG* 62.177–298**. *NPNF* (1) xiii. 184–398 (E.T.).
(*Hom. Laz.*) *Homilia in quatriduanum Lazarum*, ***PG* 50.641–4**.

Council of Chalcedon
(*Ges. Chal.*) *Gesta concilii Chalcedonensis*. ***ACO* 2.1.1.55–196; 2.1.2.3–42, 69–163** (text). Festugière (ed.), *Ephèse et Chalcédoine*, 659–895 (Fr.T.). *Actes du concile de Chalcedoine: Sessions 3–6 (La définition de*

la Foi), trans. A. J. Festugière, Cahiers d'orientalisme, 4 (Geneva: Patrick Cramer, 1983) (Fr.T.).

Cyril of Alexandria

(*Ep. Pasch.*) *Epistolae paschales*, ***PG* 77.401–981**. **SC 372, 392** (text and Fr.T.). Burns, William H., 'The Festal Letters of Saint Cyril of Alexandria: The Manuscript Tradition, Text and Translation (Letters 1 to 5)', Ph.D. Dissertation, University of Southampton, 1988 (text and E.T.). [Citations of letters 1–11 are from SC 372 and 392; citations of letters 12–30 are from *PG* 77.]

(*De Ador.*) *De adoratione et cultu in spiritu et ueritate*, ***PG* 68.133–1125**.

(*Glaph.*) *Glaphyra in Pentateuchum*, ***PG* 69.9–678**.

(*Com. Proph. Min.*) *Commentarius in 12 prophetas minores*, *PG* 71.9–1061, 72.9–364. ***Sancti patris nostri Cyrilli archiepiscopi Alexandrini, in 12 prophetas***, ed. P. E. Pusey (2 vols.; Oxford: Clarendon Press, 1868) (text).

(*Com. Is.*) *Commentarius in Isaiam prophetam*, ***PG* 70.9–1449**.

(*Thes.*) *Thesaurus de sancta et consubstantiale trinitate*, ***PG* 75.9–656**.

(*Trin. Dial.*) *De sancta trinitate dialogi 7*, *PG* 75.657–1124. **SC 231, 237, 246** (text and Fr.T.).

(*De Incar. Vnigen.*) *De incarnatione unigeniti*, *PG* 75.1189–1253. **SC 97.188–301** (text and Fr.T.)

(*Com. Johan.*) *Commentarii in Johannem*, *PG* 73.9–1056, 74.9–756. ***Sancti patris nostri Cyrilli archiepiscopi Alexandrini, in d. Joannis evangelium: Accedunt fragmenta varia necnon tractatus ad Tibersium diaconum duo***, ed. P. E. Pusey (3 vols.; Oxford: Clarendon Press, 1872) (text). *LoF* 43, 48 (E.T.). [In the parenthetical references to this work, the numbers refer to the book and chapter of the commentary, not to the chapter and verse of John's Gospel on which Cyril is commenting.]

(*Com. Paul. Ep.*) *Fragmenta in sancti Pauli epistolas*, *PG* 74.773–1006. ***Sancti patris nostri Cyrilli archiepiscopi Alexandrini, in d. Joannis evangelium***, iii. 173–440 (text).

(*Theot. Nol. Confit.*) *Contra eos qui Theotocon nolunt confiteri*, *PG* 76.256–92. ***ACO* 1.1.7.19–32** (text). Lavaud, Benoît, and Herman Diepen, 'Saint Cyrille d'Alexandrie: Court Traité contre ceux qui ne veulent pas reconnaître Marie Mère de Dieu', *RThom* 56 (1956): 688–712 (Fr.T.).

(*Con. Nes.*) *Libri 5 contra Nestorium*, *PG* 76.9–248. ***ACO* 1.1.6.13–106** (text). *LoF* 47.1–184 (E.T.).

(*De Fide Theod.*) *Oratio ad Theodosium imperatorum de recta fide*, *PG* 76.1133–1200. ***ACO* 1.1.1.42–72** (text). Festugière (ed.), *Ephèse et Chalcédoine*, 69–108 (Fr.T.).

(*De Fide Dom.*) *Oratio ad Arcadiam et Marinam augustas de fide*, *PG*

76.1201–1336. ***ACO* 1.1.5.62–118** (text).
(*De Fide Aug.*) *Oratio ad Pulcheriam et Eudociam augustas de fide*, *PG* 76.1336–1420. ***ACO* 1.1.5.26–61** (text).
(*Apol. Cap. Or.*) *Apologia 12 capitulorum contra Orientales*, *PG* 76.316–385. ***ACO* 1.1.7.33–65** (text).
(*Apol. Anath. Thdrt.*) *Apologia 12 anathematisorum contra Theodoretum*, *PG* 76.385–452. ***ACO* 1.1.6.110–46** (text).
(*Expl.12 Cap.*) *Explanatio 12 capitulorum*, *PG* 76.293–312. ***ACO* 1.1.5.15–25** (text). McGuckin, John A., *St. Cyril of Alexandria: The Christological Controversy*, Supplements to *Vigiliae Christianiae*, 23. 282–93 (Leiden: E. J. Brill, 1994) (E.T.).
(*Schol.*) *Scholia de incarnatione unigeniti*, *PG* 75.1369–1412. ***ACO* 1.5.219–31** (fragments of text). ***ACO* 1.5.184–215** (Lat.V.). *LoF* 47.185–236 (E.T.). McGuckin, *St. Cyril of Alexandria: The Christological Controversy*, 294–335 (E.T.).
(*Quod Vnus Christ.*) *Quod unus sit Christus*, *PG* 75.1253–1361. ***Cyrille d'Alexandrie: Deux dialogues christologiques*, SC 97. 302–514** (1964) (text and Fr.T.). *LoF* 47.237–319 (E.T.).
(*Con. Theo.*) *Fragmenta ex libris contra Diodorum et Theodorum*, *PG* 76.1437–52. ***Sancti patris nostri Cyrilli archiepiscopi Alexandrini, in d. Joannis evangelium***, iii. 492–537 (text). *LoF* 47.320–62 (E.T.).
(*De Dog. Sol.*) *De dogmatum solutione*, *PG* 76.1065–1132. ***Cyril of Alexandria: Select Letters***, ed. and trans. L. R. Wickham (Oxford: Clarendon Press, 1983), 180–213 (text and E.T.).
(*Resp. Tib.*) *Responsiones ad Tiberium diaconum*.Wickham (ed.), ***Cyril of Alexandria: Select Letters***, 132–79 (text and E.T.).
(*Ep.*) *Epistolae*, *PG* 77.9–390. ***ACO* 1.1.1.10–119 *passim*; 1.1.2.66–70; 1.1.3.45–101 *passim*; 1.1.4.15–32, 34–61; 1.1.5.10–13; 1.1.6.110–11, 151–62; 1.1.7.137–72 *passim*; 1.4.206–32 *passim*; 1.5.310–15; 2.1.3.66–7; 3.201–2; 4.1.87** (text). Wickham (ed.), *Cyril of Alexandria: Select Letters* (text and E.T. of Ep. 4, 17, 40, 44, 45, 46, and 55). FaCh 76, 77 (E.T. of all letters).

Diodore
(*Frag.*) *Fragmenta dogmatica*. Abramowski, Rudolf, **'Der theologische Nachlaß des Diodor von Tarsus'. *ZNW* 42 (1949): 19–69**. (Fragments of texts, Lat.V., Syr.V., and Ger.T.).

Evagrius Ponticus
(*Prac.*) *Practicus*. **SC 171** (Text and Fr.T.).
(*Keph. Gnost.*) *Kephalaia gnostica*. ***Les Six Centuries des 'Kephalaia gnostica' d'Évagre le Pontique***, ed. and trans. A. Guillaumont, Patrologia Orientalis, 28 (Paris: Firmin-Didot et Compagnie, 1958) (Syr.V. and Fr.T.).

Irenaeus of Lyons

(*Adu. Haer.*) *Aduersus haereses*, *PG* 7.4371224. **SC 100, 153, 211, 264, 294** (fragments of text, Lat.V., and Fr.T.). *ANFa* 1.315–567 (E.T.).

(*Dem. Praed.*) *Demonstratio praedicationis apostolicae*. **SC 62** (Fr.T. of Arm.V.). *St. Irenaeus: The Demonstration of the Apostolic Preaching*, trans. J. Armitage Robinson (London: Society for Promoting Christian Knowledge, 1920) (E.T. of Arm.V.).

John of Antioch

(*Ep. Nes.*) *Epistola ad Nestorium*, *PG* 77.1449–57. ***ACO* 1.1.1.93–5** (text). Festugière (ed.), *Ephèse et Chalcédoine*, 139–43. (Fr.T.).

(*Ep. Cyr.*) *Epistola ad Cyrillum*, *PG* 77.169–73. ***ACO* 1.1.4.7–9** (text). Festugière (ed.), *Ephèse et Chalcédoine*, 474–6 (Fr.T.).

(*Ep. Six.*) *Epistola ad Xystum episcopum Romae*. ***ACO* 1.1.7.158–60** (text).

(*Ep. Or.*) *Epistola ad omnes episcopos Orientis*, *PG* 84.573–5. ***ACO* 1.1.7.156–7** (text).

Leo

(*Ep.* 28) *Epistola ad Flavianum Constantinopolitanum (Tomus)*, *PL* 54.755–82. ***ACO* 2.2.1.24–33** (text). *ACO* 2.1.1.10–20 (Gk.V.). Festugière (ed.), *Actes du concile de Chalcedoine*, 32–7 (Fr.T.). *NPNF* (2) xii. 38–43 (E.T.).

Leporius

(*Lib. Emend.*) *Libellus emendationis*, *PL* 31.1221–30. **CCSL 64. 111–23** (text).

Nestorius

(*Ep.*) *Epistolae*. ***Nestoriana: Die Fragmente des Nestorius***, ed. Friedrich Loofs (Halle: Max Niemeyer, 1905), **165–202** (fragments of texts and Lat.V.). Norris, Richard A., Jr. (ed.), *The Christological Controversy* (Philadelphia: Fortress Press, 1980), 135–40 (E.T. of *Ep.* 5).

(*Ser.*) *Sermones*. ***Nestoriana*, 225–350** (fragments of texts and Lat.V.). Norris (ed.), *The Christological Controversy*, 123–31 (E.T. of *Ser.* 9).

(*Lib. Her.*) *Liber Heraclidis*. Nestorius, ***Le Livre d'Hérclide de Damas***, trans. F. Nau (Paris: Letouzey et Ané, 1910) (Fr.T. of Syr.V.). Nestorius, *The Bazaar of Heracleides*, ed. and trans. G. R. Driver and Leonard Hodgson (Oxford: Clarendon Press, 1925) (E.T. of Syr.V.).

Origen

(*De Princ.*) *De principiis*, *PG* 11.115–414. **SC 252, 268** (fragments of text, Lat.V., and Fr.T.). *Origen: On First Principles*, trans. G. W. Butterworth (Gloucester, Mass.: Peter Smith, 1973) (E.T.).

Prosper of Aquitaine

(*Con. Collat.*) *De gratia Dei et libero arbitrio liber contra collatorem*, ***PL* 51.213–76**. ACW 32.70–138 (E.T.).

Tertullian

(*De Car.*) *De carne Christi*, *PL* 2.751–92. ***Q. Septimii Florentis Tertulliani De Carne Christi Liber***, ed. and trans. Ernest Evans (London: Society for Promoting Christian Knowledge, 1956) (text and E.T.). SC 216 (text and Fr.T.).

(*Adu. Prax.*) *Aduersus Praxean*, *PL* 2.153–96. ***Q. Septimii Florentis Tertulliani Adversus Praxean Liber***, ed. and trans. Ernest Evans (London: Society for Promoting Christian Knowledge, 1948) (text and E.T.).

Theodore

(*De Incar.*) *De incarnatione*, *PG* 66.969–94. ***Theodori Episcopi Mopsuesteni in epistolas b. Pauli Commentarii: The Latin Version with the Greek Fragments, ii: 1 Thessalonians—Philemon, Appendices, Indices***, ed. H. B. Swete (Cambridge: University Press, 1882), 290–312 (fragments of text, Lat.V., and Syr.V.). Norris (ed.), *The Christological Controversy*, 113–22 (E.T. of some fragments).

(*Hom. Cat.*) *Homiliae catecheticae*. ***Les Homélies catéchétiques de Théodore de Mopsueste: Réproduction phototypique du ms. Mingana Syr. 561***, trans. Raymond Tonneau and Robert Devreesse (Vatican City: Biblioteca Apostolica Vaticana, 1949) (Syr.V. and Fr.T.). *Woodbrooke Studies:* Christian Documents Edited and Translated by A. Mingana, v. *Commentary of Theodore of Mopsuestia on the Nicene Creed*; vi. *Commentary of Theodore of Mopsuestia on the Lord's Prayer and on the Sacraments of Baptism and the Eucharist* (Cambridge: W. Heffer & Sons, 1932–3) (Syr.V. and E.T.).

(*Pecc. Orig.*) *Contra defensores peccati originalis*, *PG* 66.1005–12. ***Theodori Episcopi Mopsuesteni in epistolas b. Pauli Commentarii*, ii. 332–7** (fragments of text, Lat.V., and Syr.V.).

(*Frag. Gen.*) *Fragmenta in Genesim*, ***PG* 66.635–46**.

Theodoret

(*Ep.* 151) *Epistola ad eos qui in Euphratesia et Osrhoena regione Syria, Phoenicia et Cilicia uitam monasticam degunt*, ***PG* 83.1416–40**. *NPNF* (2) iii. 325–32 (E.T.).

SECONDARY LITERATURE

For purposes of alphabetization of the bibliographical references, the particles 'de', 'du', and 'van' are considered to be part of the surname; the particle 'von' is not. In the case of multiple works by a single author, works are listed in chronological order by the date of the first edition, although I generally cite the latest edition. Works edited by a given author follow works written by that author, regardless of chronological sequence.

Abramowski, Luise, 'Zur Theologie Theodors von Mopsuestia', *ZKG* 72 (1961): 263–93. [E.T. by L. R. Wickham in *Formula and Context: Studies in Early Christian Thought* (Great Yarmouth: Variorum, 1992), 1–36.]

—— *Untersuchungen zum Liber Heraclidis des Nestorius* (Louvain: Corpus Scriptorum Christianorum Orientalium 242, Subsidia 22, 1963).

Amann, Émile, 'Nestorius et sa doctrine', *DThC* 11 (1931): 76–157.

—— 'Semi-Pélagiens', *DThC* 14 (1939): 1796–850.

—— 'L'Affaire Nestorius vue de Rome', *RevSR* 23 (1949): 5–37, 207–44; 24 (1950): 28–52, 235–65.

Angstenberger, Pius, *Der reiche und der arme Christus: Die Rezeptionsgeschichte von 2 Kor 8,9 zwischen dem zweiten und dem sechsten Jahrhundert*. Hereditas: Studien zur Alten Kirchengeschichte, 12, ed. Ernst Dassmann and Hermann-Josef Vogt (Bonn: Borengässer, 1997).

Arnou, R., 'Nestorianisme et Néoplatonisme: L'Unité du Christ et l'union des "Intelligibles" ', *Gr.* 17 (1936): 116–31.

Azkoul, Michael, 'Peccatum originale: The Pelagian Controversy', *PBR* 3 (1984): 39–53.

Bauer, Walter, *A Greek–English Lexicon of the New Testament and Other Early Christian Literature*, trans. and adapted by W. F. Arndt and F. W. Gingrich (Chicago: University of Chicago Press, 1957; revised and augmented by F. W. Gingrich and F. W. Danker, 1979).

Bethune-Baker, James F., *An Introduction to the Early History of Christian Doctrine to the Time of the Council of Chalcedon* (London: Methuen, 1903; 8th edn. 1949).

—— *Nestorius and his Teaching: A Fresh Examination of the Evidence* (Cambridge: University Press, 1908).

Blanchette, Oliva, 'Saint Cyril of Alexandria's Idea of the Redemption', *ScEc* 16 (1964): 455–80.

Boulnois, Marie-Odile, 'Le Souffle et l'Esprit: Exégèses patristiques de l'insufflation originelle de *Gn* 2, 7 en lien avec celle de *Jn* 20, 22', *RechAug* 24 (1989): 3–37.

—— *Le Paradoxe trinitaire chez Cyrille d'Alexandrie: Herméneutique, analyses philosophiques et argumentation théologique*, Collection des Études Augustiniennes, 143 (Paris: Institute d'Études Augustiniennes, 1994).

Braaten, Carl E., 'Modern Interpretations of Nestorius', *ChH* 32 (1963): 251–67.

Brand, Charles, 'Le *De Incarnatione Domini* de Jean Cassien: Contribution à l'étude de la christologie en Occident à la vielle du concile d'Éphèse', Ph.D. dissertation, Université de Strasbourg, 1954.

Brown, Robert F., 'On the Necessary Imperfection of Creation: Irenaeus' *Adversus Haereses* iv, 38', *SJTh* 28 (1975): 17–25.

Burghardt, Walter J., *The Image of God in Man According to Cyril of Alexandria*, Studies in Christian Antiquity, 14 (Woodstock, Md.: Woodstock College Press, 1957).

Campenhausen, Hans von, *The Fathers of the Greek Church* (London: Adam & Charles Black, 1963; German 1st edn. 1955).

Cappuyns, Maïeul, 'Cassien (Jean)', *DHGE* 11 (1949): 1319–48.

Chadwick, Henry, 'Eucharist and Christology in the Nestorian Controversy', *JThS* NS 2 (1951): 145–64.

Chadwick, Owen, 'Euladius of Arles', *JThS* 46 (1945): 200–5.

——*John Cassian*, 2nd edn. (Cambridge: University Press, 1968).

Charlier, Noël, 'Le "Thesaurus de Trinitate" de saint Cyrille d'Alexandrie: Questions de critique littéraire', *RHE* 45 (1950): 25–81.

Chesnut, Roberta C., 'The Two Prosopa in Nestorius' Bazaar of Heraclides', *JThS* NS 29 (1978): 392–409.

Chitty, Derwas J., *The Desert a City: An Introduction to the Study of Egyptian and Palestinian Monasticism under the Christian Empire* (Oxford: Basil Blackwell & Mott, 1966).

Christophe, Paul, *Cassien et Césaire: Prédicateurs de la morale monastique*, Recherches et synthèses: Section de morale 2 (Paris: Éditions J. Duculot, 1969).

Clavis Patrum Graecorum, ed. M. Geerard and F. Glorie (Brepols-Turnhout: Editores Pontificii, 1979), iii.

Codina, Victor, *El Aspecto Christologico en la Espiritualidad de Juan Cassiano*. Orientalia Christiana Analecta, 175 (Rome: Pontificum Institutum Orientalium Studiorum, 1966).

de Durand, G. M. (ed.), *Cyrille d'Alexandrie: Deux dialogues christologiques* (Paris: Éditions du Cerf, 1964).

de Vogüé, Adalbert, 'Monachisme et Église dans la pensée de Cassien', in *Théologie de la vie monastique: Études sur la Tradition patristique*, Théologie, 49 (Aubier: Éditions Montaigne, 1961), 213–40.

——'Pour comprendre Cassien: Un survol des *Conférences*', *CCist* 39 (1977): 250–72. [E.T. by J. B. Hasbrouck, 'Understanding Cassian: A Survey of the Conferences', *CistS* 19 (1984): 101–21.]

Devreesse, Robert, *Essai sur Théodore de Mopsueste* (Vatican City: Biblioteca Apostolica Vaticana, 1948).

de Vries, Wilhelm, 'Der "Nestorianismus" Theodors von Mopsuestia in seiner Sakramentenlehre', *OCP* 7 (1941): 91–148.

Dewart, Joanne McWilliam, *The Theology of Grace of Theodore of Mopsuestia*, Catholic University of America Studies in Christian

Antiquity, 16 (Washington, DC: Catholic University of America Press, 1971).

DEWART, JOANNE McWILLIAM, 'The Notion of "Person" Underlying the Christology of Theodore of Mopsuestia', *StPatr* 12 (1975) [*TU* 115]: 199–207.

—— 'The Influence of Theodore of Mopsuestia on Augustine's *Letter 187*', *AugSt* 10 (1979): 113–32.

DHÔTEL, JEAN-CLAUDE, 'La "Sanctification" du Christ d'après Hébreux, 2: 11. Interprétation des Pères et des Scholastiques Médiévaux', *RSR* 47 (1959): 515–43.

DIEPEN, HERMAN M., *Aux origines de l'anthropologie de saint Cyrille d'Alexandrie*. Textes et études théologiques (Bruges: Desclée de Brouwer, 1957).

—— 'L'*Assumptus Homo* patristique', *RThom* 63 (1963): 225–45, 363–88; 64 (1964): 33–52, 365–86.

DILLON, JOHN, *The Middle Platonists: A Study of Platonism, 80 B.C. to A.D. 220* (London: Gerald Duckworth & Co., 1977).

DRATSELLAS, CONSTANTINE, 'Questions of the Soteriological Teaching of the Greek Fathers with Special Reference to St. Cyril of Alexandria', *Theol(A)* 38 (1967): 579–608; 39 (1968): 192–230, 394–424, 621–43. [This article has been reprinted in book form and published in Athens, 1968.]

—— 'Man in his Original State and in the State of Sin According to St. Cyril of Alexandria', *Theol(A)* 41 (1970): 441–55, 545–56; 42 (1971): 519–47. [This article has been reprinted in book form and published in Athens, 1971.]

DU MANOIR DE JUAYE, HUBERT, *Dogme et spiritualité chez saint Cyrille d'Alexandrie* (Paris: Librairie Philosophique J. Vrin, 1944).

FLOROVSKY, GEORGES, *The Byzantine Fathers of the Fifth Century*. Collected Works of Georges Florovsky, 8 (Vaduz: Büchervertriebsanstalt, 1987; Russian 1st edn. 1931–3).

FREND, WILLIAM H. C., 'Popular Religion and Christological Controversy in the Fifth Century', *SCH* 8 (1972): 19–29.

GALTIER, PAUL, *L'Unité du Christ: Être, personne, conscience*, 2nd edn. (Paris: Beauchesne, 1939).

—— 'Saint Cyrille d'Alexandrie et saint Léon le Grand à Chalcédoine', in *Das Konzil von Chalkedon: Geschichte und Gegenwart*, i. *Der Glaube von Chalkedon*, ed. A. Grillmeier and H. Bacht (Würzburg: Echter-Verlag Würzburg, 1951), 345–87.

—— 'Saint Cyrille et Apollinaire', *Gr.* 37 (1956): 584–609.

—— 'Théodore de Mopsueste: Sa vrai pensée sur l'incarnation', *RSR* 45 (1957): 161–86, 338–60.

GEBREMEDHIN, EZRA, *Life-Giving Blessing: An Inquiry into the*

Eucharistic Doctrine of Cyril of Alexandria, Acta Universitatis Upsaliensis. Studia Doctrinae Christianae Upsaliensia, 17 (Uppsala: University of Uppsala, 1977).

GIBSON, EDGAR C. S. (ed.), 'The Works of John Cassian', in *Sulpitius Severus, Vincent of Lerins, John Cassian, NPNF* (2) xi (New York: Christian Literature Company, 1894).

GOULD, GRAHAM, 'Cyril of Alexandria and the Formula of Reunion', *DR* 106 (1988): 235–52.

GRAY, PATRICK, 'Theodoret on the "One Hypostasis": An Antiochene Reading of Chalcedon', *StPatr* 15 (1984): 301–4.

GREER, ROWAN A., *Theodore of Mopsuestia: Exegete and Theologian* (Leighton Buzzard: Faith Press, 1961).

—— *The Captain of our Salvation: A Study in the Patristic Exegesis of Hebrews* (Tübingen: J. C. B. Mohr, 1973).

—— 'The Analogy of Grace in Theodore of Mopsuestia's Christology', *JThS* NS 34 (1983): 82–98.

GREGORIOS, PAULOS MAR, 'The Relevance of Christology Today', in P. Fries and T. Nersoyan (eds.), *Christ in East and West* (Macon, Ga.: Mercer University Press, 1987), 97–112.

GRILLMEIER, ALOYS, *Christ in Christian Tradition*, i. *From the Apostolic Age to Chalcedon*, trans. John Bowden (London: A. W. Mowbray & Co., 1965; rev. edn. 1975).

GROSS, JULES, *La Divinisation du chrétien d'après les pères grecs: Contribution historique à la doctrine de la grâce* (Paris: Libraire Lecoffre, 1938).

—— 'Theodor von Mopsuestia, ein Gegner der Erbsündenlehre', *ZKG* 65 (1953–4): 1–15.

GUILLAUMONT, ANTOINE, *Les 'Képhalaia gnostica' d'Évagre le Pontique et l'histoire de l'Origénisme chez les Grecs et chez les Syriens*, Patristica Sorbonensia, 5 (Paris: Éditions du Seuil, 1962).

GUILLET, JACQUES, 'Les Exégèses d'Alexandrie et d'Antioche: Conflit ou malentendu?', *RSR* 34 (1947): 257–302.

GUY, JEAN-CLAUDE, 'Jean Cassien, historien du monachisme égyptien?', *StPatr* 8 (1966) [*TU* 93]: 363–72.

HAHN, AUGUST (ed.), *Bibliothek der Symbole und Glaubensregeln der alten Kirche*, rev. and expanded by G. L. Hahn, 3rd edn. (Breslau: Verlag von E. Morgenstern, 1897).

HALLMAN, JOSEPH M., 'The Seed of Fire: Divine Suffering in the Christology of Cyril of Alexandria and Nestorius of Constantinople', *JECS* 5 (1997): 369–91.

HARNACK, ADOLF VON, *History of Dogma*, vols. iii and iv, trans. from the 3rd German edition by N. Buchanan *et al.* (London: Williams & Norgate, 1897). (These are part of vol. ii in German 1st edn., 1885, and in German 3rd edn., 1894.)

HARPER, JAMES, 'John Cassian and Sulpicius Severus', *ChH* 34 (1965): 371–80.

HAY, CAMILLUS, 'St. John Chrysostom and the Integrity of the Human Nature of Christ', *FrancSt* 19 (1959): 298–317.

—— 'Antiochene Exegesis and Christology', *ABR* 12 (1964): 10–23.

HODGSON, LEONARD, 'The Metaphysic of Nestorius', *JThS* 19 (1918): 46–55.

HOLZE, HEINRICH, *Erfahrung und Theologie im frühen Mönchtum: Untersuchungen zu einer Theologie des monastischen Lebens bei den ägyptischen Mönchsvätern, Johannes Cassian, und Benedikt von Nursia (*Göttingen: Vandenhoeck & Ruprecht, 1992).

JACKSON, BLOMFIELD (ed.), 'The Ecclesiastical History, Dialogues, and Letters of Theodoret', in *Theodoret, Jerome, Gennadius, Rufinus: Historical Writings, etc.*, *NPNF* (2) iii (New York: Christian Literature Company, 1892).

JANSSENS, L., 'Notre filiation divine d'après saint Cyrille d'Alexandrie', *EThL* 15 (1938): 233–78.

JOUASSARD, GEORGES, 'L'Activité littéraire de saint Cyrille d'Alexandrie jusqu'à 428: Essai de chronologie et de synthèse', in *Mélanges E. Podechard: Études de sciences religieuses offertes pour son Éméritat* (Lyon: Facultés Catholiques, 1945), 159–74.

—— 'Une intuition fondamentale de saint Cyrille d'Alexandrie en christologie dans les premières années de son episcopat', *REByz* 11 (1953): 175–86.

JUGIE, MARTIN, *Nestorius et la controverse nestorienne*, Bibliothèque de théologie historique (Paris: Beauchesne, 1912).

—— 'La Terminologie christologique de saint Cyrille d'Alexandrie', *EOr* 15 (1912): 12–27.

KELLY, JOHN N. D., *Early Christian Doctrines* (London: Adam & Charles Black, 1958; 5th edn. 1977).

—— *Golden Mouth: The Story of John Chrysostom—Ascetic, Preacher, Bishop* (Grand Rapids, Mich.: Baker, 1995).

KLINE, FRANCIS, 'Regula Benedicti 73: 8: A Rule for Beginners', in J. R. Sommerfeldt (ed.), *Erudition at God's Service: Studies in Medieval Cistercian History 11*, Cistercian Studies Series, 98 (Kalamazoo, Mich.: Cistercian Publications, 1987), 97–108.

KOEN, LARS, *The Saving Passion: Incarnational and Soteriological Thought in Cyril of Alexandria's Commentary on the Gospel According to St. John*, Acta Universitatis Upsaliensis. Studia Doctrinae Christianas Upsaliensia 31 (Uppsala: University of Uppsala), 1991.

KUHLMANN, KARL-HEINZ, 'Eine dogmengeschichtliche Neubewertung von Johannes Cassianus *De incarnatione Domini contra*

Nestorium libri 7', Th.D. dissertation, University of South Africa, 1983.

LAMPE, G. W. H., *A Patristic Greek Lexicon* (Oxford: Clarendon Press, 1961).

LAWRENZ, M. E., 'The Christology of John Chrysostom', *StPatr* 22 (1989): 148–53.

LERA, JOSÉ MARIA, 'Théodore de Mopsueste', *DSp* 15 (1991): 385–400.

LEWIS, CHARLTON, and CHARLES SHORT, *A Latin Dictionary Founded on Andrews' Edition of Freund's Latin Dictionary* (Oxford: Clarendon Press, 1879).

LIÉBAERT, JACQUES, *La Doctrine christologique de saint Cyrille d'Alexandrie avant la querelle nestorienne*, Mémoires et travaux publiés par des professeurs des Facultés Catholiques de Lille, 58 (Lille: Facultés Catholiques, 1951).

LOOFS, FRIEDRICH, *Nestorius and his Place in the History of Christian Doctrine* (Cambridge: University Press, 1914; repr. New York: Burt Franklin Reprints, 1975).

LOSSKY, VLADIMIR, *The Mystical Theology of the Eastern Church* (Cambridge: James Clarke & Co., 1957; French 1st edn. 1944).

LOUTH, ANDREW, *The Origins of the Christian Mystical Tradition: From Plato to Denys* (Oxford: Clarendon Press, 1981).

—— 'The Use of the Term *ἴδιος* in Alexandrian Theology from Alexander to Cyril', *StPatr* 19 (1989): 198–202.

LIDDELL, HENRY G., and ROBERT SCOTT, *A Greek-English Lexicon*, rev. and augmented by H. S. Jones and R. McKenzie (Oxford: Clarendon Press, 1843; 9th edn. 1940, suppl. added 1996).

MCGUCKIN, JOHN A., 'The Christology of Nestorius of Constantinople', *PBR* 7: 2–3 (1988): 93–129.

—— 'Did Augustine's Christology Depend on Theodore of Mopsuestia?', *HeyJ* 31 (1990): 39–52.

—— 'The Influence of the Isis Cult on St Cyril of Alexandria's Christology', *StPatr* 24 (1993): 291–9.

—— *St. Cyril of Alexandria: The Christological Controversy*. Supplements to *Vigiliae Christianiae*, 23 (Leiden: E. J. Brill, 1994).

MCKENZIE, JOHN L., 'Annotations on the Christology of Theodore of Mopsuestia', *TS* 19 (1958): 345–73.

MCKINION, STEVEN A., *Words, Imagery, and the Mystery of Christ: A Reconstruction of Cyril of Alexandria's Christology*, Supplements to *Vigiliae Christianae*, 55 (Leiden: E. J. Brill, 2000).

MCNAMARA, KEVIN, 'Theodore of Mopsuestia and the Nestorian Heresy', *IThQ* 19 (1952): 254–78; 20 (1953): 172–91.

—— 'Theodoret of Cyrus and the Unity of Person in Christ', *IThQ* 22 (1955): 313–28.

Mahé, Joseph, 'Les Anathématismes de saint Cyrille d'Alexandrie et les évêques orientaux du patriarchat d'Antioche', *RHE* 7 (1906): 505–42.

—— 'La Sanctification d'après saint Cyrille d'Alexandrie', *RHE* 10 (1909): 30–40, 469–92.

—— 'Cyrille (saint), patriarche d'Alexandrie', *DThC* 3 (1923): 2476–527.

Mandac, Marijan, 'L'Union christologique dans les œuvres de Théodoret antérieures au concile d'Éphèse', *EThL* 47 (1971): 64–96.

Markus, R. A., *The End of Ancient Christianity* (Cambridge: University Press, 1990).

Meunier, Bernard, *Le Christ de Cyrille d'Alexandrie: L'Humanité, le salut, et la question monophysite*, Théologie historique, 104 (Paris: Beauchesne, 1997).

Meyendorff, John, *Christ in Eastern Christian Thought* (Crestwood, NY: St. Vladimir's Seminary Press, rev. ed. 1975; French 1st edn. 1969).

Michel, Otto, *'οἶκος κτλ', TDNT* 5 (1967): 119–59.

Munz, Peter, 'John Cassian', *JEH* 11 (1960): 1–22.

Norris, Richard A., Jr., *Manhood and Christ: A Study in the Christology of Theodore of Mopsuestia* (Oxford: Clarendon Press, 1963).

—— 'Toward a Contemporary Interpretation of the Chalcedonian *Definition*', in R. A. Norris, Jr. (ed.), *Lux in Lumine: Essays to Honor W. Norman Pittenger* (New York: Seabury Press, 1966), 62–79.

—— 'Christological Models in Cyril of Alexandria', *StPatr* 13 (1975) [*TU* 115]: 255–68.

O'Keefe, John J., 'Impassible Suffering? Divine Passion and Fifth-Century Christology', *TS* 58 (1997): 38–60.

O'Keeffe, Dunstan, 'The *Via Media* of Monastic Theology: The Debate on Grace and Free Will in Fifth-Century Southern Gaul', *DR* 112 (1994): 264–83; 113 (1995): 54–73.

Olphe-Galliard, Michel, 'Cassien (Jean)', *DSp* 2 (1953): 214–76.

Ortiz de Urbina, Ignacio, 'Das Symbol von Chalkedon: Sein Text, sein Werden, seine dogmatische Bedeutung', in A. Grillmeier and H. Bacht (eds.), *Das Konzil von Chalkedon: Geschichte und Gegenwart*, i. *Der Glaube von Chalkedon* (Würzburg: Echter-Verlag Würzburg, 1951), 389–418.

Parvis, P. M., 'The *Commentary on Hebrews* and the *Contra Theodorum* of Cyril of Alexandria', *JThS* NS 26 (1975): 415–19.

Peasants, Phyllis Rodgerson, 'Making Christian the Christians: The Baptismal Instructions of St. John Chrysostom', *GOTR* 34 (1989): 379–92.

Pelikan, Jaroslav, *The Christian Tradition: A History of the Develop-*

ment of Doctrine, i. *The Emergence of the Catholic Tradition (100–600)* (Chicago: University of Chicago Press, 1971).

PHAN, PETER C., *Grace and the Human Condition*, Message of the Fathers of the Church, 15, ed. Thomas Halton (Wilmington, Del.: Michael Glazier, 1988).

PRESTIGE, GEORGE L., *Fathers and Heretics: Six Studies in Dogmatic Faith with Prologue and Epilogue* (London: Society for Promoting Christian Knowledge, 1940).

PRISTAS, LAUREN, 'The Theological Anthropology of John Cassian', Ph.D. dissertation, Boston College, 1993.

PUSEY, PHILIP EDWARD (ed.), *Sancti patris nostri Cyrilli archiepiscopi Alexandrini De recta fide ad Imperatorum, De incarnatione Unigeniti dialogus, De recta fide at principissas, De recta fide ad augustas, Quod unus Christus dialogus, Apolgeticus ad imperatorum* (Oxford: Clarendon Press, 1877).

RAMSEY, BONIFACE (ed.), *John Cassian: The Conferences*, ACW 57 (New York: Paulist Press, 1997).

RAVEN, CHARLES E., *Apollinarianism: An Essay on the Christology of the Early Church* (Cambridge: University Press, 1923).

REA, ROBERT F., 'Grace and Free Will in John Cassian', Ph.D. dissertation, St Louis University, 1990.

RICHARD, MARCEL, 'L'Introduction du mot "Hypostase" dans la théologie de l'Incarnation', *MSR* 2 (1945): 5–32, 243–70.

ROMANIDES, JOHN S., 'Highlights in the Debate over Theodore of Mopsuestia's Christology and Some Suggestions for a Fresh Approach', *GOTR* 5: 2 (1959–60): 140–85.

—— 'St. Cyril's "One Physis or Hypostasis of God the Logos Incarnate" and Chalcedon', *GOTR* 10: 2 (1964–5): 82–107.

ROUSSEAU, PHILIP, 'Cassian, Contemplation and the Coenobitic Life', *JEH* 26 (1975): 113–26.

—— *Ascetics, Authority, and the Church in the Age of Jerome and Cassian* (Oxford: University Press, 1978).

RUSSELL, NORMAN (ed.), *Cyril of Alexandria*, The Early Church Fathers (London: Routledge, 2000).

SAMUEL, VILAKUVEL C., 'Some Facts about the Alexandrine Christology', *IJT* 11 (1962): 136–42.

—— 'One Incarnate Nature of God the Word', *GOTR* 10: 2 (1964–5): 37–53.

SCHWARTZ, EDUARD, *Konzilstudien I: Cassian und Nestorius*, Schriften der Wissenschaftlichen Gesellschaft in Straßburg, 20 (Strassburg: Karl J. Trübner, 1914), 1–17.

—— *Cyrill und der Mönch Viktor*, Sitzungberichte der Akademie der Wissenschaften in Wien, Philosophisch-historische Klasse, 208.4

(Vienna: Hölder-Pichler-Tempsky A.-G., 1928).

SCIPIONI, LUIGI I., *Nestorio e il concilio di Efeso: Storia, dogma, critica* (Milan: Vita e Pensiero, 1974).

SELLERS, RICHARD V., *Two Ancient Christologies: A Study in the Christological Thought of the Schools of Antioch and Alexandria in the Early History of Christian Doctrine* (London: Society for Promoting Christian Knowledge, 1940).

SIDDALS, RUTH M., 'Logic and Christology in Cyril of Alexandria', Ph.D. dissertation, University of Cambridge, 1984.

——'Logic and Christology in Cyril of Alexandria', *JThS* NS 38 (1987): 341–67.

STEWART, COLUMBA, *Cassian the Monk* (Oxford: Oxford University Press, 1998).

STUDER, BASIL, '*Una Persona in Christo*: Ein augustinisches Thema bei Leo dem Grossen', *Aug.* 25 (1985): 453–87.

SULLIVAN, FRANCIS A., *The Christology of Theodore of Mopsuestia.* Analecta Gregoriana, 82 (Rome: Universitatis Gregorianae, 1956).

TORRANCE, THOMAS F., *Theology in Reconciliation: Essays Towards Evangelical and Catholic Unity in East and West* (London: Geoffrey Chapman Publishers, 1975).

TRAKATELLIS, DEMETRIOS, 'Being Transformed: Chrysostom's Exegesis of the Epistle to the Romans', *GOTR* 36 (1991): 211–29.

TUGWELL, SIMON, 'Evagrius and Macarius', in Cheslyn Jones *et al.* (eds.), *The Study of Spirituality* (London: Society for Promoting Christian Knowledge, 1986), 168–75.

TURNER, H. E. W., 'Nestorius Reconsidered', *StPatr* 13 (1975) [*TU* 115]: 306–21.

——*Jesus the Christ* (London: A. W. Mowbray & Co., 1976).

VAN BAVEL, TARSICIUS J., *Recherches sur la christologie de saint Augustin: L'Humain et le divin dans le Christ d'après saint Augustin*, Paradosis 10 (Fribourg: Éditions Universitaires, 1954).

VANNIER, MARIE-ANNE, 'Jean Cassien a-t-il fait œuvre de théologien dans le *De incarnatione Domini*?', *StPatr* 24 (1993): 345–54.

VÖOBUS, ARTHUR, 'Regarding the Theological Anthropology of Theodore of Mopsuestia', *ChH* 33 (1964): 115–24.

WEAVER, REBECCA HARDEN, *Divine Grace and Human Agency: A Study of the Semi-Pelagian Controversy*, Patristic Monographs Series, 15 (Macon, Ga.: Mercer University Press, 1996).

WEIGL, EDUARD, *Die Heilslehre des hl. Cyrill von Alexandrien*, Forschungen zur Christlichen Literatur- und Dogmengeschichte 5.2–3, ed. A. Ehrhard and J. P. Kirsch (Mainz: Verlag von Kirchheim & Co., 1905).

——*Christologie vom Tode des Athanasius bis zum Ausbruch des*

Nestorianischen Streites (373–429), Münchener Studien zur historischen Theologie, 4 (Munich: Joseph Kösel & Friedrich Pustet, 1925).

WELCH, LAWRENCE J., *Christology and Eucharist in the Early Thought of Cyril of Alexandria* (San Francisco: Catholic Scholars Press, 1994).

—— 'Logos-Sarx? Sarx and the Soul of Christ in the Early Thought of Cyril of Alexandria', *SVTQ* 38 (1994): 271–92.

WICKHAM, LIONEL R., 'Symbols of the Incarnation in Cyril of Alexandria', in Margot Schmidt and Carl Friedrich Geyer (eds.), *Typus, Symbol, Allegorie bei den östlichen Vätern und ihren Parallelen im Mittelalter*, Eichstätter Beiträge, 4 (Regensburg: Friedrich Pustet Regensburg, 1981), 41–53.

—— 'Pelagianism in the East', in R. Williams (ed.), *The Making of Orthodoxy: Essays in Honour of Henry Chadwick* (Cambridge: University Press, 1989), 200–13.

—— (ed.), *Cyril of Alexandria: Select Letters* (Oxford: Clarendon Press, 1983).

WILKEN, ROBERT L., 'Tradition, Exegesis, and the Christological Controversies', *ChH* 34 (1965): 123–45.

—— *Judaism and the Early Christian Mind: A Study of Cyril of Alexandria's Exegesis and Theology* (New Haven, Conn.: Yale University Press, 1971).

—— 'St Cyril of Alexandria: The Mystery of Christ in the Bible', *ProEccl* 4 (1995): 454–78.

YOUNG, FRANCES M., 'A Reconsideration of Alexandrian Christology', *JEH* 22 (1971): 103–14.

INDEX